PENGUIN BOOKS

The **Liar**

Luke Harding was born in Nottingham in April 1968. He was educated at University College, Oxford, where he edited the university newspaper *Cherwell* and graduated with a double first in English. He began his professional career in journalism at the now defunct *Sunday Correspondent*, later working at the *Daily Mail* between 1993 and 1996 as a senior writer and as the *Mail*'s West of England correspondent. He joined the staff of the *Guardian* in November 1996 as a home-news reporter and covered the Jonathan Aitken trial from the press benches.

David Leigh, now Comment Editor at the *Guardian*, was a producer at *World in Action*, where he made 'Jonathan of Arabia' in 1995. He was previously a TV reporter with *This Week* and head of investigations at the *Observer* 1981–9, where he won Granada TV's Investigative Reporter of the Year Award in 1985. He has also won three British Press Awards for campaigning journalism, and was one of the team who won another British Press Award for their reporting in the *Guardian* of the downfall of ex-minister Neil Hamilton. He has authored or co-authored books on sleaze, the Matrix Churchill case, MI5, Labour leader Michael Foot, the drug smuggler Howard Marks, Chernobyl, the Jeremy Thorpe case and Government secrecy.

David Pallister has been an investigative reporter with the *Guardian* since 1974, specializing in civil liberties, miscarriages of justice, South Africa under apartheid, and the arms trade. He has travelled extensively for the paper, covering Nigerian politics, the Ethiopian famine, civil wars in Sri Lanka and Lebanon, and the Irish Troubles. He is co-author of a book investigating the Oppenheimer gold and diamond empire, *South Africa Inc.* He helped Gerry Conlon of the Guildford Four write his autobiography, *Proved Innocent*. He was one of the *Guardian* journalists who won the British Press Awards Team Reporting Award for the Neil Hamilton affair, and was a contributor to *Sleaze*, the book of the case.

Luke Harding, David Leigh & David Pallister

*The*Liar

The Fall of Jonathan Aitken

PENGUIN BOOKS

PENGUIN BOOKS

Published by the Penguin Group
Penguin Books Ltd, 27 Wrights Lane, London w8 5tz, England
Penguin Books USA Inc., 375 Hudson Street, New York, New York 10014, USA
Penguin Books Australia Ltd, Ringwood, Victoria, Australia
Penguin Books Canada Ltd, 10 Alcorn Avenue, Toronto, Ontario, Canada m4v 3b2
Penguin Books (NZ) Ltd, 182–190 Wairau Road, Auckland 10, New Zealand

Penguin Books Ltd, Registered Offices: Harmondsworth, Middlesex, England

First published 1997
10 9 8 7 6 5

The moral right of the authors has been asserted

Set in 10½/12pt Monotype Garamond
Typeset by Rowland Phototypesetting Ltd, Bury St Edmunds, Suffolk
Printed in England by Clays Ltd, St Ives plc

Contents

Acknowledgements

We owe a debt of gratitude to the individuals who came forward to tell us their stories on the record and who courageously agreed to become witnesses in the libel trial, despite attempts to frighten or dissuade them: Valerie Scott, Jo Lambert, Robin Kirk. Thanks, too, to the others, particularly the former officials of the Independent Broadcasting Authority, who provided statements for the *Guardian* and Granada TV's defence. Many people kindly gave us information, but preferred to remain anonymous. The journalists involved in this case would like to thank Alan Rusbridger, the editor of the *Guardian*, and Steve Boulton and Ian McBride, at *World in Action*, for their resolution in sticking with the story to the end.

Foreword by Peter Preston

The point about daily journalism is that, each morning, it wipes away the toil of the day before; a new blank sheet of paper, fresh forgetfulness. But, even for the most hardened daily journalist, there are moments you guess will stay with you for as long as you live. I shall always remember the look on Jonathan Aitken's face as the affidavits from British Airways and Geneva arrived in the High Court, a look of bemusement and then of stone. A life changed for ever in fifteen seconds.

If you're lucky enough to edit a paper like the *Guardian* for twenty years, you accumulate a few such moments: none, though, really match the power – the sheer melodrama – of the Aitken denouement. It had the classic structure of Greek tragedy; that first, small lie long ago, rolling forward, building, creating an edifice of mendacity which suddenly collapsed under its own weight. It had George Carman as Perry Mason.

The temptation, of course, is to crow and to caricature. Jonathan would have taken his broadsword to the *Guardian* if he'd won. Why not exult a bit in victory? But, for myself, I've never been able to feel that so simply. This was a ripping yarn, a tale of perfidy in high places only brought into the open by a team of dedicated professionals. Yet I also found it curiously sad. Why should someone so gifted, so charming, so revered by his own civil servants, do these things, peddle these lies? It tells us something we always need reminding of – about the human condition. And I think it tells us something broader.

Jonathan Aitken was not some bit-part MP on the make. He was, and wished to be, a great player. When he tripped, he pulled himself upright again. He came, at last, to control the detail of all British public spending. We, as a society, had no defences. On the contrary, the system creaked and pottered blindly to his defence. It was the journalists and whistle-blowers who were the enemy. Their final victory was hardly, desperately won.

Journalists should not expect to be loved. That is not their role. But we have a role in a free society as – sometimes stumbling – protectors of that freedom. When I saw that look of stone on Jonathan's face, I felt that the *Guardian* had managed to do something, for all of us, which needed to be done.

'Watergate was a Shakespearean tragedy for Richard Nixon
. . . Even the most generous explanations for his conduct
do not bring him exculpation. In his frenzied efforts to fight
his way out of the quicksand of Watergate, Nixon made
himself guilty of many "crimes" – among them deceit,
negligence, bad judgement, mendacity, amorality,
concealment, and a disastrous reluctance to face up to the
individuals who were creating the worst problems.'
Jonathan Aitken, *Nixon: A Life*

'Bounders can be capital fellows; don't you agree, Colonel
Sidebottom?' **(Mr Prendergast), Evelyn Waugh,
*Decline and Fall***

'If it falls to me to start a fight to cut out the cancer of bent and twisted journalism in our country with the simple sword of truth and the trusty shield of British fair play, so be it. I am ready for the fight.' **Jonathan Aitken, 10 April 1995, Conservative Central Office**

··

Prologue: **Sword of Truth**

At 5 p.m. exactly the Right Honourable Jonathan Aitken, Cabinet minister, Tory MP and incorrigible liar, swept into Conservative Central Office for the biggest gamble of his political career. Aitken strode purposefully across the platform, which had been made available for his use by the Tory Party Chairman Jeremy Hanley with the blessing of the Prime Minister, John Major. Since Major's unexpected election victory three years earlier, fifteen members of his administration had been carried off by the gurgling tide of sleaze. Now one man in a pin-striped suit was to stand heroically against the flow.

Aitken gripped the podium firmly with both hands. Before him, the assembled ranks of Britain's press corps waited expectantly. They had been promised an 'explosive' response to front-page allegations in that morning's *Guardian* newspaper that the minister had procured prostitutes for Arabs, allowed a shadowy Arab friend to pay his hotel bill, and indulged in an improper relationship with two arms dealers. That night, a *World in Action* programme which was the basis of the *Guardian* article would repeat the allegations. Aitken was determined to have the damning film pulled off the air. 'This is going to be the best circus in town,' one television producer murmured hopefully. Seated in the front row were Aitken's wife Lolicia and fourteen-year-old daughter Victoria. Minutes earlier they had fidgeted and giggled as if waiting for the first model to shimmy down the catwalk at a fashion show. Their nervous anticipation was infectious. Now they fell silent.

Aitken, the Chief Secretary to the Treasury, was in grim mood. Or so it seemed. He glowered briefly around the auditorium in a look that mixed anger with contempt. Then, reading from an autocue, he launched into a tirade. 'I was shocked and disgusted by the very serious allegations made against me in the *Guardian* newspaper this morning,' he intoned. The very picture of injured innocence, Aitken went on: 'I have no hesitation in stating categorically that these allegations are wicked lies. I have therefore today issued a writ for defamation, against the *Guardian*, its editor-in-chief Mr Peter Preston, and the journalist who wrote the story, Mr Pallister.' Sitting directly in his line of sight through the autocue at the back of the hall, the *Guardian* reporter David Pallister listened uncomfortably. The *Guardian* claim that Aitken had tried to procure girls at a health farm, Inglewood, was an 'outrageous falsehood', the minister thundered. 'I must also mention,' he added gravely, 'that the former matron who has made this allegation was dismissed by Inglewood following a police investigation.'

Early snippets of Aitken's sensational speech were already flashing up on the wires of the Press Association. Across the newsrooms of what was once Fleet Street, senior executives gawped, then made an instant decision to clear the following day's front page. Aitken, meanwhile, continued his invective. His stay at the Ritz Hotel in Paris had not breached ministerial guidelines, he declared. 'The total picture of the *Guardian*'s report is therefore one of deliberate misrepresentations, falsehoods and lies, and is clearly part of the paper's long campaign of sustained attempts to discredit me.' The cameras were rolling. What a story! And then Aitken began to wrap himself in the flag of St George. 'My sense of shock has not in any way weakened my sense of determination to fight this matter to a finish in the courts and elsewhere,' he began. 'I came into politics for the purpose of making a contribution to public service in my constituency, in Parliament and in Government.'

With the metaphorical flag now flapping round his shoulders, Aitken issued a declaration of all-out war – against newspapers, newspapermen and television journalists; against all those who 'abuse media power'. 'Here in Britain we have both the best media in the world and the worst media in the world,' he said. 'That small latter element is spreading a cancer in our society today, which I will call the cancer of bent and twisted journalism.' At this stage, music was called for – perhaps the opening bars of 'I Vow to Thee My Country' – but none, sadly, was forthcoming. Like a stern revivalist preacher,

Aitken's gaze never faltered as he looked the TV cameras firmly in the eye. 'I have done nothing wrong,' he added, pausing for a second. And then, a vivid and baroque conclusion: 'If it falls to me to start a fight to cut out the cancer of bent and twisted journalism in our country with the simple sword of truth and the trusty shield of British fair play, so be it. I am ready for the fight.'

As a former member of the scruffy tribe of journalists he now despised, Aitken had always been fond of metaphors, particularly lavish ones. Later he would have cause to regret his rococo phraseology. The 'sword of truth' and the 'trusty shield of British fair play' were memorable phrases, which combined the cadences of florid Arabic with a hint of the old Crusader image that appeared daily on the front page of his great-uncle Beaverbrook's *Daily Express*. The tall figure behind the podium thundered on against the Conservative Party's blue backdrop.

As he stood there, declaiming, Aitken knew he was playing a giant game of poker with his accusers in the media. His lofty rhetoric bore no resemblance to the cards in his hand: a couple of twos. He knew the allegations printed by the *Guardian* were true. To admit as much, though, would be political suicide. Aitken was clever, ruthless, formidable, ambitious and – most lethally – charming. His boyhood ambition of becoming Prime Minister – stalled by a foolhardy liaison with Margaret Thatcher's daughter – still burned brightly.

That morning on a plane back from Switzerland Aitken had decided to embark on the cynical survival strategy which had served him well in the past: the Great Bluff. Over the next two years the tactic would take him further and further down a dark road of deceit, concealment and finally perjury; a mendacious journey that led all the way through the portals of the High Court and into the witness-box. To save his own skin, Aitken would drag those closest to him down into the mire: his wife, teenage daughter, and his close friend Said Ayas. At his request, they would all lie for him. In the course of this journey, Jonathan Aitken's own secrets of sexual deviancy dating back to his days at Eton and his dependency on Saudi money would be catastrophically revealed.

Richard Nixon, the subject of a flattering 600-page biography by Aitken, had embarked on a similar strategy when confronted with the growing crisis of Watergate. What was astonishing, as the extraordinary political melodrama unfolded that April late afternoon, was that Aitken should have learned so little from his unusual political hero. Aitken was, after all, a talented and brilliant man. He must have been aware of the risks he was taking. Nor was he ignorant of the sharp frontiers between truth and fiction. 'The best definition of a biographer is that he should be an artist on oath,' he observed. But he was to ignore the fundamental lesson of the Watergate scandal: beware the cover-up. And, blinded by arrogance and a mythic belief in his own invulnerability, he was to underestimate the tenacity of the journalists on whom he had so flamboyantly declared war. As the cameras rolled, Aitken's synthetic outrage rose ever higher. 'I am ready for the fight,' he said. 'The fight against falsehood and those who peddle it. My fight begins today. Thank you and good afternoon.'

In all, there had been ten minutes of explosive theatre. He had not disappointed. Aitken swept rapidly out of the briefing room, refusing all questions. The journalist who shouted out, 'Are you going to resign, Sir?' was left with his words addressed to an empty platform. Gripping the smiling Lolicia and Victoria by each hand, Aitken exited Tory Central Office in Smith Square and stormed into an overcast Westminster afternoon. As he walked the hundred yards to his grand house in Lord North Street, Aitken was mobbed by photographers and television camera crews. The extravagant speech duly led the early-evening news bulletins. The minister must have been well pleased.

That evening Aitken watched the *World in Action* documentary 'Jonathan of Arabia' go out regardless of his blustering scare tactics. The Chief Secretary then temporarily switched tack from outrage to an attempt to play matters down. Loud laughter, it was claimed, could be heard coming from his room at the Treasury as he watched the film. His friends said he had been amused by the documentary's 'amateur theatricals': pictures of actors dressed up as Arabs plodding along what was in fact a drab Merseyside beach. The change of tone proved to be far too late, however, to rescind Aitken's public declaration of war to the death with the 'liberal' media. The image of father, daughter and wife leaving Conservative Central Office was tartly celebrated on the front cover of the following week's satirical magazine, *Private Eye*. An imaginary bubble from Aitken said: 'I do not procure girls to help my career.' Victoria replies: 'Can I go now, Dad?'

The following day Lolicia Aitken flew out to Geneva for a secret rendezvous with the son of the King of Saudi Arabia, Prince Mohammed bin Fahd bin Abdulaziz. Over two decades, Aitken had grown rich through his friendship with the impulsive billionaire Prince. Unbeknown to most of his constituents, the MP had acted as Mohammed's obsequious London 'fixer' since the late 1970s, providing him with anything he desired. Now it was payback time.

Lolicia slotted a copy of the 'Jonathan of Arabia' documentary into a video recorder. The Prince sat down stony-faced and watched. The programme included mocked-up footage of Mohammed cruising through London in his white Rolls-Royce in pursuit of an undercover reporter posing as a prostitute. Mohammed hit the roof. Enraged, he tossed over a holdall full of cash. According to impeccable sources, the bag contained between $100,000 and $200,000 – small change for the Prince. The money would be used by Jonathan Aitken over the next two years to launch his libel action to the death against the *Guardian* and Granada Television. This was the same action in which he would categorically – and with a straight face – deny being dependent on Saudi largesse. And from the Prince, there was the promise of more cash to come. 'Get Fayed,' he snarled, determined that Aitken should crush his opponents in the courts. The Fayed in question was Mohamed Al Fayed, the mercurial Egyptian tycoon and the owner of the fabled Ritz Hotel in Paris.

It was here, on a balmy Friday evening, that the astonishing saga first began.

··

One: **Spaghetti Puzzle**

In the autumn of 1993, when John Major was Prime Minister, and the Conservative Party had been in power continuously for fourteen years, one of his ministers made a secret trip to Paris. Jonathan Aitken, the Old Etonian politician in question, was a suave figure. Lankily tall, a notorious heart-throb with a gaucho's high cheekbones, a dimpled grin, eyes that seemed coal-black, and wavy hair that was only slightly too chestnut to be natural, he added a touch of glamour to the stale regime of John Major, who looked and talked like a dreary bank manager. The clandestine visit began in the late evening of Friday 17 September 1993 when Aitken, the Minister of State for Defence Procurement, strode into the reception of the Ritz Hotel and tossed over his passport.

Back home Aitken's political leader was in trouble. The latest opinion poll in the *Guardian* newspaper placed John Major eighteen points behind John Smith's Labour Party. The previous night Norman Lamont – the embittered ex-Chancellor sacked four months earlier – had twisted the knife with some unkindly remarks about the PM on BBC1's *Question Time*. In the corridors of Whitehall, and in the discreet eateries around Westminster where journalists and politicians conspire over bottles of Pinot Grigio, there were treasonous whispers about leadership contests. The political honeymoon after Major's surprise election victory in April 1992 had been cut short by the surreal fiscal pantomime of Black Wednesday, when the pound was forced out of the European currency system by speculators. Meanwhile, the unbrotherly war within the Conservative Party over its attitude to Europe showed no signs of abating.

Aitken, though, was rather enjoying being a minister after eighteen long years on the back benches. Under the heading 'Title' on the

Ritz's *bulletin d'arrivée* he was booked in grandly as 'Ministre'. It had been a tiring twenty-four hours for Aitken, the man in charge of British arms sales. The previous day he had flown to Poland on a diplomatic chore which had fallen to him at the last minute. The Government had agreed to return the bones of the Polish war hero General Wladyslaw Sikorski to the new democratic Polish regime of Lech Walesa. Sikorski had perished in an air crash in 1943 and was buried in Newark in Nottinghamshire. What was left of him was now going home, to be reburied with some pomp.

The mandarins back at the Foreign Office had initially pencilled in Douglas Hogg to do the honours. But the fedora-wearing junior foreign minister was unavailable. So it was Aitken who earlier in the day had trooped behind General Sikorski's coffin with due solemnity as it was wheeled on a gun-carriage up to a castle near Cracow. And it was Aitken who had listened to an interminable sermon by Cardinal Glemp. Eventually the general's remains were interred in a gloomy catacomb. The Duke of Edinburgh, who had represented the Queen at the ceremony, gave Aitken a lift home. As the Queen's Flight plane droned over Germany, Aitken must have reflected that being a minister was not all glamour. 'We seem to be doing a lot of praying and a lot of flying today,' the Duke remarked gloomily, getting off at Balmoral. Aitken was dropped at RAF Northolt air base at 6 p.m., and was whisked by Government car to Heathrow, where he boarded a 7.10 p.m. Air France flight. Its destination was Paris, a city which was to become as central to Aitken's mythological account of his movements as Dublin was to James Joyce's *Ulysses*, another great work of fiction.

The Right Honourable Jonathan Aitken MP was later to give a detailed explanation of his infamous weekend at the Ritz Hotel in Paris. It was, he said, 'the story of complicated but innocent muddle'. As Aitken hovered over the reception counter of the Ritz that evening two different versions of reality shimmered and diverged. One was true – what actually happened – and the other was not true. Aitken was to polish and perfect the untrue version over the next three-and-a-half years into a gleaming edifice of falsehood designed to fool the public, his lawyers, his colleagues and an elderly High Court judge. The untrue account was vastly more entertaining than the real one.

Aitken was to perform a dizzy ontological conjuring trick. He would pluck his wife Lolicia from the Swiss Alps and dump her at the counter of the Ritz Hotel in time to pay his bill and rescue him from his political foes, who were to accuse him, correctly, of ministerial impropriety. The sole purpose of his trip to Paris, according to his divertingly false version of events, was to meet up with his wife and daughter Victoria in Paris, and then to install Victoria at a new school in the Swiss Alps. Victoria had inherited her mother's dyslexia, Aitken explained. It was thought unlikely she would pass the entrance exam for King's College, Canterbury, which her twin sister Alexandra was due to attend. Instead, Victoria was destined for the less academically exacting Aiglon College.

Aiglon, set among pastoral meadows and high Alpine peaks in the Swiss ski resort of Villars, attracted students from across Europe. Its core values, though, were about as English as the county of Berkshire. Aiglon had a friendly English head, Philip Parsons, an English school church ('Worship Sundays at 6 p.m.') and an unflappable English matron. Victoria was due to start her first term at Aiglon the following day, Saturday. Jonathan Aitken had hoped to join his wife and daughter in Paris on Friday afternoon. They had originally intended to make a 'long weekend of it', he claimed. But Aitken was unavoidably delayed by the lengthy obsequies for General Sikorski in Poland. By the time he finally arrived at the Ritz, a majestic *fin-de-siècle* gilt palace looking out on a statue of Napoleon, it was 10 p.m. Victoria and Lolicia had already departed for Geneva.

Of course, in this shimmering alternative reality, Jonathan Aitken had always intended to pay his own bill at the Ritz Hotel. His Arab friend Said Ayas had booked the upstanding Conservative MP into the hotel for two nights. Ayas was himself staying in room 626/627. Aitken was in 526. Because Ayas had made the booking, Aitken's bill was wrongly debited to Ayas's account. When he arrived to check in, so the story goes, Aitken produced his American Express card but had it waved away by the receptionist who told him: 'That won't be necessary.' He put the card back in his wallet. Aitken later explained that he was suffering at the time from the kind of delusion which might have befallen the fictional sitcom politician Jim Hacker: the 'arrogant disease' of 'Yes Ministeritis'. 'I was addressed as "M. Ministre",' he told a hushed High Court much later. 'I thought perhaps grand hotels somehow greet guests who they think grand in this very respectful way.'

According to the alternative version of events, Aitken met up with his millionaire friend Said Ayas in a restaurant. The two men talked not about business but about Victoria's 'pre-school nerves'. Ayas informed Aitken that his wife and daughter had impulsively departed for Geneva earlier in the day. The hiatus was typical of the 'Murphy's Law syndrome' which 'prevailed all weekend', Aitken was to explain with a twinkle. After his exhausting schedule of 'flying and praying' the Minister of State for Defence Procurement was tired. He slept late the next day. He was roused by an excited telephone call from his wife and daughter. They had reached Aiglon College. Lolicia, whose Slavic origins made her prone to impulsive moods, announced she wanted to return to Paris that evening for a romantic dinner with her husband. Aitken then had a quiet day, he was to claim. He had lunch with Said Ayas in a bistro. A keen runner, he went for a jog in the Jardin des Tuileries, the grand rectangular park south of the Ritz Hotel. As he puffed along, Aitken would have passed the elderly *pétanque* players at the Place des Pyramides enjoying the weekend sunshine and the small boys at the round pond prodding their model sailing boats hopefully into the water with sponge-tipped rods. Aitken had a nap in the afternoon in his room, and did some reading, he explained.

In the early evening there was another despatch from the Aiglon front. Lolicia telephoned to say that Victoria was not settling at all well into her new school. She was the only English girl in her dormitory and felt 'lonely and overwhelmed' by the preponderance of Russian, Italian and South American girls. (She eventually lasted a term at Aiglon, before settling at Rugby.) Their romantic dinner, Lolicia told him, was off: she was feeling too tired. But she would get up, so Aitken was to claim, early the next morning and come back and join him at the Ritz on Sunday morning. 'She is a mildly eccentric creature of romantic, positive and negative, impulses,' Aitken said later of his ethereal wife.

The evening of Saturday 18 September 1993 was a dull one for Jonathan Aitken. Or at least in the convenient alternative universe he was to create it was. He sat alone in his room, with its gilt-and-marble fireplace, mock-marble minibar full of champagne, and pastel blue walls decorated with neo-classical bas reliefs of lutes and laurel leaves. He tinkered with the US edition of his biography of Richard Nixon. He sent down for a snack from room service, read for a couple of hours, and crashed out. Alone. The following morning he telephoned

Victoria, who said she felt miserable, and promised to see her later in the day. In the late morning Lolicia arrived at the Ritz. They met in the foyer and returned to Aitken's room, arms entwined perhaps. 'We had a happy husband-and-wife reunion and a good talk,' Aitken was to say mistily. Worried about his daughter, Aitken decided to depart for Aiglon as soon as possible. He set off at '1.30ish', leaving his wife behind steaming in the bath, according to his meticulously crafted narrative. Aitken took a taxi to the station, and was whizzed down to Switzerland by TGV. Mrs Aitken, meanwhile, finished her bath and had lunch with friends. Crucially, she paid her husband's hotel bill at around 3 p.m. at the Ritz reception. The following morning Lolicia had a doctor's appointment in Paris. A note purporting to prove it was later shown to the High Court. Model father. Model husband. Model minister.

There was only one problem with Jonathan Aitken's hyper-elaborate account of his stay at the Ritz during the fateful weekend of 17–19 September 1993, which he was later to ventilate at some length on oath: it was not true. A pack of lies, in fact. His wife never paid his hotel bill. She was never in Paris. She was never, even, in France. Neither was his daughter. There was no family weekend. Nor was there any model minister. Neither was Aitken quite the model husband, nor indeed the model father. Quite the reverse, in fact.

Jonathan Aitken had a much darker purpose as he took off on his Air France flight to Paris, sinking into his club-class seat as the plane flew over the Channel. When he touched down at 9.30 p.m. local time, he had no expectation of seeing his wife or daughter at all that evening. If they had turned up to greet him, he would have been flabbergasted. Aitken had come to Paris to see someone else. Prince Mohammed, the son of King Fahd of Saudi Arabia, was in town. For at least the last fifteen years Mohammed had been Aitken's generous Arab patron. Like other members of his retinue, Aitken had benefited financially from his association with the Prince. Money would flow from the Saudi royal to those around him as a reward for their services and loyalty, usually in the form of brown envelopes. Other members of the Prince's charmed inner circle were also in Paris. Said Ayas, whom Aitken was to paint, disingenuously, as just an old friend, worked as the Prince's business manager and right-hand man. Ayas had grown exceedingly rich through his association with the Saudi royal family. Wafic Said, a Syrian-born millionaire and Conservative Party donor, was also in Paris, although he insists he never met Aitken during that weekend. Wafic had been an intermediary in one of the world's largest arms deals: the controversial £20-billion agreement in 1985 to sell British Tornado fighter aircraft to the Saudi Government. Dr Fahad Somait, a director of the Prince's company Al Bilad whom Aitken also knew, had just checked out.

These astonishingly wealthy men were at the centre of the web of financial intrigue which surrounded the Saudi royal family. Every summer the Saudi élite would escape the heat of Riyadh and decamp to Europe's cooler capital cities. There, in luxurious surroundings, they would mix business with an awful lot of pleasure. In September 1993 this constellation of influential businessmen gathered together at the Ritz Hotel in Paris. The hotel had been restored into an opulent *belle-époque* temple and was popular with wealthy guests from the Middle East. The Arabs treated the gourmet restaurant as a canteen. The Prince, who had been occupying the £3,000-a-night royal suite at the Ritz, had moved out by the time Jonathan Aitken emerged into the futuristic perspex dome of Charles de Gaulle airport and jumped into a taxi. But he had not gone far. Prince Mohammed was now staying in his lavish family villa near by. His entourage, including Said Ayas, remained at the Ritz. Wafic Said, meanwhile, had taken over the Prince's royal suite while his own sumptuous apartments in Paris were being refurbished.

In the months leading up to Aitken's secret trip, the royal family of Saudi Arabia and its representatives had been involved in some truly enormous arms deals with Britain. The most recent Saudi contract to buy weapons from British private firms had been signed by John Major early that year, and was worth almost £5 billion. Another big potential deal, to sell off some British submarines to the Saudis for several hundred million pounds, was in the offing. These Saudi deals were very murky affairs. They were generally achieved by the arms manufacturers agreeing to distribute enormous secret bribes to key members of the large royal family and their favoured friends. The money, 20 per cent, or more sometimes, of the contract price, was sent to secret bank accounts in places like Bermuda, held in the name of mysterious companies anonymously registered in the British Virgin Islands. From there, the cash was moved to Swiss banks in Geneva, and disappeared. The total in 'commissions' on the most recent contract was in the region of £1 billion. The details of these stupefyingly large deals were generally kept secret from the British and the Saudi public.

What was odd about the trip to Paris in September 1993 was that Jonathan Aitken apparently felt the need to keep its purpose secret not just from the public but from his own colleagues. On the morning of Wednesday 14 September 1993, as soon as his Government car deposited him in Horseguards Avenue at Defence Ministry head-quarters, Aitken told his officials he was going abroad. As a minister with a security-sensitive post, Aitken was obliged to request clearance from his boss, Defence Secretary Malcolm Rifkind. Parliament was in session. John Major was himself about to embark on a six-day world trip to Japan, Malaysia and Monaco, aimed at bolstering his tenuous statesman-like credentials. The Whips Office, the Foreign Secretary and the security co-ordinator in the Cabinet Office had to be informed. One of Aitken's assistant private secretaries, Miss Kemp, apologized for what she called the 'extremely short notice' of the minister's trip arranged only 'this morning'. Aitken told Miss Kemp he was going on a 'private visit' to Switzerland 'via France'. His personal firm of travel agents, Commodore Travel, sorted out the tickets, which cost him £364. He was due to return, however, not from Paris, but Geneva.

While Aitken listened to a lengthy mass in Cracow Cathedral for the departed soul of General Sikorski, his wife and daughter were 35,000 feet above sea-level aboard a British Airways flight direct from London Heathrow to Geneva. Mrs Aitken liked flying. (She was later to be accused by her mother-in-law of spending her 'entire life' in airports and health farms.) Lolicia was taking her daughter to Aiglon College for the new term. At the arrivals hall of Geneva airport on Friday morning, other passengers might have spotted Victoria and her imperious mother wheeling a wobbling mountain of luggage towards the desk of Budget Rent-a-Car. Just after midday Mrs L. Aitken and Miss V. Aitken (the names on their flight coupons) set off in a hired Volkswagen Golf on a two-hour drive round Lake Geneva and into the mountains. At Villars they checked into the Hotel Bristol, a new four-star lodge that resembled a giant log cabin. That night, mother and daughter snugly shared a room at the hotel.

Back in Paris, Jonathan Aitken woke in the sumptuous surround-ings of the Ritz Hotel. His bill provides a few forensic clues as to how he spent his time. He had breakfast in his room. He handed over some clothes to the maid for cleaning. (It appears on his bill as 'Blanchisserie'.) Late morning he phoned his London home in Lord North Street and probably chatted to his other daughter Alexandra. The rest of the day is a mystery. In the evening he made several attempts to phone his wife at the Hotel Bristol. Eventually he got through. The Aitkens almost certainly had a late-night conversation about Victoria. Intriguingly, Aitken spent twenty minutes on the phone on Saturday evening to the Labour MP Diane Abbott at her home in Hackney. What they talked about remains unclear. As night fell over Villars, Lolicia Aitken tucked herself up in room 234 of the Hotel Bristol and nodded off, alone. She had asked for, and got, a reduction of 70 Swiss francs for 'single occupancy' of the room. Lolicia had always been thrifty about money; some might say mean. Later she would regret her parsimony. Meanwhile, in Paris, her husband did some damage to his minibar.

The next morning Aitken woke again in the Ritz. His wife was 500 miles away in Villars. At 10.15 a.m., her phone rang. It was her husband. To judge by subsequent events, they made plans for a rendezvous in Switzerland later in the day. Aitken also placed a call to his house in London, presumably to touch base with Alexandra. Before the day was out, Aitken finally achieved what one must assume had been his real purpose in coming to Paris. A call was put through to his room. He made contact with Prince Mohammed bin Fahd and, he was to claim, they had a private conversation. The likelihood is they had a face-to-face meeting. It had taken all weekend to bring about. The Prince was always difficult to pin down: he was a billionaire creature of whim, as Aitken knew well. In the past Aitken had spent hours waiting for the Prince to turn up, only to discover he had decided to play tennis instead. Unbeknown to most of his electors, Aitken had actually worked in the employ of the Saudi Prince since the late 1970s, 'fixing' for him as manager of the Prince's London office. Indeed, although MPs were required to resign all other positions on becoming Government ministers, Aitken's personal secretary still continued to work out of the Prince's office in Great Peter Street, just around the corner from Aitken's own house.

The fact that Aitken went to Paris to talk to Prince Mohammed was a secret. His officials did not know of it. No record of any kind was made about it by any of the minister's officials, before or after, although Aitken was to claim later that the conversation had been on legitimate Government business. Everything of note that happens legitimately in Whitehall is punctiliously written down. This was not.

On Sunday lunch-time, the Prince's party moved on. Aitken, who had been installed as part of the Prince's entourage, moved on as well. Minutes before he left, he phoned his acidic mother Lady Aitken at her glorified granny flat next to his home. The Conservative MP's bill – some 8,010 French francs or £1,000 – had been debited to Ayas's account but was ultimately paid for by Prince Mohammed. Later that afternoon one of the Prince's functionaries, the French assistant Manon Vidal, called round at the Ritz reception desk as usual and settled the bills for all of the Saudi royal group. The total cost of the stay was about £15,000. This was very small change for the Prince, who was prone to forget just how much was in his groaningly large bank account.

The Ritz files show that Aitken handed in his key at 1.54 p.m. The minister then probably got a taxi to the railway station at the Gare de l'Est and caught the TGV, the fast train, down to Geneva. In the course of the day Lolicia checked out from the Swiss hotel up in the mountains, paying as usual by American Express. After a tearful farewell with her daughter, she drove back round the lake to Geneva in the hired Golf. Victoria retired to her dormitory in Aiglon College, and penned the first in a series of homesick letters to her parents. These Aitken later calculated, with typical cynicism, might produce a 'favourable result' if read to a jury. Lolicia dropped off her hire-car in downtown Geneva at 6.25 p.m. That would have been just in time for a rendezvous between the Aitkens, who went off to stay the night at Said Ayas's luxury premises in Geneva.

Aitken rose at dawn on Monday 20 September and caught the 8.10 a.m. Swissair plane from Geneva airport back to London, where he resumed his ministerial duties with a bracing tour of military bases in Scotland. Lolicia stayed on in Geneva for much of the day and did not catch her own British Airways flight back to London until 6 p.m. At Heathrow, as usual, the immigration staff stamped Lolicia's passport with the date of her return: she retains her Swiss nationality, and that is one of its small inconveniences.

And so, the weekend was over. It had apparently passed off successfully, and as planned. The minister's secret mission had been accomplished. What he and Prince Mohammed so urgently needed to talk about remains a secret to this day. His trip was, however, quite clearly against the regulations governing ministerial behaviour. He had taken undeclared private hospitality from a foreign ruler. Furthermore, the ruler in question was someone with whom Aitken had a long and continuing commercial relationship. Even if Aitken had meticulously declared all his activities, his position would still have been unsatisfactory. To keep the meeting secret in the way Aitken had done was a resigning matter, were it ever discovered.

Unfortunately for the Minister of State for Defence Procurement, his discreet stay at the Paris Ritz had in fact been observed. The owner of the hotel had noticed. He too was an Arab, from Egypt: Mohamed Al Fayed. Fayed was a tempestuous character. Those who fell foul of him described a personality veering unpredictably between Father Christmas and a vengeful despot. The owner not only of the Ritz in Paris but also of the famous Harrods store in London, Fayed beamed around like a fairy godfather, showering his friends with presents and bribes. He also swore like a stoker, liked his wishes gratified on the spot, and bore grudges for a long time.

Fayed was fed up with the British Government for reasons of his own. He had also developed contacts with a British newspaper – the *Guardian*. It was not long, therefore, before he mentioned, obliquely, and very confidentially, to the *Guardian*'s then editor, Peter Preston, that he had seen a British Minister of the Crown consorting in Paris with the Saudis. Challenged about his actions as a result, Aitken was to spend the next three years piling lie upon lie.

He very nearly got away with the whole thing. For Jonathan Aitken's underlying premise throughout this astonishing saga was that, in modern Britain, a brazen and litigious liar with powerful friends can always defeat the efforts of investigative journalists.

It was one of the major lessons the 'Right Honourable' English gentleman in the beautifully cut Savile Row suits believed he had learned during what had seemed for years to the envious mortals around him to be a remarkably charmed life.

'Your father is a good man, but a dull man. You must stir up mischief.' **Lord Beaverbrook to his great-nephew Jonathan Aitken**

....

Two: **Mischief Maker**

The privileged spires of Eton College stand within a convenient twenty miles of London, watching over successive tailcoated generations of the British Establishment. It was the class of 1959 that included Jonathan Aitken, and here, among the charming lawns and the chapel, is a clue to the Aitken tactics that were later to work so gratifyingly well for him in the great wall game of life.

As a schoolboy Aitken and two friends, James Aykroyd and Micky Nevill, had a fine little wheeze involving Mr Starling, the local bookie. The boys would regularly meet him to place five-shilling bets on horse-races, something certain to cause consternation among house masters if they had known. The three often had to fake illness and rush out of lessons to meet 'their man at the racecourse' in time for the next race.

The young Turks thought they had a foolproof system called 'doubling-up your losses'. Whenever one of their horses failed to romp home first they would simply place double the bet on the next race until, eventually, if you had the financial stomach for it, a winner would come home and all debts would be cleared. The boys would regularly build up bets of £10, a small fortune for a teenager in the late 1950s, but Aitken was always keen to go further. Just one more bet. Just one more.

Jonathan William Patrick Aitken was born on 30 August 1942 in Dublin to a family straight from the pages of *Who's Who*. His maternal grandfather was Lord Rugby, a distinguished colonial civil servant. The son of an Italian shopkeeper, he had changed his name from Maffei to Maffey to sound a little more English. Lord Rugby used to send the young Aitken clippings from *The Times* with pictures of

Denis Compton and the latest cricket scores, a shared obsession. Play life with a straight bat, Aitken was earnestly, if fruitlessly, told.

Aitken's father was a Conservative MP, Sir William Traven Aitken. His mother was Lady Penelope Aitken, the daughter of the 1st Baron of Rugby, and the woman who in the future would defend 'her boy' through thick and an awful lot of thin. The cherry on Aitken's family cake was Max Aitken, his great-uncle. He was the famous Lord Beaverbrook, the millionaire Canadian media baron, proprietor of the *Daily Express* in its great days, and confidant of Bonar Law, Lloyd George and Winston Churchill.

Jonathan's start in life was unpropitious. At the age of three he was found to have tuberculosis of the lungs which had spread to his bones. The medical profession offered alternative diagnoses: 'This child may live but will never walk,' said one. 'This child will not live,' said another. He was saved by a Dr Macaulay of Dublin, who prescribed three years immobilized from head to foot in plaster, strapped to a crucifix-shaped board. Bedridden for long periods of time, his was a lonely existence. During the war Aitken's father had enlisted in the RAF and served as a fighter-pilot. In 1942 his Spitfire was shot down and he was severely injured. Aitken's mother spent long periods nursing her husband. Once, on her return, the young Jonathan failed to recognize her.

Aitken's slightly distanced manner, the good-humoured stoicism that seems to hover just behind his gaze, these are said to be the legacy of that ordeal. So, too, friends suggest, are the difficulties Aitken had in maintaining intimate relationships. 'It gave me a sense that the strains and difficulties of life could be overcome,' he said. 'And a certain patience and fatalism, and quite a deep religious faith.'

Back in England, Aitken was taught Latin, French and poetry by his grandfather Lord Rugby in a hut at the bottom of the family's Suffolk garden. The lessons were shared with his younger sister Maria, later to become a successful actress. Rugby would also teach the boy to catch by hurling a squash ball at him from behind an enormous beech tree. 'He made me believe that anything was possible,' Maria said later of their eccentric grandfather, who liked to read aloud the works of Robert Browning.

Eton was a logical choice for the gilded young Jonathan. This was a world of male arrogance, fetishistic floggings by both prefects and masters, and an education in the art of politics: the well-considered phrase and the elegant put-down. Oh yes, and that little wheeze involving Mr Starling. 'Admittedly, not everybody liked him,' said Sir James Aykroyd, the Eton friend and baronet. 'But I found his company most enjoyable. His interest in politics was already clear, he was a fine debater and became President of the Political Society.'

From the beginning, there was extreme self-confidence. Only the very senior boys in his house were allowed regular use of the library. Aitken and Aykroyd invited Tim Card, their private tutor, there to a tea of toast crêpes Suzette and a splash of wine. Card reported the boys for a flagrant abuse of house rules and they were barred from the library for several weeks. Aitken thought it all a jolly fun jape.

His talents shone. He was invited to join the Eton Society, the self-perpetuating élite of twenty boys whose brocade-trimmed jackets marked them out above the mass of 1,400 pupils. Aitken was in exalted company and was of it. Between the grey, slightly dog-eared covers of the book listing the members of the Old Etonians, his name appears after that of the Earl of Airlie, close friend of the royal family. A few pages further on appear the names of contemporaries Sir Ranulph Fiennes, the explorer, whom Aitken used to thrash as a prefect with a bamboo cane; David Gore-Booth, the future ambassador to Saudi Arabia; and Nicholas Bonsor, future minister at the Foreign Office.

Aitken moved predictably on to Christ Church, Oxford, to read Law. His father had fallen out with Beaverbrook over a business dispute. Boldly, Aitken wrote to the great man at Cherkley, his Surrey home, asking whether he might visit him. 'Come lunch Sunday. Beaverbrook,' was the reply. The old man warmed to him. Wracked by gout, his leg resting on a cushioned footstool, a neat swathe cut out of the side of one of his gleaming leather pumps to ease the pain, Beaverbrook would read Aitken passages from his three books about the intrigues of the Lloyd George era. 'Your father is a good man, but a dull man,' Beaverbrook confided. 'You must stir up mischief.'

Aitken was allowed to play in the corridors of power. During the 1962 summer vacation, he became speechwriter to Selwyn Lloyd, Harold Macmillan's Chancellor of the Exchequer. Lloyd, a repressed homosexual, was very taken with his new, young friend, who was already developing the looks a hundred profile writers in the future would describe as 'matinée idol'. Lloyd wrote him a series of affectionate letters.

While his Oxford contemporaries toiled away at less glamorous summer jobs of hop-picking and shop work, Aitken was invited to Chequers to discuss 'youth issues' with Macmillan over a spot of luncheon. One day Macmillan's private secretary, Tim Bligh, arrived at the Treasury and said to Aitken: 'My master has bad news for your master. I would like you to break it to him.' Lloyd was to be the most senior of seven Cabinet ministers sacked by the politically insecure Macmillan in his Night of the Long Knives.

Aitken replied: 'I think it's a disgrace. Bloody well tell him yourself!' He nursed Lloyd through the shock, taking him to Spain to recover. Two years later Lloyd appointed him his private secretary. By his mid-twenties Aitken was dining at the best Tory tables.

Macmillan's successor Alec Douglas-Home made Lloyd Leader of the House and Aitken was introduced to the new Prime Minister. Aitken showed a capacity for the Wildean riposte: he advised Douglas-Home that if Harold Wilson, the opposition leader, persisted in calling the Prime Minister 'the 14th Earl Home' then he should retort: 'No doubt he is the 14th Mr Wilson.' Douglas-Home loved it. The young man was noticed.

At the age of twenty he was asked by Randolph Churchill, the Conservative fixer, if he would like to contest the safe Tory seat of Sudbury, in the process breaking the rules on age qualification, as Aitken pointed out. Churchill thundered: 'Don't be a silly billy. Be steady on parade, these country bumpkins will take it.' Aitken politely declined.

At twenty-one the *Economist* had marked him out as one of fifty young parliamentary hopefuls whose success was essential to the nation's future. By the age of twenty-two he was romping around America with Michael Beloff (subsequently a distinguished QC) on a debating tour. The young men, one from the right of politics, one from the left, co-authored *A Short Walk on the Campus*, one chapter dedicated to sex, 'the most popular of the extra-curricular activities on the American campus', another to New York and another to race. No subject was too complex for these two young men, pictured on the back cover: one, Beloff, in casual light-coloured jacket with ruffled hair; the other, Aitken, in sombre overcoat with hair so perfectly combed the parting is as if drawn by a ruler.

'He was the boy who had everything,' wrote the journalist Hunter Davies of Aitken's 1960s life. 'Tall and handsome and charming . . .

The world was not simply at his feet but lying on its back, waiting and panting to be taken.'

At Oxford, Aitken was President of the University Conservative Association. Only one glittering prize was to elude him. He failed three times to win the presidency of the Oxford Union. A position, almost a position by right, had been denied him, and it rankled. 'It was class hatred, pure and simple,' he said later, remembering the speeches he had made while the audience booed and hissed and threw toilet rolls at him. 'It was unfair because my family is not aristocratic. They're parvenus if anything.'

Others were not so sure that it was simply a matter of class. 'He just wasn't liked,' said Tariq Ali, an Oxford contemporary who did make it to be president. 'He was always showing off. We regarded him as a thick rich kid. The old Tories regarded him as *nouveau riche*.'

Aitken's father succumbed to his wartime injuries and died in 1964, aged fifty-six. Jonathan was twenty-one. Six months before his own death the same year, Beaverbrook, a multi-millionaire, told the young man he was making his will. 'I've been thinking about you,' he growled. 'You're a very bright boy with a very bright future. In some ways you're the best of the bunch. I'm going to pay you the greatest compliment – I'm not going to give you a single cent.' He handed him £150, saying: 'Now here's your fare back to Oxford.'

The anecdote served Aitken well in later years, as he tried to paint himself as an entirely self-made man. Friends suggested his frenzied efforts to make cash came from an insecurity born of living a wealthy life with no Old Money. It is true that Aitken was surrounded by the wealthy Beaverbrook dynasty but was not quite part of it. Max Aitken's children, Maxwell and Laura, lived a life of sumptuous comfort, travelling between homes in Leatherhead, Surrey, a flat in central London and a yacht on the Isle of Wight. If Aitken wanted that life, and he did very much, he knew he would have to work for it.

In fact, Aitken was given more of a leg-up than he liked to admit. He often explained that a stock-market crash and high death duties had wiped out the family fortune and that when his father died he was left the rather trifling amount of £5,000. What he failed to mention was that he had also inherited property and business interests in Canada, including a substantial shareholding in some local newspapers in Quebec. He sold his interest and was in a comfortable-enough position by the early 1970s to invest £50,000 in a luncheon-vouchers business in Australia.

Aitken joined one of the family papers, the *Evening Standard*. Its editor Charles Wintour, who took a bleak view of nepotism, was surprised to discover he had hired a talented correspondent. The young, well-connected writer set off to gauge the pulse of swinging London in the 1960s. Aitken wrote his second book, *Young Meteors*, about the new generation poised to seize the reins of power. He picked out Norman Lamont, then at the Conservative Research Department, John MacGregor, head of Edward Heath's private office, and Roy Hattersley, a young Labour MP.

With a crashing self-confidence he devoted two pages to a group called the Honeycombs, but made only passing reference to the Beatles. Leon Brittan, David Frost and John Selwyn-Gummer, who were all put in to be flattered, may now be household names, but history has not been so kind to Garth Pratt or Jim Ramble. Aitken devotes a chapter to 'non-meteors' – the type of people you wouldn't bother inviting to parties. The vain subtext of the book was clear: its author Jonathan Aitken was the greatest meteorite of them all. 'A thin and vulgar book,' the critic Michael Davie wrote in the *Observer*, complaining of Aitken's 'premature worldliness'.

As the poet Philip Larkin dourly wrote of the liberated 1960s, sexual intercourse was invented in 1963. Aitken's contribution to the new era of sex 'n' drugs 'n' rock 'n' roll was a puzzlingly lengthy chapter on prostitutes specializing in sado-masochism. He also took LSD as 'an experiment' with *Evening Standard* medical journalist Dr Christine Pickard. They later slept together. Deploying his well-honed maverick streak he argued for the legalization of cannabis, signing an advert in *The Times* calling for laws on the drug to be relaxed. 'Having no particular interest in or liking for marijuana myself, I nevertheless find the case for legalizing marijuana for adults a convincing one,' Aitken wrote. In those heady times, many youngsters were throwing bricks at the police and preaching world revolution. Even Aitken, while at Christ Church, thought about dumping the family connection with the Conservatives, telling friends that 'somebody had to stop the rot'. He went so far as to consider joining the Liberals.

Christine Keeler, the famous call-girl who caused the resignation and disgrace of Conservative Secretary for War John Profumo, came to his book-launch party. It must have been a glorious period in a world 'waiting and panting to be taken'. Jenny Fabian, author and 1960s good-time girl, met him at a Young Conservatives talk:

I thought he was pretty racy in his pin-stripe suit and waistcoat, standing there on the platform, laying down the law on the changing moral codes of our new society. He took me to this boring restaurant. I had to listen to him going on about what he got up to at university, the menus he had eaten his way through and the fact that he had a fridge to keep his champagne in. By pudding he was talking about sex.

Later that night, back at his flat, he asked Jenny if she would like to be whipped with an electric cable and then tied her hands to the bedposts with the cord from his maroon silk dressing-gown. 'His body, which was white and amorphous, fell on me like a sack of dough,' she recalls, ungallantly. For the good-looking Aitken, sex was invariably available, if rarely a release.

He went into the glamorous new world of TV. For the extra exposure offered by the camera lens Aitken moved to Leeds for a job on *Calendar*, an about-to-be-launched news programme. After the first opening credits rolled and the lights had gone up on the young man from the south, Aitken greeted his audience in typical style: 'Hello world, this is Yorkshire TV.' It might have worked better had the set not fallen down around his ears.

The confident young presenter and Conservative candidate was soon on the documentary circuit, travelling to Nigeria to report on the bloody civil war which had been raging for two years. Aitken rapidly plunged into a typical drama of his own. His intrigues over the hopeless Biafran cause were to land him in the dock at the Old Bailey, and cost him his nomination he had won in 1967 for the safe Yorkshire seat of Thirsk and Malton, defeating Christopher Soames and Julian Amery. The Biafra affair was to reveal what was to become Aitken's most marked character trait – the way he told lies.

In December 1969 Aitken went to dinner with Major-General Henry Templar Alexander, a bluff figure who had served in Nigeria as a military observer. Alexander trusted the young Conservative candidate; the fellow had, after all, escorted his daughter to a dance. Over port at Alexander's baronial pile in Brandsby, Yorkshire, once the ladies had retired, the conversation grew heated. Alexander, a supporter of the Federal forces who were busy shelling the rebel Biafrans using British military hardware, handed Aitken a confidential report which showed that the Federal troops were on the brink of a breakthrough.

Aitken realized the report was explosive, for it also showed that Britain was arming the Nigerian Government forces to a greater extent than that admitted by Harold Wilson, the Labour Prime Minister.

Aitken photocopied the document, written by a British official at the High Commission in Lagos, Colonel Robert Scott. He sent it to his mentor Hugh Fraser, a Conservative MP who had taken a keen interest in the war, then dropped the original back at Alexander's home. Through his literary agent Aitken then sold the report to the *Sunday Telegraph*. The paper put the story on the front page under the stentorian headline: SECRET BIAFRAN WAR PLAN REVEALED: MUDDLE, CORRUPTION, WASTE.

The Nigerian Government was furious, and Colonel Scott was expelled. The police were called in to investigate breaches of the Official Secrets Act and Alexander was told that he would be interviewed. Aitken went to see the old man to try and smooth things over. Sitting in the drawing room, next to a blazing log fire, Aitken decided to shift the blame for the leak in a method that he was to perfect over the next twenty years. Hugh Fraser had given the report to the *Sunday Telegraph*, he lied. Unbeknown to Aitken, the wily general was secretly tape-recording their conversation.

Aitken was to admit he had indulged in 'private verbal subtleties' with the general, a term which would stand alongside future admissions of 'lack of candour' and 'dissembling' for what was simply one thing: not telling the truth. 'It never occurred to me that General Alexander would be such a superior exponent of the art of self-extrication,' Aitken wrote.

During his trial at the Old Bailey in London the facts of Aitken's 'private verbal subtleties' became clear. Fraser, a friend, had been put in the firing-line as Aitken tried to save his own skin. But fortune was to smile on Aitken. He was acquitted after Mr Justice Caulfield, unsympathetic in equal measure perhaps to the interests of the previous Labour Government and to the antique Official Secrets Act, said the act ought to be 'pensioned off'. With one bound, the deceitful young politician was free.

But the affair had already cost him the nomination for the safe Thirsk seat. 'Was he trustworthy?' local Conservatives murmured. Abruptly unemployed, Aitken wrote a self-serving account of the trial, *Officially Secret*. The book contains a plethora of words which may have later spun around Aitken's mind as he pondered his downfall. 'In the campaign against officialdom's credibility gap, the truth is the best weapon,' he wrote. 'If the results of this one battle cause an eventual victory in the war for freedom of speech against the dark forces of bureaucratic over-secrecy then the ordeal will seem very much worthwhile.' All Aitken's words. He just forgot their meaning once on the other side of the fence.

Not only did Aitken lie about Fraser's role in the Scott Report fiasco, he also had a notorious affair with his wife Lady Antonia Fraser. It was one of many relationships, as he cut a picaresque swathe through London society. The names of his girlfriends read like a list from an aristocratic wedding: Lady Charlotte Curzon, the blonde daughter of Earl Howe; Elizabeth Harrison, former wife of actors Richard Harris and Rex Harrison; Arianna Stassinopoulos, the Greek broadcaster and writer; Germaine Greer; Soraya Khashoggi, the ex-wife of the Saudi arms dealer Adnan Khashoggi; and, simultaneously, Soraya's maid.

'Charming but unreliable' was the envious verdict in the House of Commons smoking room as, having beaten John Wakeham and Michael Howard for the nomination, Aitken was finally triumphantly returned as Conservative MP for Thanet East in 1974, the seat whose voters were respectfully to return him for the rest of his political career. During the campaign in the Kent constituency he started sleeping with his 23-year-old secretary Valerie Scott. Another affair was with Jackie Leishman, a reporter with the *Guardian*. That he slept around seemed to be common knowledge, but each woman – like each voter in his loyal constituency – was convinced that Aitken found in them that certain something special.

One lady only was cold. Shortly after Margaret Thatcher became Tory leader in 1975, Aitken made a quip to a Cairo newspaper that he would later regret. 'I wouldn't say she's open-minded on the Middle East so much as empty-headed. She probably thinks Sinai is the plural of sinus.' *Private Eye* picked it up, and he was accosted in the Commons by Airey Neave, head of Thatcher's private office. Aitken offered to drop Thatcher a note.

'I'm afraid that won't do,' Neave replied. 'She wants a personal apology. She will be in the Members' Lobby at 10.15. She will be wearing a green dress.'

If the mother was impervious, then Aitken would try the daughter. He embarked on a romance with Carol Thatcher, more than ten years his junior. During the 1979 election campaign Carol Thatcher went to his constituency to knock on doors for her Lothario. As a piece of practical politics, this relationship misfired spectacularly for Aitken. In his mind the liaison with Carol did not exclude others: he installed a blonde of Yugoslav extraction, Lolicia Azucki, in the bedroom at his Phillimore Gardens flat. Shortly afterwards he married Lolicia, with distressing accompanying publicity for Mrs Thatcher's daughter. 'The man who made Carol cry,' as Mrs Thatcher reportedly put it, did not get any further for a long time in his dream of becoming Prime Minister. He was to spend the next thirteen years marooned on the back benches.

In business, however, Aitken appeared to be making a great deal of money. He and Tim Aitken, Beaverbrook's grandson, started a company to manage unit trusts, purchased a small bank from Jacob Rothschild, brought in some Saudi Arabian shareholders and in 1981 formed Aitken Hume, a financial-services group. Using secret Saudi money, the Aitkens also became major shareholders in TV-am, the breakfast-television franchise. Boardroom custard-pie comedies at TV-am soon hit the headlines. Aitken, faced with a commercial flop, engineered a ruthless coup. TV stars Peter Jay and Anna Ford were ousted. Ford was so disgusted by what had happened she famously threw a glass of wine in his face. Asked to review Ford's book, *Men*, Aitken subsequently barbed: 'Anna Ford handles her subject with such tedium that she emerges as the WPC Plod of Agony Auntville.' In one of his typically bad guesses, Aitken said of the Anna Ford spat: 'I live with it to this day. In my obituary far more space will be devoted to it than to me being Minister for Defence Procurement.'

Jonathan, again revealing a ruthless streak, soon ousted Tim as chairman of Aitken Hume. Tim Aitken later told friends he had got a 'knife between his shoulder-blades from his cousin', saying that Aitken was 'the last person I had expected it from'. But for Aitken, family ties counted for little. Only when the secret Saudi holdings in

TV-am were revealed in 1988, to the dismay of the TV regulators, was Jonathan Aitken himself forced to resign from the board. As with the Biafra affair and the Carol Thatcher affair, it seemed he had not been quite a gentleman. But, as usual, the long-term consequences were not at all serious. Aitken was the quintessential insider, who led a charmed life.

During the long Thatcher years, in which there was no realistic prospect of advancement, Aitken did not waste his political time. Over a wide range of subjects his non-conformist wit and in-depth knowledge marked him out as one of the most sparkling members of the Conservative Party. He built the oddest alliances; he opposed the poll tax, the Channel Tunnel, and Rupert Murdoch's take-over of *The Times*; he supported the reform of the Official Secrets Act, the tightening of abortion law, and televising the Commons. He fought incursions into press freedom and called for tougher controls on the security services, backing an inquiry into MI5's efforts to destabilize Harold Wilson. He called for more open government, saying that 'whistle-blowers' – those who leak Whitehall documents – should have a public-interest defence. His pair, the Labour MP Diane Abbott, no stranger to a little controversy herself, asked him to become the godfather to her child. The *Guardian* and the *Spectator* voted him Troublemaker of the Year and Back-bencher of the Year respectively, and he was described as a 'spot of life-enhancement on the back benches'. By now, Aitken was on a roll.

When Thatcher was deposed in 1990, and John Major became Prime Minister, Aitken's long wilderness years were soon at an end. A veteran Eurosceptic, his belated move into the Government was partly earned when he worked the Westminster corridors persuading anti-European MPs to vote in the Maastricht Treaty. In 1992, at the age of forty-nine, he was made Minister of State for Defence Procurement by a Prime Minister unexpectedly victorious at the polls. The appointment was welcomed by Saudi Arabia and defence salesmen looking forward to the £5-billion contract to supply more Tornado fighter aircraft due to be signed in Riyadh. But in Whitehall there were mutterings of consternation. Senior officials were well aware of his close association with the Saudi royal family and arms dealers; and knew that there was a clear potential for problems. Major, it appears, did not. Even Tory friends of Aitken said that they were mystified by the appointment.

But for this newly appointed master of his universe it was simply a step, admittedly delayed, on the ladder. Twenty years before, over dinner with his friends Joanna Lumley and Austin Mitchell at Yorkshire Television, he had detailed his life plan. Make a fortune, get into parliament, become a minister, become Prime Minister – with dates attached. So, there had been some blips – official secrets, TV-am, Carol Thatcher – but now he was back on track again. A successful tenure at the Ministry of Defence, big arms deals and an applauded defence review kept him rising in the clear blue sky. In July 1994 he was promoted to the Cabinet as Chief Secretary to the Treasury. The position came with another glittering bauble, the office of Privy Councillor, which allowed him to add the words 'Right Honourable' to his name. Up and up he went.

For the moment, Aitken's dubious connections and faint grasp on the truth were matters that floated beneath the surface. Aitken was a man at the height of his powers. His Westminster home at Lord North Street developed a reputation for lavish functions, with the blonde Lolicia revealing at least one talent, the art of the dinner party. Leafing through files which contained more than a thousand names from the world of politics, business and journalism, she would meticulously prepare seating arrangements, keeping records even of what the main topics of conversation were.

These were heavyweight events, one regular guest saying that some people appeared to be there 'just to show Aitken's pulling-power in front of his business contacts'. As convenor of the Conservative Philosophy Group, Aitken entertained an array of speakers including Lord Blake, the Conservative Party historian, Roger Scruton, the philosopher, Lord Rees-Mogg, the former editor of *The Times*, Henry Kissinger and Richard Nixon, whom Aitken first met in 1966. He also attracted the dog-like devotion of the journalist Paul Johnson, who fawned on him in the tabloids, describing him as 'charming, handsome, successful and rich'.

The Cabinet minister manifested a devout love for the Church of England, becoming churchwarden at St Margaret's, the Westminster church. There were those who suggested, given Aitken's *louche* private morals, that this must have been something of a façade, to help his standing in Conservative circles. Whatever the reason behind his discovery of God, certainly every brick – political, financial, social, spiritual – now appeared to be in place.

Yet the foundations of Jonathan Aitken's palatial house had been dug when he first encountered the Arab world, more than twenty years before. And those foundations were rotten.

Three: **Arabian Knight**

Twenty years before his clandestine visit to the Ritz, in the late summer of 1973, Jonathan Aitken attended a lunch in Paris which would change his life for ever. Over a glass of vintage Château Lafite Rothschild, perhaps, the thirty-year-old would-be financier was introduced to a Saudi prince wearing an impeccable Western suit, shirt and tie. Prince Mohammed bin Fahd spoke excellent American English, was fond of tennis, and had a weakness for chocolate cake – and women. He was especially keen on blonde ones. A year at the University of California, where the campus was full of nubile, unveiled girls, had whetted young Mohammed's appetite for life's more secular pleasures.

As the mustachioed grandson of King Ibn Saud, the conqueror of modern Saudi Arabia, the Prince occupied an exalted position in Saudi society. He was spoilt, self-centred and rich; but curiously devoted to his friend and 'business manager' Said Ayas.

Ayas was a dapper, rather elfin man with dark, mischievous eyebrows and a mop of thick black hair. In later years he would conceal his receding hairline with a baseball cap. He spoke French, English and Arabic, and hailed from a well-to-do family in Beirut. Ayas had abandoned his medical studies in Lebanon after more urgent business cropped up: helping the Prince spend his family fortune. Over the next two decades his assistance to the Prince would transform him into a multi-millionaire with homes in Houston, Paris, London and Riyadh and his own £20-million luxury yacht.

Ayas's friend Prince Mohammed had inherited most of his father's vices – tardiness, a love of gambling, blondes and fast cars. One hereditary fault was excepted – Fahd's chronic obesity. King Fahd was appointed Crown Prince in 1975 when the Saudi King Faisal was assassinated by a deranged nephew. Fahd, a man so fat that the steps down from his private 747 jet had to be specially reinforced to cope with his vast bulk, became King himself in 1982. 'Come and call on me in Riyadh,' Mohammed said to Aitken, after a friendly chat. The Prime Minister Edward Heath was on the brink of announcing an election in which Aitken would stand as a candidate, but he privately resolved to take up the Prince's offer as soon as possible.

Jonathan Aitken was not the first adventurer to be attracted to Arabia. In the early years of the century British explorers roamed its deserts in caravans and armies. Cartographers mapped the boundaries of countries hitherto known only by tribe and faith; while civil servants converted them by treaty into nation states. In the First World War, the British famously encouraged a revolt by tribes along the eastern shores of the Red Sea.

The myth of Arabia was cemented by T. E. Lawrence, whose romantic account of the uprising against the Turks and the Ottoman Empire during the First World War, *Seven Pillars of Wisdom*, became the stuff of legend. The Arab revolt led by Lawrence and Sherif Hussein of Mecca routed the Turks, Germany's sickly ally. In Lawrence's imagination, the vast Arabian peninsula, with its date groves and undulating deserts, its bitterly cold nights and searing days, became a grandiose synonym for purity, manliness, dignity and honour. 'We were a self-centred army,' Lawrence wrote, 'without parade or gesture, devoted to freedom ... a hope so transcendent that our earlier ambitions faded in its glare.'

But by the 1920s the British had sold out Lawrence's friends. They conceded domination of Arabia to Sherif Hussein's rival Ibn Saud, Prince Mohammed's satyric grandfather who founded the modern Saudi state in 1932, siring forty-two sons (and an unknown number of daughters) along the way.

With the discovery of oil in the same year, a more venal tradition emerged. Production took off after the Second World War. During the 1960s Arabia saw the real beginning of oil revenues which would turn the kingdom's deserts into a gurgling black lake of money. The country's rulers were persuaded that much of their new income would be wisely spent on Western guns, missiles, tanks and planes. Adnan Khashoggi, the son of a devout Muslim from Mecca whose father was physician to King Ibn Saud, made his fortune by brokering these huge arms deals, earning millions in commission. As a young journalist, Aitken visited the Gulf port of Abu Dhabi and saw at first hand the intoxicating impact of oil – and the greasing of palms. In February 1967 he wrote in the *Evening Standard*:

If you visit the only and hopelessly overcrowded hotel, where the cheapest room is £10 a night, the bar is packed with Klondike-like characters shooting big lines about the contracts they hope to win, spreading libellous rumours about anyone else who looks like a potential competitor, engaging in every conceivable form of intrigue and openly offering large bribes to local Abu Dhabians to act as middlemen.

The hundreds of Western entrepreneurs and traders who gathered at the Saudi trough quickly learned the one golden rule: to do serious business in the kingdom it was necessary to have a sponsor with influence. That meant one of the several thousand princes of the House of Saud, preferably one as close to the tight-knit ruling clique as possible. Some were educated sophisticates like Prince Mohammed; others were lazy incompetents. All of them expected a piece of the cake, through land, oil and contract commissions. Their personal extravagances became a byword in the West for Arab excess. Not surprisingly the poor Arab citizens despised them. While their rulers indulged in a sybaritic lifestyle, the unforgiving feudal state punished lower transgressors with amputations or public executions in a Riyadh open space that was blackly dubbed 'Chop Square'.

Between 1973 and 1978 Saudi Arabia's annual oil revenues soared from $4.35 billion to $36 billion. The country was awash with money, and resembled a giant building site. At the ports on the Gulf and Red Sea coasts, there were scenes of unimaginable chaos. Scores of merchant ships clogged up the harbours for months on end. Food rotted on quays; American helicopters were hired at extraordinary expense to off-load the cement ships; real-estate prices rivalled those in Manhattan. Western businessmen who failed to bribe their way into one of the few hotels had to pay $100 a night to stay in a doss-house, or $50 to kip down in the back of a taxi.

At the time of his useful meeting with Prince Mohammed, Aitken was keen to exploit this twentieth-century Klondike. In late 1972 he had joined Slater Walker, the eponymous merchant bank founded by Jim Slater, a chartered accountant turned financial whizzkid, and Peter Walker, a Conservative politician later to become Welsh

Secretary. Aitken had written fawningly about both men in *Young Meteors*. They, in turn, approved of his right-wing politics and thrusting parliamentary ambitions. Aitken joined the company as Slater's personal assistant. Slater had decided it was time to explore new possibilities in the booming Gulf. His motive was simple: greed. 'We wanted to get locked in to the oil money, to find a conduit to tap into that wealth,' he recalled. Aitken set about the project. At a cocktail party he recruited the Lebanese-born entrepreneur Naim Attallah, a consultant to Asprey, the London jewellers. Attallah's job was to take Asprey's exhibitions to the Gulf, and Aitken became his travelling companion to Kuwait and Abu Dhabi via Beirut. They set up an office in the Lebanese capital, then a sparkling Mediterranean playground, with Aitken as managing director of Slater Walker Middle East.

At the end of 1974, during the parliamentary recess, Aitken – now MP for Thanet East – flew to Riyadh to look up his new friend Prince Mohammed. He also called round at Said Ayas's house for dinner. Back home Aitken boasted of the 'valuable contact' he had made to his secretary and mistress Valerie Scott. Ayas was the door to Mohammed, Aitken realized. And Mohammed, who was rapidly earning a name for himself as a commission-taker *extraordinaire*, was the door to a huge pile of money. How could he ingratiate himself with Ayas? Aitken asked his secretary to buy a present for Ayas's newborn daughter May. Valerie Scott chose a blue rabbit. Jonathan then wrote the message: 'To match your beautiful blue eyes' on the card accompanying the rabbit, which was duly despatched to Riyadh.

Six months later Ayas's brother Mimo turned up at Aitken's Slater Walker office. He wanted to go to Cambridge to do an MA, but his American degree was not recognized by the university. Could Jonathan help? Aitken put his formidable charm to work, and Mimo was subsequently accepted at Downing College. Aitken's stock with Said Ayas soared. Here was a man at the heart of the British Establishment who could seemingly open a few useful doors himself.

By the middle of 1976, Jonathan Aitken was effectively on Prince Mohammed's payroll. Aitken had been laid off from Slater Walker as the firm became embroiled in a scandal surrounding its Far Eastern share dealings. Unemployed, the politician looked around for other ways of maintaining an upper-class lifestyle. The indebted Said Ayas offered Aitken a new job, working for Ramzi Sanbar, a fabulously rich Palestinian entrepreneur who had made his fortune in the Saudi construction business acting as Mohammed's 'agent' in Lebanon. In 1975, when warring Muslim and Christian militias started to shell downtown Beirut into rubble, Sanbar evacuated his busy company to London.

Aitken, an opposition back-bencher during Harold Wilson's second Labour premiership, installed himself in Sanbar's plush premises in the most famous street in Mayfair, Park Lane. The Arabs had long been obsessed with this now shabby quarter overlooking Hyde Park – with its prestige car dealerships, Arab banks and major hotels.

Sitting in a wood-panelled ground-floor office, with his feet up on a mahogany desk, Aitken must have felt a cut above his parliamentary colleagues, making do with cramped offices in the Gothic labyrinth of the House of Commons. There was a price, however, to this Faustian arrangement. From now on, Valerie Scott recalls, this junior Conservative back-bencher was obliged to do 'whatever' made the Arabs happy.

In the Commons, Aitken joined the British–Saudi parliamentary group, later becoming chairman, which offered the prospect of free travel to the kingdom. On his return from a trip to Riyadh, he spoke lyrically of the new concrete 'Eldorado' being built on the Arabian peninsula. 'I wish I had some interests to declare in this area, so fantastic are those opportunities,' he had trilled.

In fact Aitken developed plenty of interests to declare. But mysteriously these never found their way very clearly into the newly drafted Register of MPs' Interests. The Register required declaration of 'any pecuniary interest or other material benefit which a member receives which might reasonably be thought by others to influence his or her actions, speeches or votes in parliament'. Over the next two decades, Aitken was to treat this rubric in the spirit of cynical evasion.

The Register had been set up in the wake of the Poulson scandal. John Poulson, the Yorkshire architect, was at the centre of a web of bribery which included three MPs who had received financial favours. The Register was a response to a perennial problem in the supposedly incorruptible British House of Commons: sleaze.

Besides his salary and bonuses for his job as part-time chairman of Sanbar, Jonathan Aitken acquired a dark blue Jaguar XJ6. 'The Prince is buying me a car,' Aitken declared in May 1976, breezing into his Phillimore Gardens flat, where Valerie Scott was opening his constituency mail. A few days later the Jaguar arrived. An excited Aitken celebrated, as any boy would with a new toy, by taking the automatic for a spin round the block. 'Don't tell anybody the Prince has bought me this car,' Aitken confided to Valerie Scott. He was particularly anxious his constituents (whom he was to describe fondly as 'peasants') knew nothing of his sudden good fortune. 'Don't tell anybody at all,' he said. Gifts of expensive cars from princes to hangers-on were routine in those heady days. A joke doing the rounds in Riyadh was that princely Cadillacs were dumped when the ashtrays were full.

There were regal visits from Prince Mohammed bin Fahd bin Abdulaziz al Saud, to give him his full title. Like many newly rich Middle-Easterners, the Prince was enamoured of Britain. He liked its temperate climate, its quaint monarchy, its green parks and its high-rolling West End casinos. He liked Savile Row and Asprey. Most of all he liked the opportunities it afforded to let off steam 4,000 miles away from home, and the puritanical edicts of Riyadh's grim official Muslim sect, Wahhabism.

The Prince came to Britain five or six times every year, and stayed between ten and fifteen days. A keen tennis fan, he would also descend for Wimbledon fortnight. His entourage would wait at the airport, often for hours at a time, to greet him on his arrival. Hovering uncomfortably in the background was the British Member of Parliament: Jonathan Aitken. 'Jonathan would dance attendance on him,' Valerie Scott recalls. 'Jonathan would behave in an extraordinary way when Prince Mohammed was present. As a general rule Jonathan was very arrogant and liked to be in control. With Prince Mohammed he was not in control. Jonathan would always behave in a subservient way and do the Prince's bidding.'

During his visits, Mohammed would use the tall, thin block of Sanbar offices at 96 Park Lane as his London HQ. He stayed on the other side of Hyde Park at his lavish Knightsbridge home in Bolney Gate, while his entourage were accommodated in the Dorchester Hotel, a favourite Park Lane Arab-owned haunt. The Prince usually arrived at Sanbar's in the early evening. (He slept late.) His white Rolls-Royce, upholstered in blue velvet, would pull up on the cobbled forecourt. A retinue of followers would throng into the rather sombre office. It was always a moment of high excitement for Sanbar's staff. The office butler had laid in sandwiches and the Prince's favourite chocolate gâteau from a local patisserie. At the end of each visit Said Ayas would get out the envelopes. Sometimes it was £250; if the Prince was especially generous it might be £1,000 – the equivalent of three months' wages. The envelopes were handed out to everybody – the receptionist, butler and secretaries.

Eyeing their distribution was Jonathan Aitken, whose own much fatter *douceurs* were almost certainly handed over out of the gaze of prying lower staff. 'Jonathan took great interest in who received what,' Valerie said. 'I got the impression he was similarly rewarded by the Prince. It was Prince Mohammed's way of thanking those who worked for him.'

And Jonathan did work very hard to please his new master. He made efforts to ingratiate himself by learning the Arabic for 'your Royal Highness'. When Mohammed felt the urge to visit a private room at one of the West End casinos, Aitken would tag along, even though roulette bored him. Constituency commitments would be juggled around the Prince, and Aitken took advantage of pairing arrangements which meant he only had to vote in the Commons if there was a three-line whip.

Every summer Mohammed would decamp to his pink castle in Cannes decorated in a giddy Arabian style. As a key member of his entourage, Aitken would follow, somewhat resentfully, and put up in the Majestic Hotel near by. At the end of his stay the bill would be paid by Said Ayas, on behalf of the Prince. The pattern would repeat itself over the next two decades, to culminate in 1993 in the traumatic soap opera at the cash desk of the Paris Ritz Hotel.

Mohammed pulled off one spectacular coup which confirmed his reputation as the Arab world's Mr Commission. The Dutch telecommunications giant Philips had retained Mohammed as its local agent, knowing his father, Crown Prince Fahd, was the real power in the land. Philips was consequently invited to make a sole bid to modernize the creaking Saudi telecommunications network: a huge project. But the price of about £3.5 billion was six times that estimated by the Saudis' own consultants. Much of the preparatory work was done at the Park Lane offices of Ramzi Sanbar who acted as an adviser to the Prince, with Aitken at his elbow.

Rival US bidders – forbidden, nominally at least, by their country's laws to pay bribes – were furious. Fahd, faced with widespread protests, cancelled the bid in February 1977 and put the contract out to purportedly open tender. Although he had apparently deprived his son of an astronomical commission, Fahd was, however, not about to let him lose out entirely. Philips put in a revised bid eventually totalling £1.7 billion and were awarded the contract in December 1977. It was widely reported that Prince Mohammed was to pocket $500 million of this – still a tidy sum for a favoured son.

Among the jubilant Prince's gang in Riyadh that month was Jonathan Aitken. His euphoria, one can assume, was not for selfless reasons.

And there was more lolly to come. Local subcontractors were to be awarded £545 million of work. A good slice of that went to a company called Saudi Arabian Management and Engineering Research. SAMER just happened to be a joint-venture company between Prince Mohammed bin Fahd and Ramzi Sanbar. Aitken personally recruited British engineers for the job. His helpfulness knew no bounds.

In the booming Saudi Arabia of the 1970s it was a truth universally acknowledged that an Arab prince in possession of a large fortune must be in want of a jet.

During the summer of 1977 the British MP helped Mohammed buy the ultimate executive accessory: a private airliner. Fahd, the Prince's father, already had his own flying palace, curiously decorated in the style of a British manor house. His Boeing 747 jumbo even boasted its own tinkling fountain.

After lunch, at the Paris air show, Aitken introduced Mohammed to Sir Kenneth Keith, the chairman of Rolls-Royce, whose engines powered a used BAC 1-11 jet which was for sale. 'I'll have it,' the Prince said. Aitken's role was to fix up the purchase. The asking price was £3.5 million. Buying an aeroplane is no simple business, but Aitken put his contacts to work, finding two Old Etonian cronies: a lawyer, Mark Vere Nicholl, to help draw up the contract, and a peer, Lord Pearson of Rannoch, to arrange insurance. Aitken travelled on a proving flight to the Middle East, organized British Caledonian to supply the pilots, and personally interviewed and recruited some of the air-hostesses. 'They have to be blonde and beautiful,' he told a pursed-lipped Valerie Scott.

'Fix it,' the bored Prince would murmur at Aitken, when the plane required maintenance to rigid schedules: 'Fix it.'

This toil was all done, he swore to the High Court twenty years later, for not a single bean. However, Prince Mohammed's new toy was suitable only for short hops, not transatlantic flights, and was abruptly sold off after a couple of years.

In 1978, sitting on his growing petro-dollar mountain, Mohammed equally abruptly dispensed with the services of Ramzi Sanbar. The Prince decided to set up his own company in London, Al Bilad UK. 'Al Bilad' means 'The Nation'. Who better to run it, Mohammed thought, than Jonathan Aitken, the Prince's very own passport to the British Establishment?

Mohammed's love affair with Mayfair continued. He thumbed his nose at Ramzi Sanbar by having Aitken purchase a new office only fifty yards away from his old one. More than £1 million was lavished on the four-storey property. On 1 January 1979 Aitken became managing director of Al Bilad, with Mohammed as chairman. Said Ayas was appointed a director, together with Mark Vere Nicholl, Aitken's Eton chum, Sheikh Fahad Al Athel, one of the Prince's more sullen aides, and Dr Fahad Somait, a wealthy Saudi contractor.

With its neo-classical entrance pillars and oval upper windows, 21 Upper Grosvenor Street provided a grandiose base for a young MP rising rapidly in the opposition Conservative Party. Aitken took over the huge ground floor and used it as his parliamentary office. There were hidden perks for the MP, which never found their way into the MPs' Register. Valerie Scott, Aitken's secretary, was on the Al Bilad payroll. The rules allowed him to pocket almost all of his parliamentary 'secretarial allowance'. In a typically grasping gesture, Aitken would fill up with petrol at the Fountains garage in Park Lane before driving to his Kent constituency. The petrol would be charged to Al Bilad. When the invoices arrived Aitken, sitting happily in the splendour of his ground-floor office, would authorize the payment.

Jonathan Aitken acquired his wife through these Saudi connections. In 1977 Olivera Lolicia Azucki, Serbian by birth, now living in Switzerland, sold tacky trinkets to Middle Eastern princes, the same princes to whom Aitken was attempting to sell investment deals. Said Ayas's mother, Fariah, introduced Aitken to Lolicia as a friend from Geneva. At first Aitken showed little interest in this short, slightly dumpy, blonde-haired woman who used to barge into his office unannounced, hoping to make sales. More often than not he refused to take her calls. But Lolicia, who said she hailed from simple agrarian Slavic stock, was persistent. She avidly read the *Lady* magazine in an attempt to understand the finer points of British society. She whispered to him as they danced under the flashing lights of Annabel's in London that he was the man she was going to marry.

So, a courtship of sorts began. During the Christmas of 1977, when Aitken went out to Riyadh to see the signing of Prince Mohammed's telephone contract, he contracted typhoid. Lolicia was in the Middle East too, plying her wares. Sensing her moment, perhaps, she devotedly nursed the prostrate MP. When he recovered, they flew to Lausanne and skied together.

It was a big wedding. Lolicia, a woman who would later travel to Buddhist retreats for sixteen hours of prayer and a night spent sleeping upright in a wooden box to keep the body's energies flowing, stopped at little to make her way in life. Forensic reading of the *Lady* was supplemented by *Country Life* and *Brides*. She rang up *Harpers and Queen's* Jennifer's Diary to check on the intricacies of a society bash. She rang so many times they stopped taking her calls.

The wedding list was set up with an obscure silver firm near Sheffield. Friends would ring up Valerie Scott, who had been asked to help with the organization, and ask what was on the list for, say, £40. Valerie had been instructed to respond: 'Well, unfortunately nothing at that price, but there is a beautiful tureen at £50.' Having encouraged greater generosity from the guests Valerie would then ask for a cheque to be made payable to the Aitken wedding account, bank it and give the money to the Aitkens. Valerie said that she saw few of the presents.

Aitken may have hoped that the pews at St Margaret's Church in Westminster would be decorated with at least a few Muslim members of the Saudi royal family with whom he and Lolicia had done business, but none came. Even Said Ayas, the close family friend, did not make it.

Lolicia, though deferential to the political Great Man, was an odd choice of bride for Aitken. She readily admitted that she was a 'thick political wife' who knew little of British affairs of state. Dinner guests invited to their home at Lord North Street spoke of her as 'remarkably unappealing'.

But Lolicia certainly fitted familiarly into the Saudi milieu. She and Aitken also shared a common interest in money, of which their Saudi contacts had lots and lots and lots. All the Saudis with whom Aitken spent time at Al Bilad, as he was acutely aware, were far richer than he could dream of being.

Al Bilad, as run by Aitken, did many things for Prince Mohammed bin Fahd. Aitken shipped luxury goods to Saudi Arabia, especially the Prince's favourite Rolls-Royces and Bentleys. He came to own a total of ninety cars. When the Prince and his entourage arrived in London to let off steam Aitken arranged hire-cars, drivers and domestic staff. Some of the Saudis caught venereal diseases and needed medical appointments. Aitken's duties included looking after the rapidly extending list of properties bought by Mohammed and his cronies. Mohammed acquired two mansions on 'Millionaire's Row' in Hampstead, close to Kenstead Hall, the huge pile owned by his gigantic father.

More substantially, Al Bilad acted as a sponsor and commission agent for companies large and small wanting to do business in the kingdom. One British businessman, working for a US company, was told to contact Al Bilad to discuss details of a contract. Coolly, Aitken told him that no state contract in the kingdom was ever awarded without a backhander being paid to a member of the royal family. Al Bilad's own commission fees were 15 per cent, he explained. The businessman quickly formed an opinion of the dashing MP. 'A working man can quickly spot a spiv a million miles away. He was incredibly rude to people who worked for him and obsequious to the Arabs. He was like their messenger boy.'

It may never be possible to uncover exactly what personal benefits Aitken received from his generous Arab patrons. There is no dispute that he received plenty of flashy watches – a traditional Saudi gift. A Rolex encrusted with jewels can be worth thousands. There were London jewellers well-used to turning such presents into cash. They were merely bagatelles, however.

It was no coincidence that the young MP and his wife Lolicia were soon able to buy a place of their own. In 1980 he moved out of his self-contained second-floor flat in his mother's Kensington mansion in Phillimore Gardens and into a four-storey Georgian town house in Connaught Square, on the edge of Mayfair's Grosvenor Estate and within walking distance of his parliamentary office. The property's £183,000 price was mysteriously covered by a Northern Rock mortgage of only £25,000. Lolicia and Jonathan then lavished £50,000 on improvements. A year later, while 39 Connaught Square was still on the market, the couple bought one of the most exclusive properties in Westminster, 8 Lord North Street. In the shadow of the House of Commons and Conservative Central Office, the small row of eighteenth-century town houses was traditionally the preserve of elderly Conservative grandees. As a launch pad for a glittering ministerial career, Lord North Street could not be bettered.

Aitken's parliamentary colleagues must have been mystified and envious. How could this 38-year-old back-bencher afford it? By November 1981 Aitken had quietly paid off most of a £200,000 loan used to buy the Queen Anne house. The inevitable suspicion remains that Aitken, like the other people in the Saudi royal family's charmed circle, was hugely rewarded for his services and loyalty to them.

In 1987 Aitken acquired perhaps the grandest property of them all, the White House in Sandwich, in the genteel heart of his Kent constituency. The large detached house, bounded by sea defences and high walls, rates high in exclusivity and snobbishness. The property overlooks the golf course of Royal St George's as well as the Channel; to get there the *hoi polloi* have to pay a £3.50 toll to traverse the private roads. Occupancy of the £500,000 house, Aitken was later to claim, was 'a gift' to his wife and children from the true owner – Lolicia's generous Serbian grandmother.

Investigation reveals that the White House is in fact registered as owned by a Panamanian company, Hipper Real Estate, administered from the lawyer's office of Aitken's Al Bilad associate, Mark Vere Nicholl. Panamanian companies, the beneficial ownership of which is concealed, are traditionally used by the wealthy to obfuscate their more unsavoury business dealings. How an elderly woman living under a poor Communist regime managed to accumulate enough money to buy a sumptuous property in England via a Panama company, Aitken has never explained.

Once the London office of Al Bilad had been set up, Aitken cast around for investment projects which might separate the Prince from more of his painlessly acquired millions. He had already persuaded Prince Mohammed to sink a couple of million into sponsoring the

Frank Williams motor-racing team. (Another Old Etonian chum of Aitken, Piers Courage, had driven for Williams.) Happy times beckoned for the Prince and his friends at Brands Hatch, watching the Al Bilad logo flash by on the side of racing cars, in the company of glamorous young women.

Now, a row over a controversial TV drama-documentary, 'Death of a Princess', was brewing. The programme depicted the executions of a Saudi princess and her lover for adultery. Princess Misha'il had been shot dead while kneeling on the ground of a Jedda car park in 1977. Her Lebanese boyfriend Khalid Muhalhal was beheaded. The Saudi royal family hushed up the affair, claiming that the Princess had died in a 'swimming-pool accident'.

Screened in March 1980 on commercial TV, the film caused a mighty diplomatic row, with British ministers – Lord Carrington, the Foreign Secretary, in particular – grovelling in their apologies. The incensed Saudis threatened economic retaliation and embarked on an expensive campaign to try and buy influence in the British media.

This coincided with the Independent Broadcasting Authority inviting bids for a series of new commercial-television franchises. Jonathan Aitken had the chance to take part in one consortium which bid unsuccessfully for his old stamping-ground, Yorkshire TV, and another which was to go on and win the breakfast franchise, TV-am.

He persuaded his rich Saudi friends to stump up £2 million. The investment, he told them, would lead to some influence over the belligerent Western media, as well as large profits. While Parliament sat in February 1981 Aitken secretly flew to the Saudi capital to organize the cash. It was personally couriered by the Prince's bagman Fahad Somait in a bearer cheque from the Prince's account, to be deposited in a bank in Switzerland. From there, as soon as Aitken signed a series of agreements promising the Saudis he would promote their interests at the new TV station, the funds were released to another bank account in Amsterdam. There they were used to finance an Aitken company set up in the shadowy Caribbean tax haven of Curaçao. This company, in turn, put up 15 per cent of the cash for TV-am.

When the station launched with its shouted slogan 'Good Morning Britain!', it might thus have been more truthful to have cried: 'Good Morning Netherlands Antilles, Union Bank of Switzerland and all in Riyadh!' Except that few at TV-am, and certainly not its first chairman, the distinguished journalist Peter Jay, had any idea where the cash originated. 'I was given the impression it came from cutting down a Beaverbrook forest in Canada,' Jay now recalls.

Aitken – tongue in cheek no doubt – promised Prince Mohammed that his company, Aitken Telecommunications Holdings, could make a series entitled *Father of His Country*, which would help repair the tarnished image of the Prince's family. Among the great rulers who would be profiled – Churchill, Gandhi, Tito – was his grandfather King Ibn Saud, the lubricious founder of the Saudi state.

The TV-am saga demonstrated Aitken's mendacious business methods – and his ruthlessness. The secret Arab stake directly contravened rules which prevented non-Europeans from controlling British TV stations. Aitken knew this; but said nothing until he was found out six years later. TV-am, first transmitted in February 1983, lurched from disaster to disaster. As ratings plummeted, Aitken plotted a coup with his cousin and fellow investor Tim Aitken. With the support of institutional backers he temporarily took over as chief executive, ousting the cerebral Peter Jay. The IBA, dismayed at Aitken's presumption, forced him to resign as chief executive because he was a Conservative politician and hence scarcely politically impartial. Of the greater conflict of interest – that he was in the pocket of the Saudi royal family – the IBA continued to remain innocently unaware.

Aitken continued on the board: the ructions at TV-am abated, and the cartoon character Roland Rat gradually hiked up the ratings. But Aitken was to treat his own cousin Tim with ruthlessness at Aitken Hume. After a series of disastrous investments and an unwelcome take-over bid, Tim and Jonathan had a catastrophic falling out. Aitken ejected Tim from the board. In his place, a discreet Syrian-born entrepreneur Wafic Said emerged as a major new investor. He was to figure prominently in Aitken's later fortunes.

It was not until February 1988, when litigation between the two cousins was finally settled, that Tim Aitken got his chance to take revenge for his ousting. He leaked the existence of the secret Saudi stake in TV-am to the *Observer* newspaper. Aitken was made to resign from the board and airily apologized to the Independent Broadcasting Authority whom he had duped, for his 'lack of candour' – another synonym for lying.

Aitken was to tell many lies, too, about a further intriguing business interest funded for him by the Saudis. This was a Berkshire health farm called Inglewood, around whose doors in the 1980s a tantalizing whiff of sexual intrigue was to swirl.

GWENDOLEN Personally I cannot understand how anybody manages to exist in the country, if anybody who is anybody does. The country always bores me to death. **Oscar Wilde, The Importance of Being Earnest (Act I)**

'Why anyone should get the slightest pleasure out of having pain inflicted on them is a mystery to me.' **Jonathan Aitken, Young Meteors**

....

Four: **Inglenookie**

I n a sleepy corner of Berkshire, surrounded by fields of English wheat and softly lowing cows, an elderly Saudi sheikh was growing restless. The pleasures of the country were beginning to pall on him. Since arriving at Inglewood Health Hydro a few days earlier, the sheikh had not felt the urge to wrap himself in warm Breton seaweed or soak in the hydro's soothing peat bath. These pleasures were left for other residents. The prospect of having his skin exfoliated (or bikini line waxed) held little allure for this Arab gentleman of senior years. Nor did he want to have any part of his body electrolysed.

While female guests were happy to plunk a ball around Inglewood's sloping tennis court or stroll through its terraced garden, the sheikh preferred to stay inside Inglewood's luxurious thatched VIP villa, Falcon Lodge. The nearby village of Kintbury, where Jonathan Aitken would worship ostentatiously on Sundays, held little interest. As a strict Muslim, bell-ringing or brass-rubbing were clearly out of the question. Sketching Kintbury's canal – with its pleasure boats, ducks and trembling poplars – might have killed a few hours. But the sheikh did not sketch. He had fled the baking heat of Riyadh in the summer of 1981 for the cooler climes of Europe and now found himself trapped in a cavernous country house, tapping his fingers.

Jonathan Aitken, the man who had brought the sheikh to Inglewood, was anxious to stay his departure. The middle-aged British women who booked into this temple to Narcissus kept Inglewood's economy going, it was true. But it was 'the Arabs', as Aitken disparagingly referred to them, who were the big spenders. Some of them would pay up to £5,000 a week. If the Arabs wanted extra diversions, such as fruit machines or horse-riding lessons, these could be laid on – at a price. The bill would be bumped up accordingly. The Arabs rarely complained. They simply paid up and moved on. Limousines would arrive and they would be whisked back down the M4 to London, an hour away, to visit more stimulating Mayfair haunts. Their leisurely summer peregrination would then continue, and the entourage with its luggage would fly on by private jet to Cannes, Geneva or Washington.

But what to do about the listless sheikh? Jonathan Aitken, who had helped his Arab friends to buy the health hydro secretly the previous year, decided it was time to act. He picked up the phone and spoke to Robin Kirk, a whiskery New Zealand-born osteopath who had worked as Inglewood's principal since June 1976. Kirk was sitting in his consulting room. It was mid-morning. The sheikh, Aitken explained, was restless. He was considering leaving at the end of the week. Would it be possible to find some 'girls' for him, to entice him to postpone his departure?

'It was quite clear he was referring to prostitutes,' Kirk recalled later. 'I was surprised that he should ask me and replied something along the lines of "Where would I find girls in this area?"' Aitken then suggested Swindon. 'I said I would not know how to go about finding girls and I refused to help. Although I was surprised that Jonathan had asked me, I was not altogether surprised by the nature of his request,' Kirk said. 'I gathered from previous conversations with him his attitude to sex was fairly relaxed.'

Robin Kirk was not the only member of Inglewood's management team who was asked by Aitken to procure call-girls in an attempt to avoid any pastoral ennui on his Arab visitors' part. Jo Lambert, Inglewood's matron, recalls a visit by a pleasure-seeking prince and his entourage in the early 1980s. Aitken wanted his Arab guests to have fun. In advance of their arrival, he asked Jo Lambert to transform one of the rooms in the VIP house into an amusement arcade. She installed one-armed bandits for her guests and made arrangements for the Arab party to go riding. The health hydro was fully booked. The corridors buzzed as linen was changed. Residents padded back to their rooms from the heated indoor swimming pool in pink towelling dressing-gowns.

Aitken then phoned back with another, more unusual, request. 'He asked me how everything was going and then, out of the blue, he asked whether I knew any girls I could get for the Arabs,' Mrs Lambert said. 'I understood that he wanted me to provide prostitutes for them. There could be no misunderstanding. I told him that I did not know any "girls" but if he needed them, he should bring them with him.' She then let fly with a riposte worthy of Lady Bracknell. 'I said "Where am I going to get girls in the middle of *Berkshire*? Do you want me to put an ad in the *Newbury Weekly News*?" To which he made no reply, I'm afraid.'

These initiatives by the managing director of Inglewood did not exactly constitute 'pimping', as he was later rather frothily to complain was the charge being laid against him. Pimps take a cut of prostitutes' earnings. 'Attempted procuring' would have been more appropriate a term. It may have been no more than a host thoughtfully providing all possible diversions for his millionaire guests.

Two nurses who worked at Inglewood at the time corroborate this extraordinary story. Melanie Collins, a nursing sister, recalled how Mrs Lambert came into the Inglewood office after her conversation with Aitken in a 'most agitated state', storming: 'Who does he think I am?' Jo Lambert explained what the back-bench MP had just asked her to do. The joke then went round Inglewood staff that some of the 'young and attractive' beauty therapists might consider earning extra money by offering their services to Arab guests. Another dismayed nurse, Jane Leadbeater, recalled how she discussed Aitken's request with her colleagues over coffee. Ms Collins said: 'We tried to make light of it, but that was because we felt shocked.'

It was in the 1970s that Lolicia Azucki first started to appear at Inglewood. The 31-year-old Lolicia would regularly spend long weekends there. Staff remember her as a 'pain' who would drive them 'absolutely insane' with her demands. The future Mrs Jonathan Aitken was a fanatical enthusiast for Inglewood's many alternative therapies and would embark on a round of treatments: massage, sauna, Slendertone, mud pack, osteopathy, steam cabinet, manicure, facial and pedicure. She was preoccupied with her weight, and would fast on a gruesome diet of lemon and water six times a day.

Before motoring back to London on Monday morning, however, she would often pop into the then owner's office for coffee. Lolicia had another, more venal, reason to make the most of the facilities: she was being paid commission by the management in return for introducing wealthy Arab clients to Inglewood. Her own bill was heavily discounted.

Another of those new clients she regularly brought down to Inglewood was the handsome marathon-running figure of Jonathan Aitken, clearly open to being persuaded that his lithe body was a temple. In 1978 the *Daily Express* spotted Aitken at Inglewood and described how the 'lusty Tory MP' whose philandering was well known had shared a room with Lolicia. 'She's just a girlfriend. Nothing more,' Aitken told the *Express* coolly.

This former nineteenth-century seminary, once used by monks of the De Salle order, had been converted by an Armenian textile magnate into an affordable version of the upper-crust health farm Champney's. Manoug Nicolian, the owner, was a charming wheeler-dealer, with a dash of Del Boy about him. He had recruited Robin Kirk and Jo Lambert, then a nurse, when his previous director grew too fond of fine wine. Nicolian worked at his PR in *Vogue* and other magazines, and bookings gradually took off. When celebrities like Joan Collins or Valerie Singleton visited, he would fire off a press release.

But it was a visit from a fabulously wealthy Arab princess, Princess Nura, in 1978 which transformed Inglewood's fortunes. The Princess and a party of five, including her personal doctor and son and daughter, booked into the royal suite and stayed for several weeks. They spent lavishly – on treatments and in Inglewood's fancy boutique. Word spread among the Saudi community that Inglewood was a congenial place to stay where overweight Arab wives could discreetly shed a few pounds. Nicolian decided to consolidate his new client base by building Falcon Lodge, the five-bedroom villa in Inglewood's grounds in which the elderly sheikh would yearn for home and the desert.

By 1980 Manoug Nicolian decided to sell Inglewood and move on. Jonathan Aitken, well on the way to becoming the *de facto* MP for Riyadh West, agreed with Robin Kirk that 'the Arabs might be interested in it'. They were. After a year of negotiations, the site where the lascivious Henry VIII had courted his third wife, Jane Seymour, was bought by Prince Mohammed's front men for £1.3

million. Three Al Bilad directors secretly stumped up the money in May 1981: Dr Fahad Somait, the Saudi businessman; Fahad Al Athel, his dour colleague; and Said Ayas, Prince Mohammed's right-hand man and Aitken's pal.

The registered owner was now a company called Finchley Holdings. Despite its English sound, this company was registered in Panama where the secret of its true control remained far from prying eyes. The new Inglewood notepaper gave the impression that 'managing director' Jonathan Aitken was behind the health farm, not the Arabs.

Once the transaction had been completed Jonathan and Lolicia enjoyed Inglewood's lavish facilities for free. Like the car, the petrol and the magnificent watches, these benefits never found their way into the Register of MPs' Interests. The parishioners of Kintbury were also none the wiser about the health farm's new owners. There was a good reason for this: Aitken flagrantly lied about the acquisition to the local newspaper.

After getting wind of the change of ownership the *Newbury Weekly News* despatched reporter Mike Beharrell to talk to the dashing Tory MP about his business coup. The paper described Aitken as 'the proud new owner of Inglewood Health Hydro at Kintbury'. 'I am really a health-farm buff and believe very much in the type of treatment they do here,' Aitken declared. The epitome of public-school charm, he posed for his photograph in front of the mansion.

The photo was duly captioned: 'Master of all he surveys.' Aitken also falsely told the paper that two 'London businessmen' had helped bankroll his successful bid: Tim Gibson, the MP's grim-faced accountant; and Mark Vere Nicholl, the blue-blooded Eton chum who worked as his solicitor. The episode was a classic example of Aitken's *modus operandi*: he would distance Arab investment from outside eyes while depending on it secretly.

In the High Court Aitken resorted to the kind of twinkling verbal sophistry that had served him well in the past to brush away the Inglewood affair. 'There is no doubt I dissembled about my role, for reasons that seemed valid at the time,' he said. The reason for the 'dissembling' – that Inglewood's market resale value would fall if the identity of its real Arab owners was revealed – was entirely spurious.

Those who worked at Inglewood back in the early 1980s observed that Prince Mohammed's relationship with the biddable Tory MP was one of master and servant. Aitken was the servant. It was also apparent to staff that he was uncomfortable in this role. In the summer of 1981, on the occasion when the Prince graciously visited the hydro for Sunday lunch with his cousin Prince Saud bin Naif and a party of other Arab guests, he was shown around the five-bedroom VIP house, with its garden and inviting whirlpool bath. 'I noticed that Jonathan sat very much apart from the others and appeared to be glowering. He was not part of the entourage,' Robin Kirk recalled.

On another occasion an old Arab gentleman dropped in for tea at Falcon Lodge. 'I remember Jonathan standing in the corner of the room with no involvement in the conversation. It was clear that he did not want to be there and felt uncomfortable,' Jo Lambert said. 'He told us to respect the important Arabs – that they were like the royal family and should be treated as such. I got the feeling that he was treated as a servant by them. If they rang up and told him to pick them up and drive them anywhere, he would do it. He was extremely deferential.'

For eleven years until he was promoted to the Government Aitken took a managerial interest in the running of the health farm. Many of his Arab friends stayed there. Few of his Kent constituents could have been aware of his devotion, although he was to claim his duties as a director were 'not time-consuming'. He was in regular contact with Jo Lambert and her successor Maxine Metcalfe, who ingratiated herself with Jonathan Aitken by calling him 'Sir'. He personally answered letters of complaint and signed wage cheques. He even paid the yoga teacher. When the management of the hydro changed hands in the 1990s, it was Aitken who personally assured staff that their jobs were safe.

But by then a ferocious dispute with Jo Lambert and Robin Kirk had terminated their relationship with Aitken. It was a row which was to provide him with useful ammunition for the future, when Kirk and Lambert were to join a lengthy line-up of witnesses Aitken needed to find a way to discredit.

Sitting in the oriental splendour of his Upper Grosvenor Street office as the Arabs' new manager, Aitken had promised to pay Kirk and Lambert a generous end-of-year bonus. No contract was ever signed because, Aitken explained suavely, 'the Arabs don't give contracts'. By the time the payment was due, Aitken denied any knowledge of the conversation.

Kirk and Lambert were furious, but events were to overtake them. Police were called in to investigate allegations that Jo Lambert had stolen towels, linen, videos and furniture from Inglewood. Aitken then dismissed the couple, even though no charges were ever brought, thus saving himself a tidy sum.

After Kirk and Lambert's departure, Inglewood never quite managed to shake off its association with tarts. In 1987 the *Sun* claimed Cynthia Payne, the notorious jolly madam who inspired the film *Personal Services*, had visited. The paper dubbed the hydro 'Inglenookie'. Cynthia claimed she had merely gone there for a rest when she was feeling tired.

Three years later there was more farce. Two respectable Berkshire ladies, Eve Williams, a former hairdresser, and Mary Baldry, who runs a taxi firm, booked into Inglewood for a fortieth-birthday treat. They had intended to stay four days and enjoy a pampering break away from their husbands Robin and Rex. The exercise bike and the prospect of losing a bit of weight beckoned. On the second night of her stay, however, Mrs Williams woke up in the early hours to find her whole body 'smothered' in bugs. 'I ripped my nightie off and ran into the shower only to find that the flannel was covered in bugs, too,' she recalled. She threw on a T-shirt, roused her friend Margaret from slumber and marched down to reception. It was 2 a.m. There, Mrs Williams was greeted by a curious sight: a short, heavily overweight woman 'done up to death' in a black dress and chiffon scarf with her hair 'piled up'. She was sitting round a 'little table' in the reception area with four other heavily made-up and bejewelled girls who had squeezed into gaudy evening dresses. They all had 'neat-looking' mobile phones. 'As we passed I heard one of them say: "You're on the same game as us then?" Another said: "Are you going to join us girls, or are you doing a moonlight flit?"' Mrs Williams recalled with a shudder.

The dumpy madam plying her trade at Inglewood in May 1990 was none other than Lindi St Clair, the publicity-seeking prostitute who enjoys the tabloid sobriquet 'Miss Whiplash'. Ms St Clair, whose HH breasts weigh a stone each, claims – improbably – to have led a host of MPs through her 'dungeon rooms'.

Ms St Clair had first visited the hydro the previous year when she stayed in a luxury suite. She returned the following year – dragging two video machines, a video camera and a personal computer with her – and set up camp in room 15, overlooking Inglewood's leafy grounds. By day she tapped away at her autobiography; by night she mixed sex tapes and entertained her Arab and Bulgarian clients with leather hoods and clanking chains.

On her second visit, Ms St Clair brought several other prostitutes with her. She booked in under the name 'Lady Laxton', an aristocratic title she had picked up at auction amid great publicity. Lindi is not the most reliable of sources; and yet there is firm documentary evidence to show she stayed for several weeks. She was eventually thrown out. 'The deal was that I would go out there, posing as a regular guest, and supply sex to the Saudis and their associates,' Ms St Clair claims. 'As madam I took half the money from the girls. I would charge a fee of between £200 and £1,000. I made the fees up as I went along. Some girls stayed there under different names and some girls came down just for the day.'

The topic of Inglewood was to lead to one of the more subterraneously comic exchanges during Aitken's High Court libel case. George Carman QC asked Aitken dryly: 'Have you found over the years with your long and detailed knowledge of the Arab community that it contains those among its members who might seek the pleasure of escort girls while they are in London?'

Aitken replied: 'If they ever did, they didn't bother me with this aspect of their lives.'

In fact, prostitution – and the use and abuse of women – was at the heart of Aitken's curious connections with 'the Arabs'. After his eventual downfall there was to be some pompous moralizing in the right-wing press to the effect that a man who philandered in his private life could be expected to misbehave in his public role as well. It is perhaps more to the point to examine the ways in which Aitken and his Saudi paymasters, with whom he rubbed along so well, shared certain strange attitudes towards sex.

Call-girls held a bizarre attraction for Aitken, who, behind a courtly manner, practised a casual amorality. They allowed him to indulge in a peculiar upper-class addiction which some of his ordinary girlfriends were reluctant to share: sado-masochism. Aitken's enthusiasm for beatings was an unsurprising legacy from his days at Britain's finest public school. 'I once asked Jonathan how he had begun this interest and he said it was at Eton,' his former secretary Valerie Scott recalls.

'He would do things to invite a caning from the prefects, having discovered how much he enjoyed it.' As a prefect himself, Aitken also administered punishment with a long bamboo cane.

The athletic Conservative MP expressed a long-standing personal interest in prostitution as far back as the 1960s. He interviewed eight girls 'earning from £5,000 to £26,000 a year' for his book *Young Meteors*, written when he was twenty-four. In *Young Meteors* Aitken writes knowingly of 'correction', which he categorizes as a 'vice peculiar to Englishmen'. With typical disingenuousness, Aitken expresses bafflement as to why 'anyone should get the slightest pleasure out of having pain inflicted on them'. But with thinly veiled self-reference he notes that 'a rapidly increasing number of young men are indulging in this practice', offered by drolly titled women like 'Miss Swish and Miss L. Ash'. 'All men are equal under the whip, dear,' one veteran madam tells him.

The year after Aitken married in 1980, his new wife Lolicia had twin daughters, born prematurely after a difficult pregnancy. The babies had to be kept in intensive care in the hospital in Lausanne where they were born, with Lolicia, also seriously ill, in a nearby ward. 'The next few days I lived day and night by the incubators as things got steadily worse,' Aitken was to tell his High Court libel trial, all distressed husband. 'The three ladies in my life were in great danger.' He testified, a touch theatrically: 'It was undoubtedly the most traumatic and emotionally searing period of my life.'

Within days of the revived twins' Westminster christening in December 1980, medicine having saved his daughters, Aitken started sleeping with Paula Strudwick, a sometime prostitute who specialized in whippings. One can only conclude his compulsions were considerable.

Paula, a good-looking, easily sensual woman who had worked for west London madam Cherry Parish, was introduced to the MP by a mutual friend, the 1960s sex therapist and general practitioner Dr Christine Pickard. 'I was immediately attracted to Jonathan who looked handsome dressed in slacks and a cream Fair Isle sweater,' Paula recalls. 'From the start he was extremely attentive towards me and said to Christine: "Why haven't you introduced me to this lovely lady before?"'

After a boozy Islington lunch in Portofino's restaurant in Camden Passage, Christine and Paula, accompanied by the now deceased sexologist Peter Horfield, repaired to Paula's nearby home in Milner Place with Jonathan. He slept with both women. 'We took part in a three-in-a-bed sex session. Peter was not involved,' Paula explains.

Another dinner followed, this time without Dr Pickard. From then on Paula and Jonathan would meet on average twice a week. The liaisons took place in a small bedroom on the upper floor at 21 Upper Grosvenor Street, or at Paula's place. Her flat was decorated with pictures of women holding whips, and there were four leather restrainers at the corners of her bed. Aitken did not pay her, and he still maintains, ludicrously, that he had no idea she was working as a prostitute. What, one wonders, did he think the restrainers were for?

Strudwick often beat the future Minister of State for Defence Procurement with his own 'swishy canes'. 'There were no games. It was just he loved the pain. He kept asking for it harder. He could take a lot of it. My arms would ache,' Paula claims. It would be wrong, however, to regard Aitken as a passive or dominated figure. His women are agreed that he gave the orders throughout. Sometimes, for example, Paula's aim slipped while at her work. 'Oh for heaven's sake!' Aitken would complain: 'I don't believe this. At least get it straight – you're going all over the place!'

This was the period in 1981 when Aitken was acquiring the Inglewood health farm, where he was so keen to suggest 'girls' for the Arabs. In a surreal episode worthy of a Tom Sharpe novel, Aitken sent his mistress Paula down to Inglewood to lose weight. (She got a cheese-paring 10 per cent discount on her bill.) Aitken promised to meet her there for a corrective weekend.

'He rang and said he couldn't make it after all,' Paula recalls. 'But there was something I had to do for him.' He instructed her to collect birch twigs from a nearby wood. This was stressful for a town girl: she had to call up a girlfriend and ask for nature tips on identifying the birch by its leaves. Teetering unhappily on her muddy heels, Paula collected armfuls of the tree and stuffed them in the boot of her car for the drive back to London. The MP then came round for a thrashing. What Paula had not grasped was that at the Eton of Aitken's day, to be birched was a rare and special event, confined to major offenders. He must have come to regard it as a treat.

After twenty-seven months, Paula ended the relationship. 'I felt increasingly I was not getting anything out of it,' Paula said. 'Jonathan only wanted to be beaten by me, sometimes followed by sex, sometimes not. Jonathan was one of the coldest people I know because he was so controlled. He couldn't relax.'

Later, after this relationship with Paula Strudwick was exposed, Aitken put out a statement on House of Commons notepaper admitting he had cheated on his wife. The damage limitation involved a little Aitkenesque deceit. 'My wife and I were going through a difficult patch in our marriage at the time of the affair,' the Rt. Hon. MP wrote: 'We overcame these difficulties and for many years now have had a happy, fulfilled and faithful marriage.' Even by Aitken's plastic standards, it was something of an exaggeration to claim he had enjoyed a 'faithful marriage'.

It was in 1974 that Aitken had initiated a relationship with his 23-year-old secretary Valerie Scott, which continued intermittently after his marriage to Lolicia. The affair eventually fizzled out in 1986. Valerie says she first became aware of the MP's interest in 'swishy canes' during the October 1974 election campaign while they were staying at the seaside San Clu Hotel in Ramsgate, Kent. Pictures of Val during that campaign show a rather sweet-faced girl, trailing around behind the glossy-haired candidate as he addressed the crowds, her black coat buttoned up to a high neck. Not a woman of the world, she had left school at sixteen to become a secretary.

After knocking back a few drinks, they finished up in bed. Aitken asked his secretary whether she had had any 'experience of spanking'. He sometimes beat his current girlfriend but she did not enjoy it, he explained. Valerie declined the offer. Unlike most of Aitken's girlfriends in the 1970s – who believed, mistily, that they were destined to finish up as Mrs Aitken – Valerie had few illusions. She found Aitken 'interesting' and 'very charming and amusing' when he wanted to be. But she never forgot that he usually juggled several women at the same time. Once Aitken phoned her at 2 a.m. having returned from his Kent constituency. 'Guess what I've got in the boot,' he said breathlessly down his car phone. 'Birch twigs.'

In 1976 another farcical episode took place. Aitken's cleaner Mary Greenslade walked into his second-floor flat in Phillimore Gardens, the Kensington home he shared with his mother and sister. Mrs Greenslade made a strange discovery. At the bottom of the Conservative MP's brass four-poster bed she found a piece of furniture 'similar but larger than a footstool' covered in black leather. Mrs Greenslade took Valerie Scott, who worked downstairs, into her confidence and asked her to have a look. 'Apparently he used to leave his whips, canes, ropes and belts all over the floor and Mary Greenslade would have to put them away the next morning. They were all strewn about when I saw the room, and had obviously been used the previous night,' Ms Scott said. The daily noted several canes, a riding crop, 'a thing with a black leather handle and thongs hanging from it' and 'a thing which looked like a loo brush'. There were ropes and straps hanging from the footstool.

Far from running to the tabloids, Mrs Greenslade behaved with that laudable upstairs-downstairs discretion which helped build Britain an empire – carefully returning Aitken's extensive whip collection to the top right-hand cupboard of his white fitted wardrobe. The two women later peered into Aitken's study. The bookshelves contained several books and periodicals as well as a magazine beloved by chastisers everywhere, *Spanking Monthly*.

Aitken adopted a nonchalant attitude about his unorthodox sexual antics. The sense of invulnerability which first manifested itself at Eton made him careless about exposure. And, of course, his private life, in so far as it was conducted between consenting adults and caused no harm, should have remained just that – private. It was his own hysterical challenges to the media when he became a Cabinet minister that led to it all coming out.

But Aitken was also sexually predatory in a rather unattractive way. And so were his Saudi masters. It was Aitken in 1984 who pulled all the strings he knew how in an attempt to protect Prince Mohammed from the attentions of the *News of the World*.

ROYAL RAVERS FOR HIRE was the headline in the tabloid that Sunday – and under it was an account of a *News of the World* 'girl investigator'. Seeking to infiltrate a call-girl circle, she had got herself spotted by one of Prince Mohammed's aides, working in a London boutique patronized by the Saudis. He said, 'The Prince likes you,' and she was driven in a limousine to the Prince's mansion in Winnington Road in Hampstead. There she encountered an enthusiastic Prince Mohammed, dressed only in a bathrobe. In time-honoured fashion, she 'made an excuse and left'.

This was a rather half-hearted story by tabloid standards, and poorly researched – it was accompanied by a photo of the wrong man, said to be Mohammed's pimp. But what was significant was that it was Aitken who was called in to put the arm on the press. Prince Mohammed was extremely irked. So his faithful British factotum Jonathan Aitken used his contacts to complain to the Australian managing director of the paper, Bruce Mathews, that Prince Mohammed wanted something done about the story. Aitken's personal lawyer, Richard Sykes, wrote complaining to the paper on Prince Mohammed's behalf.

These tactics had only limited success – the paper apologized for its mistake over the photo, and conceded they could not substantiate the charge that the boutique-owner was running a brothel. But they did not retract the allegation that Prince Mohammed liked to have sex with Western girls.

In the winter of 1978, air-hostess Sue Hamnett (she asks for her real name not to be published) put on her best black velvet Marks & Spencer jacket and a hippy skirt and trudged towards the Mayfair office of Al Bilad. Outside it was snowing. Her boyfriend Paul had dropped her off in his Triumph van, and she crunched nervously towards the entrance lobby.

The November advert in *The Times* for a job as an air-hostess to work on a private Saudi jet had unsettled her at first; she and Paul had joked with one another about 'white slavery'. The tax-free salary of £20,000 a year seemed ridiculously high. Where, she wondered, was the catch?

But her doubts were assuaged by the fact that a young and upstanding Conservative MP was waiting upstairs in a sober meeting room to interview her. His name was Jonathan Aitken. She had heard of him, distantly, she recalled later, and felt confident he was 'legitimate'. Sue, an attractive, blonde 25-year-old New Zealander, was ushered into Al Bilad's upholstered boardroom. She recalls that Aitken was standing next to a 'fancy antique' desk and came forward to greet her. 'Umm, how do you do?' Aitken said. He then gestured towards half a dozen 'sophisticated-looking' Arab gentlemen wearing Savile Row suits, adding blandly: 'These gentlemen are sitting in.'

The interview seemed disastrous. Aitken said he had never heard of the New Zealand airline on which she had served her training. After twenty minutes the interview ended abruptly. 'I'd sensed then that I'd lost it,' she reflected later. But, curiously, she did get the job, beating off competition from several other better-qualified girls. She later discovered that one of the Arab gentlemen had stood up, as she crunched disconsolately back through the snow, and announced, 'She's the one. Thank you. It's all over.'

It was bone-chillingly cold on the Gatwick tarmac at 7 a.m. on New Year's Day 1979, when Sue Hamnett reported for duty and climbed aboard Prince Mohammed's BAC 1-11, destined for the 'nether blue yonder', as she thought of it. It was the plane Jonathan Aitken had helped the Prince buy at the Paris air show two summers previously. Ten days of hectic flying followed, to Riyadh and back round Europe, at the end of which one of the Arab group took the young air-hostess aside and gave her an envelope containing $1,000 in $100 bills. This was her tip.

In 1979 terms, the payment was 'awesome', Ms Hamnett explained eighteen years later over a cigarette and a cup of tea, sitting nervously in the living room of her suburban New Zealand home.

In the following months, a pattern emerged. The plane would only ever spend three or four weeks at a stretch in Saudi Arabia. The rest of the time the Prince and his entourage would travel frenetically to torrid pleasure spots: Cannes in France, Casablanca in Morocco, or Marbella in Spain. Sue and the rest of the plane's staff would be accommodated in the very best hotels: the President in Geneva, or the Majestic in Cannes. At the end of each trip Said Ayas would discreetly produce envelopes for all the expatriate staff.

Aitken, the young Conservative MP, hitched a lift on the Prince's plane 'lots of times'. But he was never invited to sit in the separate royal quarters at the front of the plane with the 'important people'. Instead he sat at the back. 'Without a doubt he was a servant,' Ms Hamnett said. 'He was treated as such. Your level of importance dropped as you got back. Well, Jonathan always sat at the back.'

He did, however, benefit substantially from the Prince's largesse. When the party descended on a hotel Aitken's bill was 'lumped along' with that of all the other Britons, and picked up by Said Ayas or Faisal al Sowail, one of the Prince's relatives.

Two months into her employment, when she was staying at the President Hotel in Geneva, something odd took place. Sue Hamnett and the rest of the crew had retired to their rooms, got changed and wandered downstairs for a drink in the bar. One of the Prince's Arab associates came over and gave her an envelope. 'He said: "I would just like you to have a nice time," or words to that effect.' Inside the envelope she found $5,000 in US dollars – the equivalent of more than $50,000 today.

Ms Hamnett said she felt shocked – 'I thought maybe I was getting into the position that everybody had warned me about.' Her colleagues advised her to say nothing. More envelopes followed, containing some £20,000 in all. She was also given a free first-class flight back to her family in New Zealand the following Christmas, arranged by the man who had recruited her, Jonathan Aitken. And then it happened.

In Jedda, in the 'awesome surroundings' of a palace, Sue Hamnett was invited to 'have a drink' with her original benefactor. By this stage she knew 'probably what was expected'. 'I went to the room; it was a big, huge room. There was a bed; it was very sumptuous. He came out. I seem to remember he was in his Saudi gear.' They had sex. He rapidly sodomized her. This, she said, was a 'terrible shock'.

'But it wasn't rape. I suppose I was resigned to it. He wasn't a hideous old ogre; he was an attractive young man, with enormous appeal. It was an impossible situation. A year had gone by, and I had naïvely allowed myself to think that the money had been given to me because they genuinely wanted me to have a good time.'

Two weeks after the incident, she was fired by Aitken. 'I'm just here to tell you that you are dismissed from your job,' he said curtly, after summoning her to the flat, in Emperor's Gate, London, of an air-hostess colleague with whom Sue Hamnett believes he was having an affair.

According to Ms Hamnett, there was 'no question' that the MP was aware of the real reason why she was paid thousands of dollars in cash. 'I have no doubt Jonathan arranged women for the Saudis,' Ms Hamnett said. 'But he was a sophisticate. He was a hard man, and it would have been a business thing. He wouldn't have been able to deal with the soft and gentle side of somebody like me; he wouldn't have been able to do that.'

Good-time girls, secretaries, blondes, air-hostesses – this was the sexual world of the West for which Jonathan Aitken was a *louche* tourist guide to his Arab paymasters. But the chief motor that drove their personal Anglo—Saudi relationship was never sex. It was money, and the deals where money was to be got. That meant, above all, as the 1980s wore on, the big deals in the arms trade.

Jonathan Aitken, 6 March 1996, to the Trade and Industry Select Committee investigating arms deals to Iran

....

Five: **Merchant of Death**

Gerald James wasted no time in the summer of 1988 in dictating a letter from his new chairman's office in Lincolnshire to Jonathan Aitken. The letter was sent to the MP at his Saudi paymasters' Mayfair premises in Upper Grosvenor Street. James wanted an introduction to the Saudi royal family to sell them arms, and he was prepared to pay for it. 'I do not expect this sort of advice to be free,' he wrote.

James was physically a big man, who was in a hurry to make big money. In the dog-eared Britain of the 1980s, he understood the secret recipe for making millions out of international arms sales – one part right-wing politics, two parts old-fashioned bribery, and six parts oil-rich Arabs. Then stir it all up with a war, or the prospect of war. James, the chairman of what had originally been a military pyrotechnics and fireworks firm, Astra, was one of those who used to be known, in more shockable times, as 'Merchants of Death'. He had just acquired a gun factory.

The otherwise dull borough of Grantham, on the edge of the flat East Anglian fens, is dominated by a jagged roofscape of giant sheds smack in the middle of the small town. In 1988 this was James's gun factory, one of the district's chief employers. Previously Swiss-owned, the BMARC works had been opened up there in Lincolnshire on the eve of the Second World War to provide aircraft cannon for the Spitfires and Hurricanes which did so much to win the Battle of Britain.

But those heroic days were long gone. The Grantham firm, with its ageing range of rapid-fire cannons, used as anti-aircraft guns on warships, was desperate for orders from almost any source when it

was finally dumped by its Swiss owners in 1987. Oerlikon, the Swiss
parent, sold off the firm to James, a little-known entrepreneur from
Kent.

James himself had been involved in a conspiratorial far-right
political group of the 1970s, the 'secret army' organized by George
Young, the anti-Black and anti-Jewish former deputy head of the
British Secret Service. A rightist Conservative MP, Gerald Howarth,
was already on James's firm's payroll as a consultant – and Jonathan
Aitken, the Richard Nixon fan and intimate of the Saudi royal family,
was already James's very own constituency MP in Sandwich in Kent.

Aitken was often helpful to his constituent, whose company
donated £1,000 to his 1987 re-election campaign. In February 1985,
asked by James for contacts through whom he could sell military
equipment to Saudi Arabia, Aitken had already unsuccessfully recom-
mended his own new business partners, Lebanese entrepreneurs
Fouad and Ziad Makhzoumi, who banked with Aitken Hume.

Aitken had just been appointed to the board of Makhzoumi's own
UK company and, according to Makhzoumi, was to become involved
in new ventures he introduced. There were two odd things about
Aitken's connections with this Lebanese dealer. First, the politician
appeared unenthusiastic about advertising the link: it was not regis-
tered on the MPs' Register as an interest, and Aitken also failed to
include it on his published lists of directorships at Companies House.
And second, in response to an inquiry from James about Saudi Arabia,
Aitken for some reason mentioned Makhzoumi's excellent results in
Iraq as well as in Saudi Arabia.

Iraq, run by the villainous dictator Saddam Hussein, was in the
throes of a bloody war, and the British Conservative Government
was regularly wringing its hands about it. As Aitken's Party colleague,
Foreign Secretary Sir Geoffrey Howe, piously put it: 'We are doing
everything possible to bring this tragic conflict to an end.' Aitken
later wriggled a good deal about this introduction he offered to
Makhzoumi, saying he did not realize that Astra's 'military pyrotechnics' might have been covered at the time by an unpublished arms
embargo relating to Iraq operated by his own colleagues in
Government.

The reason for James's bout of letter-writing to Aitken in July 1988
was the public announcement a couple of days earlier that a fresh

instalment had been agreed of the most gigantic arms deal in British history: to sell the Saudi royal family whole fleets of aircraft and warships, at very high prices. James hoped Aitken could get him a share of the action 'to help our group in connection with Saudi contracts'. There was, he wrote: 'Obviously a very large ammunition and weapon requirement . . . Because of your associations with the country, you could advise us.'

The original Saudi deal had been signed in 1986 by Mrs Thatcher. It was not merely a sale: it was a whole merry-go-round system of transferring Saudi oil money into new pockets. The system was charmingly christened by the Saudis 'The Dove' – 'Al Yamamah'.

Over a period of deliveries lasting more than a decade, the Saudis were to hand over oil and cash worth £1.5 billion a year to the British Ministry of Defence. The M.o.D., in turn, after taking a modest cut as a 'management fee', were to dole out the money to a single big privately owned arms firm, British Aerospace.

BAe, as 'prime contractor', were to build Tornado and Hawk war-planes at their Lancashire factories, and deliver them to Saudi Arabia, the biggest importer of weapons in the world. They were also to buy in all the guns, bombs and electronics the planes would need from 'subcontractors'. Other purchases, such as minesweepers ordered from the Southampton shipbuilders Vosper Thorneycroft, and a fleet of helicopters expected to come from the Yeovil manufacturers Westland, would be handled by BAe as well, as prime contractor. And on top of the hardware there were the spares and the hugely lucrative technical and personnel support services: the small Saudi population was simply unable to handle the vast amounts of sophisticated arms it was buying.

The prices charged were excessive. A Tornado fighter-bomber which cost NATO £20 million was to be sold to the Saudis for closer to £35 million. Some of this extra charge – the smallest part – was 'royalties' to the British taxpayer, via the M.o.D., for having paid all the money to develop the war-planes in the first place. A larger chunk was profit for the manufacturers. But the biggest extra item – ranging between 15 and 26 per cent of the price – was 'commission'.

At every stage, commission was skimmed from the process. For example, each 2,000-lb bomb that went on the planes was fitted with a sophisticated electronic fuse made by the firm Thorn-EMI, better known for their more socially acceptable role in the music business. A total of 26 per cent in commissions was paid by Thorn-EMI on each transaction. Some went direct to 'agents' in Saudi Arabia. Some went via a bank account in Bermuda, in the name of dummy companies in the British Virgin Islands, and then disappeared in various directions.

The bombs themselves, into which the fuses fitted, were made by the state-owned firm of Royal Ordnance. They, too, paid over similar commissions in excess of 15 per cent. The size of these payments, as one of their executives later testified, was classed as an 'official secret'.

And at the top of this food chain, commission of around 20 per cent was handed over on delivery of each of the £35-million BAe planes themselves on which these bombs and fuses were fitted. It was paid out along the discreet Bermuda route. Thus an underground river of money of at least £300 million a year in secret commissions began to flow, corrupting British business life. Such payments are illegal, nominally at least, in the US. Other countries have tried to stamp them out. But in the Britain of the 1980s, they were connived at by the British Government and described by complacent executives of the firms involved, as 'normal commercial practices in certain countries'.

The river of cash was of course, although no one involved cared to use the word, a river of bribes. It is flowing on in 1997, a decade later, as the Tornado deliveries still continue. This was exactly the same system of tribute, paid to members of the Saudi royal family via intermediaries, with which Jonathan Aitken was so involved in his Al Bilad engineering projects. And it was Jonathan Aitken's Arab business associates, as Gerald James was well aware of when he wrote to him in 1988, who were some of the key intermediaries in Al Yamamah.

Fahad al Athel, one of the trio of millionaire Saudi 'fixers' in Al Bilad, also ran a company called Saudi Fal. He told a US helicopter executive when offering his agency services that the Saudi Fal proceeds were divided up 40 per cent to Prince Mohammed bin Fahd, his patron, and 40 per cent to other Saudi royals, including Mohammed's sons. The remaining 20 per cent was kept by Athel himself. Athel's firm normally charged Western customers 15 per cent of the total contract price as their overall commission.

These figures enable us to see just how obscenely juicy the life of such an intermediary could be. As Aitken boasted privately, it was Athel, via Saudi Fal, who had acted as agent on the £400-million Vosper minesweeper part of Al Yamamah signed in 1986. This means that Athel personally pocketed £12 million (although he may, of course, have used some of this cash to pay off his own obligations to people who had helped him).

The Vosper deal was only a little fragment of Al Yamamah. If Athel's stunning wealth was calculated to make Aitken envious, it was as nothing compared to the truly Dionysian riches amassed by Aitken's other Arab associate. This was the key man who had brokered the entire mind-boggling Al Yamamah deal on behalf of British Aerospace, enlisting Mrs Thatcher and the British Government on the one hand, and a cluster of favoured sons and nephews of the Saudi King on the other.

Wafic Said, a hawk-nosed Syrian by birth, spread largesse wherever he went, like all the Arab fixers who turned up in Britain. He could afford it – in the years after the Al Yamamah deal first began to flow, Wafic Said also bought prize race-horses; invested in films; and acquired an Oxfordshire country estate to accompany his £9-million apartment in London's fashionable Eaton Square, a Regent's Park town house, his Paris apartment, his palatial villa in Marbella, his ski-lodge in Switzerland and his *pied-à-terre* in Monaco. He bid at auction for the late Duchess of Windsor's jewels; donated at least six figures to the British Conservative Party; and purchased paintings by Renoir, Gauguin and Monet. His most recent act of conspicuous spending in 1997 was to offer £20 million to endow a new Oxford college – the Wafic Said School of Business Studies.

Jonathan Aitken, too, was indirectly a beneficiary of Wafic Said, this very rich 'business manager' of the Saudis. In June 1985, while Wafic Said was at his busiest trying to put together the Al Yamamah deal, he offered an initial £8-million investment into the ailing Aitken Hume merchant bank, enabling it to take over Sentinel Insurance. This fresh injection of Arab funds helped Aitken in a battle for control with his cousin Tim. Wafic Said was eventually to put £15 million into Aitken's firm, and to hold a 30 per cent stake. Aitken was subsequently to boast to Gerald James that he himself had played a big part in helping bring Al Yamamah about. It was reported that he had written to the Foreign Office about this time, boosting Wafic Said's bona fides.

Did Aitken himself get a cut of the commissions on Al Yamamah? No one knows. It has been frequently suggested that he did dip his cup in this flowing river of money. Aitken did indisputably function as a representative of key Saudi royals in London at the time of the arms deals, and did become visibly rich. Knowing what one does of Saudi methods, it would have been quite unusual if Aitken had in fact not been offered some *douceurs*.

When Gerald James wrote to the well-connected politician in 1988, offering him money in return for arms-deal introductions, Jonathan Aitken jibbed at first. He wanted better terms. He asked James to make him a full director of the main Astra company instead of a mere 'consultant'. James balked in turn: he eventually proposed that Aitken could have a seat on the board of the subsidiary company, BMARC, for a nominal £10,000 a year.

They shook hands on the deal. Aitken immediately provided the name of Fahad al Athel, his business associate who had been the agent for the Vosper contract. James should write to him, he suggested, offering Athel commission if the new batch of Vosper minesweepers were to be specified with BMARC cannon. James should come to Geneva in September, Aitken suggested. Aitken would be there himself – no doubt in attendance on the Saudi royal court – and could personally introduce James to Athel.

Aitken's first attempt to earn his keep in this way misfired: it turned out that a US company, EMERLEC, was already on the inside track for the Vosper cannon deal. James's visit to Geneva was highly embarrassing for Aitken. While James fumed at the Hôtel des Bergues, or steamed about irritably on solitary trips on Lake Leman, Aitken was simply unable to produce Sheikh Athel, never mind any of the royals themselves. James had to console himself with a lunch alone with Aitken and the garrulous Lolicia.

But Aitken continued to promise he would deliver Athel. He would personally take James to Riyadh at Christmas, and they would meet there, he claimed. The BMARC files contain some rather sad correspondence in which Aitken's attempts to pin Athel down are greeted with an airy note that the sheikh is in Portland, Oregon, by the side of Prince Saud, and cannot possibly make himself available for a 'presentation of BMARC's products'.

Eventually, in the spring of 1989, Aitken successfully arranged for a BMARC salesman, David Trigger, to make contact with Athel inside Saudi Arabia. They drew up an agreement for Athel to receive his 15 per cent: Athel agreed to promote the British arms firm for a contract to 'weaponise' a fleet of Black Hawk helicopters which the Saudis were talking about buying from Westlands.

The BMARC archives contain an illuminating note from Astra's sales director John Sellens about this Al Yamamah commission: 'I am happy with the 15 per cent, which I understand would also look after Jonathan Aitken's interests.' This memo chimes with James's own recollections, that Aitken assured him he would be 'looked after' in any deal that was eventually concluded with the Saudis.

Aitken himself continued to take an active part in setting up the helicopter deal with Athel. He wrote on 29 March 1989, on his Al Bilad notepaper with the House of Commons portcullis logo:

The immediate big target is the weapon equipment for Westland helicopters. Sheikh Fahad ... will go and sell this package to the relevant military commanders and ministers. He believes that at best the weapons package could be around US$5 million per helicopter, so with a fleet of over 80 helicopters, this is clearly big money.

It certainly was big money. On a $400-million deal, Athel would hand over some £30 million to sweeten Prince Mohammed and friends. He would make £8 million himself. It would have been an uncharacteristically ungenerous fixer who could not have spared half a million or so as a thank-you to the man who had made the original introduction – Jonathan Aitken MP.

But it was Aitken's bad luck, perhaps, that the helicopter deal ran into protracted delays. The Saudis had been so profligate that they got into difficulties completing the funding for the first part of Al Yamamah. The order for helicopters was postponed into the indefinite future.

Meanwhile, Gerald James's company, too, ran out of cash after unwise take-overs. It was further discovered that British defence ministry officials were being bribed by the firm in the hope of getting orders for ammunition: Astra's chief executive was sent to jail. Astra collapsed, and Jonathan Aitken was sacked from the board.

Aitken's attempt to broker a big arms deal had ended in ignominious failure.

*

When his activities as a would-be Saudi intermediary later came under inquiry, Aitken simply told lies about them. This was, of course, his classic pattern of behaviour. In 1992 his ministerial press office were instructed to deny in a letter to Paul Foot of *Private Eye* that Aitken had unsuccessfully attempted to negotiate himself a position on Astra's main board at the time. Instead, a picture was painted that Aitken had merely agreed to do a constituent a favour.

Aitken himself claimed repeatedly that he had been offered a directorship out of the blue by Gerald James merely for his 'merchant banking experience'. This was a ridiculous untruth – merchant banking had nothing to do with it. When news began to emerge in a US court case of Fahad al Athel's involvement in a putative Al Yamamah helicopter deal revolving around the payment of enormous commissions to the Saudi royals, Aitken insisted that he knew nothing about it.

It was the abortive trip to Geneva to introduce Gerald James to Athel and the Saudi royals that Aitken found the most difficult to explain away: not only did it link Aitken to Saudi arms deals, but it also depicted him as a man who fawned on the Saudi court and its clique of bagmen.

Whenever Gerald James told the story in later years, Aitken publicly tried to pour scorn on it. He told a select committee of MPs that James was insane, and a candidate for the 'funny farm'. Finally, when it became impossible to deny that a meeting had indeed been arranged in Geneva just as Gerald James alleged, Aitken resorted to a drastic new story to explain why he had been unable to produce Athel for the promised introduction: 'The plaintiff did not introduce him to Fahad al Athel on that occasion,' Aitken pleaded to the High Court in his libel action, 'because Mr James was visibly drunk.' This was simply an invention, a fiction dreamed up on the spur of the moment, and later dropped when it had served its turn. It was characteristic of the Aitken method.

During the whole time that Aitken was a minister in charge of arms sales to Saudi Arabia – from 1992 to 1994 – these deceptive ploys succeeded. His background was concealed from public view. Aitken went to Riyadh on behalf of Her Majesty's Government in January 1993 to persuade his business associates in the Saudi royal family to sign up at last for the long-delayed second half of Al Yamamah – another £5-billion deal for more Hawks and Tornados.

(The dream of talking the Saudis into buying additional helicopters, whose 'weaponisation' Aitken had earlier hoped to arrange on his own behalf, was, however, finally abandoned.) Aitken was thus able to use the full authority of the British Government to negotiate yet another arms deal in which a river of secret commissions would flow into the pockets of his Saudi associates. And, at the same time, he succeeded in concealing his own history of dealing with those same people.

Aitken even succeeded in deceiving a judicial inquiry – the Scott Inquiry – about the extent of his business links with the Saudi royal family over arms deals. Lord Justice Scott was conducting a prolonged inquiry into yet another scandal surrounding the Government-sponsored British arms industry – the sale of supposedly banned military equipment to the Iraqi dictator Saddam Hussein, whose interminable war continued throughout the 1980s.

In theory, all significant military sales from Britain were by now banned to Saddam, who was not only conducting a bloody war against Iran, but also using poisonous gas against his domestic Kurdish opponents. The official Government view was that Saddam was a repulsive mass-murderer and torturer from whom all right-thinking Britons recoiled in horror.

The genuine Government view was quite different. Alan Clark, Jonathan Aitken's old friend, and at that time minister in charge of export-licence applications, put it well in a later interview:

It was my job to maximise exports, despite guidelines I regarded as tiresome and intrusive. Second, Iran was the enemy and still is. And it was clear to me that the interests of the West were well served by Iran and Iraq fighting each other, the longer the better.

Just as Britain covertly backed Iraq against the revolutionary fundamentalists of Iran, so did Saudi Arabia. The Saudi royal family gave Saddam money, and they helped smuggle arms to him. In one of his most sensitive discoveries, Lord Justice Scott traced 1987–8 shipments of artillery ammunition from Britain to Saudi Arabia which went straight on overland to Iraq with the assistance of a Saudi prince.

What Scott did not know was that there was also a certain amount of evidence that forty of the eighty-eight Black Hawk helicopters the Saudis were considering ordering may also have been destined for diversion to Iraq. Iraq was trying to obtain forty machines, according to Westland correspondence with Whitehall. Evidence disclosed by the US manufacturer Sikorsky, in a Washington court case, confirmed that they were considering supply to Iraq, paid for by the Saudis. And the size of the potential Saudi helicopter package was reduced by forty machines after the end of the Iran–Iraq war made them superfluous. These were all no more than straws in the wind. But they made Aitken's private involvement in the Saudi royal family's helicopter negotiations a highly embarrassing episode, were it ever to come out.

Doggedly following his lines of inquiry, the judge approached Aitken himself after magazine allegations that the arms sales minister had been involved with the Saudi royals. The article in question said:

Aitken boasts a deep and extensive knowledge of British arms exports. As a back bench MP, he listed among his interests a company named Aitken Hume International which, he said, had common interests with certain members of the Saudi royal family.

This was a sloppy and unfocused piece of journalism. But it panicked Aitken into telling lies. The reference should have been in fact to Al Bilad, which Aitken had deemed prudent to list more fully in the MPs' Register, after the 1988 TV-am exposure of Saudi funding, as a firm that had 'contracts with Saudi royal interests'. Aitken Hume was the minister's merchant bank.

Scott insisted on an Aitken response to the mentions of his name in the article. The minister could have given an honest reply. This would have said:

My merchant bank, Aitken Hume International, was partly funded at its launch by the Saudi King's son and his associates, who also held accounts there. It was subsequently supported by major investments from the business manager of the Saudi defence minister, Prince Sultan, and his son Prince Bandar. But I also worked directly for the Saudi royal family as a director in London of Al Bilad, owned by Mohammed, the King's son. Through my Al Bilad associates, I negotiated an arms deal involving the potential sale of 88 Westland helicopter gunships to the Saudi regime at a commission to the Saudi royal family's agent of 15 per cent.

Instead, Aitken comprehensively underplayed his relationships with the Saudi royals. He was deliberately throwing dust in the judge's eyes:

Aitken Hume International PLC was and is a small merchant and commercial bank specialising in US investment management . . . A small number of Saudi Arabians, two of whom were junior members of the royal family, were clients of the bank. Their deposits were comparatively modest. Aitken Hume International had no banking, investment or other commercial business resulting from arms exports to Iraq or anywhere else.

Lord Justice Scott would have concluded from this statement that the minister had never had any meaningful relationships of any kind with the Saudi royals. The words served their purpose, and deflected the judge from any further inquiry into Aitken's arms dealings.

Murky as they were, it was not, however, Aitken's would-be helicopter deals that were to land him in real trouble. In the disreputable world of arms sales, infested with bribery and smuggling, Aitken had been unwise to insist on the title of 'director' of BMARC. To be a director of a company, even a non-executive one, made Aitken legally responsible for the company's activities. One of these was Project Mango.

On his infrequent visits up from London to the provincial wilderness of Grantham for BMARC board meetings, Aitken apparently did not notice what his new colleagues were actually currently manufacturing in the huge noisy sheds with their sawtooth roofs. The workers were completing a very large order, for 140 cannon. Mounted on the decks of small patrol boats, these simple and rugged 20mm guns could be operated by one man without electric power. They could be very useful for a small belligerent nation mounting hit-and-run raids against, say, oil installations or tankers.

Such a thought never crossed Aitken's mind, however. He told inquirers subsequently that 'I was not briefed on this contract at any time.' Nor, he confessed, had he ever paid any attention when the progress of the order was discussed at board meetings under the rubric LISI. He had never taken the least notice.

This incuriousness was unfortunate. The retired General Donald Isles, deputy managing director of BMARC, who was in charge of the contract, could have told him about some exceptionally disturbing features of this cannon deal. For a start, the guns had been ordered up by BMARC's former Swiss parent Oerlikon who called the deal Project Mango.

But they were not to be sent to Switzerland. They had been ordered instead to be shipped from Britain to Singapore in partial-kit form. LISI meant Licence for Singapore. The British Government had issued official export permits for the gun 'components' to be sent there, in the belief that a Singapore state firm was to use them for its own gun industry, under a manufacturing licence.

Isles, and indeed many of his executive colleagues, knew perfectly well, however, that Singapore was not the real destination. There was a further, secret, customer beyond the Singapore company. Who was it? It was scarcely politic to ask. All British legal requirements were being complied with.

However, there was some knowledge that was inescapable. General Isles knew that Oerlikon were trading with a forbidden country. BMARC had been sent an explicit Oerlikon order for guns in 1986 for that country, which his deputy had been forced to return. Naval officers from that country had recently visited both Oerlikon's Zurich headquarters and BMARC's own premises in England. Furthermore, there had been rumours within the company as to the true destination of the naval guns for Project Mango. The rumours, as Isles knew, specifically named the forbidden country – Iran.

Of these facts about Project Mango, Aitken remained entirely unaware. His directorship, after all, was largely cosmetic. He must have almost forgotten those echoing sawtoothed sheds in Lincolnshire as his career took its exciting new twists in the 1990s – first as arms sales minister and then as a member of the Cabinet.

Yet, in the end, it was not only his Saudi deals and his trip to the Paris Ritz but also this lack of curiousness as a company director that was to catch up with him. And when it did he was to lie his head off in the usual Aitken way. In that at least, Jonathan Aitken remained consistent.

IAGO   Trifles light as air
          Are to the jealous confirmations strong
          As proofs of holy writ. ***Othello* (III.3)**
**Quoted by Jonathan Aitken in a letter to
Peter Preston, 4 February 1994**

··

Six: **Dear Jonathan**

O n the evening of 16 October 1993, after the lifts and
escalators had shut for the night, the editor of the *Guardian*
Peter Preston puffed his way up five floors to the top of
Britain's most famous department store, Harrods. He was,
as usual, a trifle weary when he got to the modest glass hole in
the wall which opened into the chairman's suite of offices. Inside
Mohamed Al Fayed, the protean Egyptian businessman with a professed love for Britain but an equally vehement contempt for its
political workings, waited impatiently, drumming his fingers.

The two men had met before. In June that year, Preston had made
the first of several bizarre pilgrimages to Al Fayed's small but heavily
ornate inner sanctum. Out of the blue, Fayed – a mobile Arab face
stuffed into an Establishment striped shirt and grey suit – had
volunteered some background information which might help Preston
with a looming libel action. The *Guardian* had published a story about
secret donations to the Conservative Party before the 1992 general
election. Over a half-hour chat Fayed had launched into a baffling,
thickly accented denunciation of Mark Thatcher, Margaret Thatcher,
arms contracts and dubious Arab princes. Almost separately, he had
also tossed in the names of the lobbyist Ian Greer and of two
ministers, Neil Hamilton and Tim Smith, who he said had been
covertly on his payroll in the late 1980s.

As back-benchers, Hamilton and Smith had been only too happy
to ask questions in the House of Commons which would help Fayed
in his vicious battle with Tiny Rowland of Lonrho for control of the
House of Fraser group and its flagship store Harrods. There was a

good reason for their helpfulness: Fayed was secretly paying them fees. They were being richly rewarded for their parliamentary services with brown envelopes stuffed full of cash. But what use had it all been? Even four years on, Fayed was still incensed about an unflattering Department of Trade and Industry inspectors' report into his take-over, which claimed Fayed had lied about his origins. 'The Government have shat on me,' Fayed sometimes raged. He presented himself as an innocent abroad, importuned by lobbyists and politicians – a lad up from the country in a Ben Jonson comedy, immediately surrounded by the smart operators.

In 1993, following the initial Preston–Fayed meeting, two *Guardian* reporters had begun investigating the murky world of lobbyists, politicians and party funding. But the story had become becalmed on a sea of denial and threatened litigation. Fayed, the Deep Throat of the sleaze saga, did not as yet want to go public.

None the less, Fayed had now come across another story which he thought might interest Preston. He had spotted another Government minister up to no good: Jonathan Aitken. In his long journey from the old quarter of Alexandria to control of the department store which sold silk pyjamas to the British upper classes, Fayed had acquired the Ritz Hotel in Paris. He bought the faded property in 1979 and was rewarded by his friend Jacques Chirac, then the Mayor of Paris, with the freedom of the French capital and some flowery speeches. Fayed set about restoring the Ritz into a twinkling rococo palace.

The previous month – the weekend of 17–19 September – Fayed said he had spotted Aitken in the hotel bar along with a Saudi wheeler-dealer called Said Ayas. And, he discovered, the supreme Syrian middle-man Wafic Said was also in residence. What, Fayed wondered, was Aitken doing with a director of Al Bilad, the trading company of Prince Mohammed, the Saudi Prince with a finger in many pies? 'Just imagine if you see the Attorney-General sitting with Al Capone, it will be exactly the same,' an exasperated Fayed later protested.

Intrigued, Fayed asked to see a copy of Aitken's account. The hotel-owner then discovered that the minister had not paid his own bill. The bill had been debited to Ayas. Fayed was astonished. Sitting in his Knightsbridge office two weeks later, Fayed pulled a copy of the bill out of his pocket. He tossed it theatrically over to Preston. There could be no doubt. Aitken's bill was for 8,010 French francs and was clearly marked: 'Débiteur A/C Mr Ayas #626/7'. Ayas had paid Aitken's bill. But why? And what was Her Majesty's Minister of State for Defence Procurement doing in such curious company?

Preston was interested but cautious. There did not seem much of a story. Unlike Hamilton and Smith, Aitken was staggeringly wealthy in his own right. The sum involved was 'piffling', Preston thought. That he had Arab links of some description was well known within Westminster circles. Preston had met Aitken several times before – they had both campaigned for a Freedom of Information Act – and had even been invited to a party at Aitken's grand Lord North Street home.

But Fayed's previous tip-off about Hamilton and Greer was slowly proving to be astonishingly accurate. The Aitken bill could not be ignored. Preston decided to haul aside two staff reporters to do some digging around the edges: David Pallister, who had spent two decades following arms dealing and Saudi affairs; and Paul Brown, who had specialist knowledge of Conservative Party funding.

Pallister's first step was straightforward: to phone Aitken at his Ministry of Defence office to try and set up a face-to-face meeting. Aitken pompously told Pallister to contact the M.o.D. press office; and complained that Pallister mumbled. On 19 October 1993 Pallister tried again and wrote formally to Aitken asking about his meeting at the Ritz with prominent Saudis and 'how it relates to your job in Government?' Aitken's heart may have thumped as he read Pallister's letter in the privacy of his M.o.D. study. His reply, though, betrayed no emotion and was glacial in tone:

Dear Mr Pallister,

Thank you for your letter of 19 October. You have been misinformed about my visit to Paris and Geneva over the weekend of 18 September.

The following facts may be of interest to you.

1. I had no meeting with Mr Ayas, Dr Somait and Mr Wafic Said in Paris over the weekend of 18 September or at any other place or time.

2. I have not spoken to Dr Somait or Mr Wafic Said for several months.

3. The purpose of my visit was to meet up with my wife and daughter – who was going to her new school that weekend.

4. I had no meetings in Paris or Geneva except for social encounters with my daughters (*sic*) godparents and other old friends. There were no substantive conversations relating to my job in Government.

If you have any enquiries relating to my job in Government in future, please deal directly with the Ministry of Defence Press Office.

Yours sincerely,

Jonathan Aitken

Thank you and good night. The letter sounded categoric enough when Preston and Pallister discussed it. But Pallister, who had made other calls, discovered one niggling fact. Said Ayas *was* Victoria Aitken's godfather. In point 1 Aitken had had no meeting with him; yet in point 4 the two men had met. The letter was disingenuous to say the least. Although the *Guardian* team did not as yet know it, the letter was to prove to be the foundation stone of a giant temple of deceit that Aitken was to erect, painstakingly and obsessionally, over the next three-and-a-half years.

The brush-off had the opposite effect to that intended. Ayas, contacted by the paper, separately confirmed that he had had dinner with Aitken *en famille* on the Friday of that weekend. So why was the minister dodging and weaving? Preston wondered whether a personal letter from him might prompt a fuller response.

It was thus that one of the more curious epistolary relationships of the late twentieth century was born. The 'Dear Jonathan' letters, as the correspondence between Preston and Aitken became known, began in politeness and ended in rancour and loathing. The novelist Samuel Richardson, author of *Clarissa*, might have enjoyed the correspondence as it ranged, often voluminously, over the dark events of the Ritz weekend. There were playful allusions on both sides; to Shakespeare, Feydeau and the Bible.

Aitken's highly literate letters to Preston begin in a spirit of intellectual gamesmanship. The lying was brazen, but the tone most of the way through was light and breezy. Later Aitken would regret having written at such length; the undulating contours of his mendacity were there for all to see. On 22 October 1993 Preston first wrote to Aitken at his home, apologizing for troubling him 'outside the ministerial loop'. Preston was a 'bit perplexed'. Was the Ritz meeting between Ayas, Aitken and Said 'a giant coincidence or an informal rendezvous of old business partners?'. Preston noted that Aitken's reply to Pallister was 'surprising in its vigour and interesting in its care'. If this letter was the last word 'then I suppose the lads will have to plough on alone', he wrote. Would Jonathan like to elaborate?

Jonathan would. Four days later almost 2,000 words of explanation, denial and Aitkenian subterfuge dropped on Preston's desk. 'Dear Peter,' Aitken began,

Thank you for your letter of October 22nd. I am grateful to you for explaining the background to those curious enquiries from Mr Pallister last week. Although I believe you have put two and two together and made about seven, at least I now understand the *Guardian*'s concerns, so I am glad to give you a fuller personal answer to your perplexities in the hope of laying this bogey to rest.

Aitken admitted he did meet Ayas in Paris, but over a dinner which was a 'casually arranged family affair'. Wafic Said had been staying at the Ritz, but he had not met him. There was no rendezvous of old business partners. As for Pallister, 'investigative reporters with controversial reputations arguably should be given careful and minimalist replies'. Aitken insisted again that his Ritz weekend was a 'family matter', dismissing the *Guardian*'s 'mysterious theories'. After five pages he signed off, 'With all good wishes, Yours ever, Jonathan.'

But Preston had seen the bill. And he was sceptical of Aitken's denials. So on 27 October he wrote again. On 2 November 1993 Aitken wrote back. He repeated his earlier denials, and amiably offered to meet Preston for an off-the-record chat 'over a drink at the Ritz' when the dust had settled 'on this non-story'. Secretly, he was also taking steps to cover his back.

Preston had already hinted that the matter of the Ritz bill could be referred up to a higher authority. Aitken ensured that copies of the correspondence were sent to the Chief Whip, Richard Ryder, the Cabinet Secretary and the Prime Minister's private secretary, Alex Allan, who were roped into his deceit. In a letter to Ryder Aitken struck a nonchalant pose. He professed to be 'mystified' rather than 'alarmed' by the *Guardian*'s inquiries for their 'complete non-story' for which 'the appropriate headline would be "Much ado about nothing."'

By this stage the reporters Pallister and Brown were feeling disheartened. They had been pounding away for three months. There was still, as such, no story. But a copy of Aitken's Ritz bill would certainly help their inquiries. Preston went back to Harrods and asked Fayed if he would help. But Fayed's key advisers Michael Cole (his silver-tongued PR man), Mark Griffiths (his aide) and Royston Webb (his lawyer) were strongly against the idea, and thought disclosure of the Aitken bill might damage the Ritz's reputation.

But Fayed did agree to a formula devised by Preston which would allow the *Guardian* to obtain Aitken's bill: the infamous 'cod fax'. The journalistic ruse was simple enough. Pallister mocked up a letter, ostensibly to the Ritz Hotel, asking for a copy of Aitken's bill. The letter purported to come from Aitken himself, and used his House of Commons letterhead. But the fax number at the top of the letter led back to the *Guardian*. It was an agreed insurance policy. The *Guardian* could now expose the Ritz connection without Fayed being implicated.

The cod fax worked. A Fayed assistant in Paris responded forty-eight hours later and sent back a copy of Aitken's bill. Preston, editor of the *Guardian* for eighteen years, had used this stratagem as a way of protecting an edgy source. It would be tricky if the ruse was ever discovered. It was, and the cod fax was to blow up extravagantly in his face. Later, though, once the extent of Jonathan Aitken's duplicity became known, the episode was to appear very much as having been in the public interest.

After a two-month gap, and now secretly armed with a copy of Aitken's bill, Preston wrote again to the minister on 11 January 1994:

Dear Jonathan,

I'm sorry to resume our fitful correspondence on that Paris weekend in September, but one further matter has arisen which I think I should put to you. A combination of circumstances and inquiries surrounding my chaps' original inquiries meant that one or two loose ends were left in the hands of others, and it has naturally taken some time for them to fall in place. But one, in particular, causes obvious bafflement.

It is now clear to me that Mr Ayas didn't merely join you for a family dinner but himself paid for your two nights at the Ritz – a bill of around £1,000. That may have been an act of extraordinary generosity between old friends; though to some it may reinforce the impression of some kind of business meeting. In any case, my team are naturally concerned to know how it fits in with section 126 of Questions of Procedure for Ministers. That seems to me a legitimate, even urgent question in current circumstances:

and, in the context of our previous exchanges, I thought I should put it to you directly.

Yours sincerely,

Peter Preston

Aitken's reply was frosty – and untrue:

Dear Peter,

Thank you for your letter of January 11th. You have again been misinformed.

Mr Ayas did not pay my hotel bill. There had been no 'act of extraordinary generosity between old friends'. There was not 'some kind of business meeting'. There has been no breach of any section of the Questions of Procedure for Ministers.

The facts of this matter are that the hotel bill was paid by my wife, with money given to her by me for this purpose, some hours after I had left Paris.

Since receiving your letter the only possible connection I have been able to discover between your wrong information and the correct facts, is that in my absence Mr Ayas (who you will recall from our earlier correspondence is an old family friend) did help my wife with some minor administrative and transportation arrangements at the time of her departure. However, these arrangements did not include any financial help with the hotel bill which, I repeat, was paid for with our own money.

I hope this makes the position clear.

Yours sincerely,

Jonathan

Aitken's letter now emerges as a truly staggering document, although at the time Preston had no idea just how deeply he was being deceived. Aitken's wife had never even visited Paris; she spent the entire weekend in Switzerland. Aitken had not paid his hotel bill. Ayas could not have helped Mrs Aitken with some 'minor' transportation arrangements because, sadly for Aitken, she was never there. A senior Conservative politician had decided, coolly and quite cynically, to emulate the tactic of Richard Nixon when confronted with the growing scandal of Watergate: the cover-up. Aitken decided to conceal the embarrassing matter of his Ritz Hotel bill by lying his way out of it. And the minister had hit upon what seemed the perfect alibi: his wife.

He wrote again to Richard Ryder, enclosed copies of the latest exchange of letters, and complained glibly of the 'quasi-McCarthyite era we are living through'. Privately though he must have been a very worried man. Aitken had gambled that the *Guardian* would never hear about his Ritz Hotel bill. It had. Now his wife was to ride to his rescue.

But for the cover-up to work Aitken's cronies had to stand by his story, now rapidly multiplying in complexity. The minister telephoned Said Ayas at his £20-million luxury yacht in the Caribbean, the *Katamarino*, in order to shore up his version of events.

But, of course, Preston knew he was being lied to. Aitken's bill had clearly been debited to Said Ayas. And so on 19 January 1994 Preston wrote again. 'I'm afraid I cannot easily accept your assurances about the Ritz bill . . .' he began. The *Guardian*, Preston wrote, was in a position to *prove* that Aitken had not paid his hotel bill for 8,010 French francs and 90 centimes. Preston also expressed bemusement, 'more mystically', at Aitken's claim that he had met up with his wife in Paris. The bill showed Aitken's room was single occupancy.

Aitken must have broken into a sweat when he read Preston's response. He was beginning to wobble. The pressure was telling. In his long reply of 20 January the minister grew increasingly heated. 'For my part I feel I have shown the patience of Job throughout this correspondence,' he wrote. He claimed the words 'Débiteur A/C Mr Ayas' had been typed in error by the Ritz, adding again, 'the bill was paid in cash by my wife with money given to her by me for that purpose'. 'Are we all bare-faced liars?' Aitken demanded to know. He went on:

These exchanges began with allegations of Ministerial impropriety centring on the Ritz hotel meeting between myself and three foreign businessmen. Although we have since been uphill and down dale into all sorts of changing theories, subjects, plots, details, locations and scenarios, the fundamental allegation remains and you evidently believe it, while I categorically deny it.

Aitken was lying, barefacedly. But instead of walking away from the table, he decided to invest in some more chips. His recklessness may well have been driven by private assurances that he would soon be promoted to the Cabinet. Aitken invited Preston to refer the matter to Sir Robin Butler, Whitehall's gentlemanly head prefect, whom he described as 'the arbiter of Ministerial Rules of Procedure'. Meanwhile, he sent another back-covering letter to Richard Ryder, complaining of this 'increasingly obsessional if not demented correspondence'.

And then he gave the roulette wheel another sharp spin. On 23 January Aitken phoned the *Guardian* newsdesk trying to get hold of Preston. The minister claimed he had 'found' his Ritz bill and located an 'independent French witness' who confirmed his wife Lolicia had paid it. On 26 January he wrote again to Preston. 'I understand that lawyers acting for Mr Ayas have received a letter from the Ritz Hotel confirming that he did not pay my bill and that my wife did pay it.' This was desperate stuff. The claim was garbage. No such letter existed.

Unfortunately for Aitken, Mohamed Al Fayed had secretly been passing copies of all relevant letters from the Ritz management to Peter Preston. Aitken signed off: 'I shall, with some difficulty, restrain myself to saying that our correspondence is at an end.' Preston replied on 27 January with a wonderful, mischievous lob. It might not be 'practical' to supply testimony from the independent French witness, but could Aitken send him a copy of the letter between Ayas and the Ritz management? Obviously Aitken could not.

Four days later Preston collated the large bundle of letters between himself and Jonathan Aitken and posted them off to Sir Robin Butler, the bicycling Cabinet Secretary and head of the Civil Service, for investigation. He also wrote a note to the Prime Minister informing him of the Ritz correspondence.

Behind the scenes, Aitken then moved into hyper-drive. He sought an exculpatory letter from Frank Klein, the Ritz Hotel's idiosyncratic polyglot president who was fond of leaving messages on his friends' answering machines in song. Klein simply and drily confirmed that Said Ayas had not 'personally' paid Aitken's hotel bill. Preston wrote back on 2 February pointing out that the Klein letter made no mention of the lovely Mrs Aitken who was supposed to have paid the minister's bill. Aitken nevertheless must have felt he was getting the upper hand. He wrote back in lyrical mood two days later:

Dear Peter,

Thank you for your letter of February 2nd, and for letting me know your characteristically dark suspicions about Mr Klein's letter. My guess is that most objective observers would regard it as a convincing rebuttal of your allegations that Mr Ayas paid my bill. However I note your eternal scepticism

of these and related matters. You certainly seem incorrigible in your enthusiasm for barking up the wrong trees.

As I indicated in my letter of January 20th I am entirely content that you
should have referred your allegations and the totality of our correspondence
to the Cabinet Secretary. This at least has the advantage of making it
unnecessary for us to write any more letters to each other.

So while I wait with baited breath to discover whether anyone outside
the *Guardian* believes that you have proved a breach of section 126 of the
Questions of Procedure for Ministers, may I terminate our exchanges on a
Shakespearean note by quoting some lines from Othello. Iago, speaking
about The Moor's oversuspicious nature says:

'Trifles as light as air
Are to the jealous confirmation strong
As proof of holy writ'

Substitute 'The Guardian' for 'the jealous' and the lines seem to be a
rather good explanation for your side of this obsessional correspondence.
Thank goodness it can now cease!

Yours sincerely,

Jonathan Aitken

Back in Whitehall Sir Robin Butler fell on Jonathan Aitken with
all the ferocity of a spaniel. Sir Robin, Harrow and University College,
Oxford, merely asked Jonathan Aitken, Eton and Christ Church,
whether he had paid his hotel bill. The minister smiled one of his
dimpled smiles and said he had.

Butler took a fortnight to reply to Preston. He concluded that since
Aitken had said he had paid his own bill no breach of ministerial guidelines could have taken place. Somewhat chummily, he showed a draft
of the letter he intended to send to the *Guardian* editor to Aitken, which
said the dispute 'seems to be a matter of his word against yours'.

Was that all right, Jonathan? It was not. Aitken suggested the
Cabinet Secretary's reply should be of a much more 'minimalist
nature' to discourage the *Guardian* from publishing a story. Sir Robin
duly wrote a 'minimalist' reply to Preston, testily complaining that
he was merely an adviser, not an arbiter of ministerial procedure.

The exercise had been a complete waste of time. The weary editor
picked up his pen again and despatched the whole bumper bundle
to the Prime Minister. If Robin Butler was not the arbiter of ministerial
probity, perhaps John Major was.

*

Six months earlier, on a pleasant Sunday afternoon, it had been a French woman wearing a smart business suit who had turned up at the cash desk of the Ritz Hotel in Paris. She had come to pay several hotel bills, including Jonathan Aitken's. Her name was Manon Vidal. A striking brown-haired former model with dusky Latin features and an almost masculine jaw line, Madame Vidal worked as private assistant to Prince Mohammed and Said Ayas.

She routinely paid the hotel bills for the Prince whose rooms were often booked in Said Ayas's name. Towards 4 p.m. on Sunday 19 September 1993, just after the Prince's group vacated the Ritz *en masse*, Vidal arrived to settle their account. She told the cashier Eric Ozere she was 'very busy' and had to rush off to the George V and Intercontinental Hotels to pay the bills of other Arab members of the Fahd party. The previous day she telephoned the Ritz and was told that 117,008 French francs were outstanding on the Ayas account. She duly turned up with a cheque for that amount.

Since then, though, the Arab party had made a few valedictory trips to the minibar, and with extra telephone calls included there was an additional 4,256.80 francs to pay. Madame Vidal reached into her capacious handbag, took out an envelope, and handed over 4,257 francs in cash. Mr Ozere then gave her 20 centimes change.

By late February 1994, as Vidal relaxed at her home in Aix-en-Provence, Aitken was desperately trying to prop up his crumbling story. He sent an optimistic fax to Klein asking him to confirm that Lolicia had 'paid' his hotel bill. Klein wrote back diplomatically stating a cash sum of 4,257 francs had been paid by a member of Said Ayas's staff. This gave Aitken a new way out. What if Lolicia Aitken had been the woman who had paid in cash that afternoon? Manon Vidal, an employee on the payroll of the Asturian Foundation, a shadowy business front for the Saudi royal family, was hardly likely to shoot her mouth off. Eureka! Aitken must have thought.

But there was a problem with Aitken's groaningly complex story. His bill at the Ritz had come to 8,010 francs, as Preston seemed to know. And yet Manon Vidal had only withdrawn 4,257 francs from her handbag, as the paperwork revealed. Aitken went back to his friend Said Ayas, and together they concocted a plan of farcical improbability to explain away the discrepancy. The Ritz had made an error, Aitken was to explain. Said Ayas's youthful nephew Abdul Rahman, who had been staying at the Ritz at the same time, had accidentally paid the other half of Aitken's bill, the story went. Aitken promptly whipped out an old Aitken Hume cheque-book and sent a cheque to Abdul Rahman for £426.88 together with a letter apologizing 'for this mix-up'. Ayas then happily corroborated Aitken's lie. In a letter to Aitken of 23 February, written for the benefit of the Cabinet Secretary, Ayas wrote that he had personally seen Lolicia pay her husband's bill, adding menacingly: 'If the *Guardian* newspaper does publish a report saying that I paid your bill, I shall get my lawyers to sue them.'

Aitken had squared the circle. His *Guardian* accusers had been beaten off by a seemingly impregnable defence. But then Aitken, as if possessed by the mischievous atavistic spirit of his dead great-uncle Beaverbrook, blew it. On his return from holiday Mr Klein interviewed Mr Ozere, the Ritz cashier who had been on duty that fateful afternoon. He then wrote a helpful letter to Aitken. Ozere's recollection was that 'a brunette lady of European aspect speaking French paid the cash sum of 4,257 francs in favour of the account of Mr Ayas'.

Manon Vidal, in fact.

A wiser man would have buried the letter in his filing cabinet. But a gloating Aitken decided to rub Preston's nose in it. On 3 March 1994 he fired off a triumphant letter to Sir Robin Butler, and sent a copy of his epistle to Preston. 'Further to our recent correspondence I thought I should pass on to you some helpful information I have just received from the Ritz Hotel in Paris,' he opened. He went on:

Mr Klein, who has himself been away from Paris, has now again written to me. The relevant passage of his letter, dated February 28th, runs as follows:–

'When I returned I discussed matters with the cashier who was on duty on 19 September and I am pleased to tell you that he does in fact remember the transaction to which you refer. His recollection is that a brunette lady of European aspect speaking French had paid the cash sum.'

The last sentence is a reasonably accurate description of my wife, who is a French-speaking Swiss national, of European parentage and appearance, and a brunette.

Even by Aitken's usual standards of mendacity, this was a whopper. Aitken had deliberately lopped off the end of the Klein paragraph

The deceitful young politician. Jonathan Aitken in March 1970, in hot water after breaching the Official Secrets Act. His most marked character trait was already evident: the way he told lies. (© the *Guardian*)

Jonathan Aitken and his new fiancée Lolicia Azucki on 26 June 1979 after announcing their engagement at a House of Commons swimming gala. (© Getty Images)

Inglewood. The Berkshire health hydro managed by Jonathan Aitken and bought using secret Arab money. A tantalizing whiff of sexual intrigue swirled around it in the 1980s. (© Associated Press)

Prince Mohammed bin Fahd, the son of King Fahd of Saudi Arabia. Aitken had worked as his obsequious London 'fixer' since the 1970s. Mohammed secretly helped bankroll Aitken's libel action. (© Patrick Kovarik/Popperfoto)

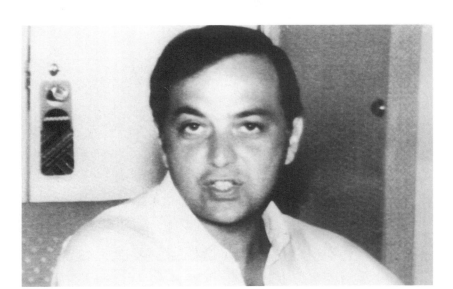

Said Ayas: Aitken's friend and co-conspirator. Friendship with Prince Mohammed turned him into a multi-millionaire. After the case collapsed he was placed under house arrest in Saudi Arabia. (© Granada Television)

Roosting triumphantly at the heart of the Major Government: Jonathan Aitken, Chief Secretary to the Treasury, leaves 10 Downing Street on 31 March 1995 with his Cabinet colleagues Michael Portillo, Jeremy Hanley, Peter Lilley and John Redwood. (© Martin Argles/ the *Guardian*)

The fabled Ritz Hotel in Paris owned by Mohamed Al Fayed. Aitken made a secret trip to the Ritz in September 1993 while Minister of State for Defence Procurement. For nearly four years he lied to his colleagues about the trip and claimed his wife had paid the bill when she was in fact in Switzerland. (© Sean Smith/the *Guardian*)

Mohamed Al Fayed. The mercurial Egyptian tycoon who tipped off the *Guardian* after spotting Jonathan Aitken secretly consorting with prominent Saudis at the Ritz Hotel. (© Martin Argles/ the *Guardian*)

A stagey family photo of Jonathan Aitken and his wife and children at the minister's Lord North Street home. The photo accompanied a flattering article by Roy Hattersley describing Aitken as a future Prime Minister. (© Tiddy Maitland/Solo Syndication)

Jonathan Aitken making the Sword of Truth speech at Conservative Central Office, 10 April 1995, in which he attacked the 'cancer of bent and twisted journalism'. (© Martin Argles/the *Guardian*)

Jonathan Aitken exits Conservative Central Office with his wife Lolicia (left) and daughter Victoria after declaring war on the media in his infamous Sword of Truth speech. He was forced to resign from Cabinet three months later after his affair with a prostitute was exposed. (© Martin Argles/the *Guardian*)

Jonathan Aitken arriving at the High Court with his 17-year-old daughter Victoria. At his instruction she would lie for him. (© Photo News Service)

George Carman QC: Britain's greatest jury advocate leaves court after the collapse of the Aitken trial.
(© Martin Godwin/the *Guardian*)

Doodle of the Aitken trial judge Mr Justice Popplewell by *Guardian* editor Alan Rusbridger on the first day of the trial. Popplewell – a cricket enthusiast – decided to hear the case without a jury.

Victory: Alan Rusbridger (left) and Peter Preston on the steps of the High Court, 20 June 1997, after Aitken is exposed as a liar and withdraws his libel action. (© Kippa Matthews)

Jonathan Aitken reappears in public after fleeing the country for more than three weeks following the collapse of his court case. He is mobbed by photographers outside his Lord North Street home. (© Martin Argles/the *Guardian*)

which made clear that only 4,257 FF – half the bill – had been paid. He had lied to the Cabinet Secretary. In the High Court he loftily dismissed the episode as 'sharp editing', and said he felt justified in using subterfuge because of the deadly cat-and-mouse game Preston was playing with him.

Aitken had also created another problem for himself: his wife, according to her passport at least, had blonde hair. A few days later Preston sat in his office in a state of stupefaction. Fayed had given him a complete copy of the Klein letter, which had been sharply edited by Aitken. The lies were getting more and more flagrant, he reflected.

John Major, meanwhile, had been a little troubled by the Preston dossier. If everything was all in order, could Aitken not simply send the wretched Preston a copy of the Ritz bill, Major wondered? On 17 March Sir Robin, Alex Allan, John Major's private secretary, and Aitken sat down together and scratched their heads over the mysterious Ritz receipt. Allan produced a pocket calculator and, rather like a clever grammar schoolboy about to sit an exam for a class prize, tried to make the sums add up. 'I'll just work this out, I enjoy this sort of puzzle,' he said. But his efforts did not explain away the fact that the bill was debited to Ayas. 'The production of the bill will not dispose of the questions from the *Guardian*,' Allan reported back to his boss.

On friendly and confidential terms, Preston wrote once more to the Cabinet Secretary imploring him to take a second look at the affair. He got a sniffy reply instead from Allan: 'The Prime Minister regards these as private matters for Mr Aitken and sees no grounds for what you describe as "inquiry" or "arbitration" on his part.' In a triumphant piece of braggadocio, Aitken scribbled on a draft copy of the letter, shown to him by Allan: 'This is all such baloney – but over to the conspiracy theorists!'

Preston was not content to leave it there. And he was not a conspiracy theorist. On 10 May 1994 the bizarre saga of Jonathan Aitken and his Ritz Hotel bill burst into print for the first time. Preston, despairing of the Prime Minister's inertia, wrote a detailed article for the *Guardian* tabloid section entitled THE MINISTER, THE MANDARIN, THE PREMIER AND THE EDITOR. 'I was trying to reflect my extreme worry that something was going on I didn't understand,' Preston explained.

The piece introduced the main players in the odd Ritz drama and, crucially, reproduced Aitken's Ritz Hotel bill. Back at the House of Commons Aitken dismissed the article as 'interminably boring'. But that same day the cod fax episode came back to haunt Preston. Frank Klein, who had seen the *Guardian* article, wrote a stiff letter to Aitken and promised a full investigation into how the *Guardian* had obtained a copy of his hotel bill. The cod fax was duly dug up from the Ritz vaults and shown to Aitken, who in turn showed it to Butler, Allan and Major. Butler wrote a tart private note to the editor referring to the 'margins of criminality'. But nothing was said openly by either the Cabinet Secretary or Aitken; the fax simply lay in their files for use if Preston caused trouble again.

Two months scudded by, and then in July 1994 Jonathan Aitken, the defence minister who had spent the last few months lying to his political superiors, was rewarded with a job in the Cabinet. Showing the kind of poor judgement which contributed to the Conservatives' later electoral meltdown, John Major offered Aitken the post of Chief Secretary to the Treasury. With it came the new rank of Privy Councillor, and the gentlemanly prefix 'Right Honourable'.

For the next two months, Aitken immersed himself in the ministerial spending round. And then, in September 1994, the saga took a fresh twist. Mohamed Al Fayed heard that he had lost his case in the European Court of Human Rights, which might have had the damning DTI report into his Harrods take-over declared in breach of the Convention. Fayed went ape. At his penthouse suite in Harrods the air hummed with expletives as Fayed stomped and chafed.

On the evening of 19 September 1994 Preston went to Harrods and saw the Egyptian multi-millionaire alone. Mohamed looked a little dishevelled, shirt undone, jacket discarded, grim and upset. They drank whisky. There was, as he saw it, no justice. He had decided to go public with his allegations against four Government ministers: Tim Smith, Neil Hamilton, Jonathan Aitken and Michael Howard. That meant the grubby story of Hamilton, Smith and Greer taking money from Fayed to lobby – one on which the paper had done so much digging work – could at last be told.

The *Guardian* printed it. Tim Smith resigned on 20 October. Five days later Hamilton, kicking and screaming, was made to walk the plank. The Prime Minister grimly announced he was setting up a new committee to clean up standards in political life chaired by a quietly rigorous Roman Catholic judge, Lord Nolan. In the corridors of Westminster there was consternation and panic in the Tory ranks.

Jonathan Aitken, meanwhile, was following the strategy of ex-President Richard Nixon and 'hanging tough'. On 27 October 1994 the *Guardian* went on the offensive. In a front-page article, Aitken's sharply edited letter to Klein was published for the first time. Preston wrote again to Butler observing: 'I happen to think that ministers should not lie to Cabinet secretaries. And I cannot think why this minister should lie to you.' Butler replied coolly, saying Aitken had showed him a copy of the full Klein letter. He added: 'We sucked the orange dry in correspondence earlier in the year.'

In the House of Commons the political temperature reached boiling-point. Gordon Brown, the Shadow Chancellor, joined the attack. Was any part of the Chief Secretary's bill for his stay at the Ritz Hotel paid by Mr Ayas? On the Tory benches, there was indignant uproar. Betty Boothroyd, the Speaker, interrupted. But Aitken wanted to respond. 'I would very much welcome a chance to answer the question,' he began, 'not least because it is the first chance to clear myself of the scurrilous allegations that had been made.' Aitken denied the allegation 'completely' and flourished Sir Robin Butler's letter, which 'confirmed' he did not regard Aitken as having lied to him. 'I hope that the House . . . will accept both my assurance and the Cabinet Secretary's assurance and put an end to the hysterical episode of sleaze journalism by the *Guardian*,' he declared.

It was melodramatic stuff. Aitken could now add a new entry to the long list of institutions he had lied to over the years: the House of Commons. Preston wrote again to Aitken on 24 October 1994 and complained of his sharp editing: 'I now see it was not Sir Robin who was being seriously misled in that article – but myself.'

And then the empire struck back. Aitken planted the fatuous Abdul Rahman story on the *Daily Mail*. The paper gullibly splashed it under the headline: AITKEN DID PAY THAT RITZ BILL. Meanwhile John Major, having lost two ministers to sleaze disclosures, was white with rage. In a briefing paper written for his lawyers, and never previously revealed, Aitken made an intriguing but unlikely claim: Major had personally authorized the Downing Street press office to leak the existence of the cod fax to the Tory-supporting *Sunday Telegraph*.

On 30 October 1994 the *Telegraph* duly published a front-page story revealing the *Guardian*'s 'forgery'. Conservative MPs who had watched helplessly as the sleaze crisis carried off two of their own howled and ululated with anger. They wanted Preston's head, preferably on a big plate. In an emergency debate in the House of Commons, several fist-waving Tory MPs called for Preston to be arraigned for contempt. They wanted the cod fax and the unauthorized use of House of Commons notepaper referred to the Privileges Committee, the group of MPs who are the supreme guardians of Commons behaviour.

Aitken's constituency neighbour Roger Gale MP, a former *Blue Peter* producer and self-appointed judge of media standards, frothingly described Preston as 'the whore from hell'. Preston listened phlegmatically to the absurd spectacle from the Public Gallery. Outside Aitken's house in Lord North Street the press were encamped. But support for the minister both inside the Cabinet and in his constituency was holding up. Aitken confessed privately he did indeed have a discussion with Prince Mohammed during the Ritz weekend. This, of course, appeared to have no connection with who paid his hotel bill. Aitken had paid it himself. The Prime Minister no doubt calculated losing yet another minister to sleaze would deal a fatal body-blow to his sickly administration. 'As we all know, his integrity and his moral and Christian standards are above reproach,' Aitken's Conservative association chairman Major John Thomas trilled.

By the end of 1994 Jonathan Aitken was congratulating himself that he had ended the year 'bloody but unbowed'. He had appeared in a co-star role with the Chancellor Kenneth Clarke in the November Budget and put up what he regarded as 'strong debating performances' in the House of Commons. By contrast, he told his friends, his 'mortal enemy' Preston had come off badly. After three hectic months, it was true that Preston felt exhausted and personally depressed. Six months before the affair exploded, in the quiet of summer, he had told Hugo Young that twenty years' editing under pressure was enough. Young was the *Guardian*'s chief political columnist and chairman of the Scott Trust, the body which owns and guards the paper. Preston said he wanted a change. His obvious successor, deputy editor Alan Rusbridger, was waiting in the wings. In January 1995 Preston became editor-in-chief of the *Guardian* and the *Observer*, and Rusbridger took over the editorship of the *Guardian*. His main foe out of the game, Aitken must have imagined himself home and dry.

But, once again, he had underestimated the tenacity of his 'cancerous' enemies in the media; in particular a dented-Volvo-estate-driving journalist by the name of David Leigh.

'Look, when I retired, the Saudis gave me this house. And they bought me that Volkswagen Golf outside. And when I said I had hearing trouble, they bought me a set of spectacles with a built-in hearing-aid. *And* they paid for my prostate operation. I'm not going to go on TV now and slag them off.' **Anonymous ex-chauffeur to the Saudis**

....

Seven: **Jonathan of Arabia**

Perched high above London, the producer David Leigh had a glamorous view through his picture window whenever he glanced up from his computer screen on the 17th floor of the South Bank Television Centre. The great white dome of St Paul's, the bravura skyline of the Lloyds building and the distant bulk of Canary Wharf tower in Docklands were all spread out along the busy Thames to the east – while to the west, the mass of Big Ben and the Houses of Parliament lay exposed. Eyeing this panorama like a modern Canaletto, it was easy for a journalist like Leigh to make the mistake of believing he could see exactly what was really going on in Britain. Leigh certainly failed at first to grasp that he was about to face one of the most stubborn and testing enigmas of his career.

Simply by lying, over and over again, the Cabinet minister Jonathan Aitken had by now achieved a sort of stalemate over his trip to the Ritz. He was roosting triumphantly at the heart of the Major Government. An old friend from his *Young Meteor* days, the Labour politician Roy Hattersley, even wrote a profile for a Sunday paper predicting that Aitken might be the next Tory leader. He said Aitken was a 'family man', who was 'without an enemy' in politics. The piece of flattery was accompanied by a stagey group photo of all the Aitkens – Jonathan, Lolicia and the three children – lined up on a sofa in Aitken's overweening Lord North Street drawing room in early 1995.

This was the point in Aitken's fortunes at which Leigh, the investigative journalist, came on the scene. He had had a long and combative track record, and was currently producing documentaries at *World in*

Action. After thirty years, this half-hour programme, which went out on Monday nights, was still the most belligerent documentary series on British television, getting audiences of six million or more on the populist commercial channel for exposures that had spanned in their time the story of the bribes paid by corrupt architect John Poulson in the 1970s, and the dogged campaign to free the wrongfully convicted Irishmen, the Birmingham Six, in the 1980s.

Despite the highly regulated condition of British broadcasting, and the long dominance of the Conservative Government, *World in Action* was a programme that prided itself on going where some of its rivals feared to tread. The programme's Liverpudlian editor Steve Boulton was perfectly prepared to do battle with a Cabinet minister, if the evidence materialized.

David Leigh knew a lot of people at the *Guardian*. He had worked there himself as a young reporter, and was intrigued by the paper's clash with a politician who seemed unwilling to sue. 'It was perfectly obvious Aitken was lying to Peter Preston about the Ritz,' Leigh now says: 'I thought I must be able to find out why.'

Over three months, having secured the co-operation of Preston, he started to dig up Aitken's history: 'When you're looking for the truth about politicians, the best tactic is often to go back a long way in time, and see what they were up to before they became careful.' Leigh started to pursue where Aitken's first bag of money came from. When did Aitken first meet Said Ayas? he asked himself. What was their relationship all about?

One of the first things Leigh stumbled on was a series of hints about Aitken's sado-masochistic aberrations. To his surprise, half the dinner-tables of London seemed to know about them. They were the kinds of things that, had the Party whips, or MI5, been aware of them, would have raised at least a question mark over his suitability for ministerial office, on grounds of potential blackmail. One journalistic couple mentioned tantalizingly that they had a French friend who had had a sexual relationship with the politician: 'Aitken used to tie her up, of course. He said she was the woman he wished he had married.' They were unwilling to reveal her identity. Other colleagues implied that Aitken insisted on being whipped himself. One of Aitken's many girlfriends, the glamorous Jackie Leishman, had actually been a *Guardian* reporter herself at the time. This seemed a promising lead. But, traced with difficulty to the Sussex countryside where she was now the partner of a rich Greek, she, too, was far from forthcoming about specifics.

Much more directly to the point were the leads on Aitken's business relationships with the Saudis and other Arabs. Leigh did a deal with David Pallister of the *Guardian* – an old colleague and friend. Pallister would have advance sight of the script of the *World in Action* film that was made. He could have the exclusive story. In return, Pallister offered to share the fruits of his own independent digging – and any new witnesses he uncovered – with *World in Action*. It was an agreement that both parties were to honour punctiliously three months down the line, although it turned out to be an 'exclusive' that would land both *World in Action* and the *Guardian* in a huge legal battle.

There were four off-the-record sources available from the *Guardian* – all individuals who had tentatively come forward after the Ritz row had blown up the previous October. The first – 'Stan' – Leigh found in a cab-company restroom down a City back alley. He didn't want his name revealed, he said hoarsely: 'The Saudis will get me.' He had been driving Saudi royals on their visits to London throughout the 1970s and 1980s, he said. He had fetched call-girls for them from an escort agency in Kensington, and also taken them to casinos. Stan eventually produced a dog-eared letter belonging to another driver. It concerned a trivial dispute over how much Prince Saud bin Naif, the young son of the much-feared Saudi interior minister, had been due to pay for chauffeurs and cleaners during one of his visits to London. What was interesting was the signature: 'Jonathan Aitken'.

It seemed that, while on one level the Conservative politician had been very much the high society figure, on another plane he had simultaneously been rather a mundane, even lowly, fixer for rich Saudis. Companies House records showed that Aitken was in this Prince's employ: he was a director of a service company called SNAS, which looked after Prince Saud's London interests, including a gigantic mansion off Hyde Park, Cleeve Lodge, bought with paperwork organized by Aitken's Old Etonian lawyer friend, Mark Vere Nicholl. SNAS certainly did not appear in Aitken's *Who's Who* entry. Nor did it appear on the Register of MPs' Interests.

There was a second source – 'Randolph'. He was even more nervous. Over scallops and Chablis with Leigh at Novellis, a chi-chi brasserie in Clerkenwell, Randolph revealed that Aitken had been promoting some little arms deals in 1994 at the Ministry of Defence, while arms sales minister himself, which involved a Lebanese businessman called Fouad Makhzoumi. Randolph did not want to say too much: but it was made plain that the armoured-car firm Alvis were involved – and that the minister had met Makhzoumi for private talks about the deals at his Lord North Street house. The *Guardian* had already checked and found, to their puzzlement, that Aitken had actually been a director of a Makhzoumi company while an MP, but had never declared it on the MPs' Register. Nor had he even listed the directorship – as company law required – on the records of his other companies. The whole relationship with Makhzoumi – like so much else concerning Aitken's links with the Middle East – seemed never to have been made visible.

Up a creaking lift in a cavernous warren of offices just by London Bridge, Leigh found the *Guardian*'s third off-the-record lead – in the consulting rooms of Robin Kirk, the osteopath. Fifteen years after he had fallen out with Aitken, the mild-mannered and slight New Zealander, his hair and moustache grey with the years, could still be transformed by the memory of his Inglewood days into a considerable rage. 'Jonathan was a shit,' he says, 'and I told him so.' Kirk had been contacted by the *Guardian* after they ran their 1994 exposures. But the osteopath, who ran a successful private practice and lectured at the College of Osteopathy, was only willing to talk, like the others, off the record. For a TV documentary Leigh needed live witnesses who were prepared to go on camera. He had to turn timid people into brave ones.

Over the succeeding months, Leigh eventually persuaded Robin Kirk to appear on camera. Kirk was to go 'over the parapet' with a slight tremor in his voice, in an act of signal courage. Like a few others who would do the same, he had to face a torrent of invective from Jonathan Aitken as a consequence.

It was a few days after his meeting with the osteopath that Leigh stepped off a charter flight full of winter sunseekers in Lanzarote, the biggest of the Canary Islands, near the coast of Africa. There was a large, not-quite-extinct volcano in the middle of the island, and a jazzy strip of Rolex-watch-and-gold-chain bars and eateries which defaced the coast. It was a place for people who needed to stay away – the ones who felt the cold and, indeed, the ones who felt the heat elsewhere. Set back from the garish strip, in the plusher area, the TV producer found an estate agent's office selling villas and time-shares. There, running it, was the feisty, but jumpy, Irishwoman who had been Robin Kirk's lover and the matron at Inglewood fifteen years before.

Jo Lambert, too, was nervous – and understandably so. She had been arrested after a police investigation that had certainly been authorized, if not encouraged, by Jonathan Aitken, which had ended in her being ignominiously thrown out of Inglewood. She insisted that, although she had been accused of pilfering, not only had she never been convicted of making off with Inglewood's spare towels and old chests of drawers, but she had also never been charged in the first place. The whole 'police investigation' had been trumped up. What struck Leigh, as they talked it over that evening in a small restaurant on the island, was that Jo Lambert was not trying to conceal her brush with the law. On the contrary, she was indignantly volunteering the details of it as evidence of what a rotter Aitken could be.

She was eventually to agree to appear on the film under her own name. She described Aitken's efforts to have his Arab associates diverted with girls at Inglewood. But what was most gripping was her account, which confirmed that given by Robin Kirk, of the true ownership of Inglewood. Aitken the MP was very much the 'front man', who gave the impression that he controlled, if not owned, the health farm outright. But the firm's shares were held anonymously by a Panamanian company – and that disguised control by the Saudis.

Kirk and Lambert knew exactly what had happened, they explained. They had been instrumental in persuading Aitken, the 1970s visitor to the health farm with his Swiss girlfriend Lolicia, to step in. Aitken's friends the Saudis had put up the money. Furthermore, the whole Inglewood operation was run from the office of another Saudi prince – Saud's cousin and the King's son. This was Aitken's own employer, Prince Mohammed bin Fahd. Day-to-day control was in the hands of the Prince's aides – Fahad Athel and Said Ayas. Jo Lambert knew all this for a fact – at one point she had personally been required to go and work on Inglewood's affairs out of the lavish Saudi offices at 21 Upper Grosvenor Street. But Aitken kept the Saudi ownership secret.

Kirk and Lambert had an explanation for Aitken's clear deceit – the Jewish matrons who patronized the health farm would have been put off their lucrative slenderizing if they had known Inglewood was owned by Arabs. 'I said that to him myself,' said Kirk. This excuse was all very well – but the picture that was emerging was rather shocking. The Inglewood directorship was yet another one that Aitken had kept out of the Register of MPs' Interests. A Conservative MP simply could not go around concealing his business links with the Saudi royal family without the gravest doubts arising about his probity. And this name – Prince Mohammed bin Fahd – was occurring ever more frequently in the recollections of Aitken's circle. Who was he?

The staff at Inglewood did not really know. Jo Lambert said: 'I'm sorry. One Saudi looked much the same as another to me. Jonathan simply used to refer to them as "the Arabs".'

Back in England, Leigh started trying to trace other drivers from the large pool of chauffeurs who had been engaged to take the high-rolling Saudis around town on their frequent holiday escapes from the Islamic rigours of Riyadh. The investigative journalist got short shrift from most of them – and the reason why was revealing. 'Look,' said one grizzled cabbie, gesturing around his suburban home, 'when I retired, the Saudis gave me this house. And they bought me that Volkswagen Golf outside. And when I said I had hearing trouble, they bought me a set of spectacles with a built-in hearing-aid. *And* they paid for my prostate operation. I'm not going to go on TV now and slag them off.'

There were many such rebuffs. But, approached patiently, one man eventually threw out a phone number. And, that evening, Leigh's Volvo drew up outside a terrace house in an obscure west London side-street in Acton. A frantic yapping and barking greeted his tentative ring on the bell, and the woman who opened the door seemed to thrust aside quantities of dogs and cats, at which she shouted vigorously, as she cleared a way to her front parlour.

Valerie Scott was slightly eccentric. She was charming, too, with a voice that was alternately melodious and earthy – although the dark circles round her eyes suggested a life that had not been exactly easy. She was now running a social services nursery after putting herself through a Psychology degree course as a mature student. Yes, she said, she had been Jonathan's personal secretary all the way through the period when he had first met Prince Mohammed, Said Ayas, and all the other Arabs, twenty years ago. She had worked six years for

Aitken, and six more after that for Said Ayas himself. No, she didn't mind in the least answering questions.

'What was Aitken's relationship with Prince Mohammed exactly?' said Leigh.

'Well, he bought him a plane,' Valerie Scott replied. It was the first of many startling recollections Valerie Scott came out with, which painted a picture hitherto more or less completely unknown to the general public – that of a playboy Saudi prince, wallowing in the bribes slipped to him by Western firms as commissions, with an obsequious British MP helping him to spend the cash.

Virtually Aitken's entire life-style, it seemed from Valerie's account, had been lubricated by Prince Mohammed's millions. The MP ran his political office from Prince Mohammed's plush premises off Park Lane; he filled up the Jaguar given to him by the Prince with petrol on the Prince's account; he persuaded the Prince to sponsor a motor-racing team associated with one of his Old Etonian chums; and he used the Prince's money to parlay himself into positions at Inglewood, TV-am, and at his cousin Tim's merchant bank, Aitken Hume. In return, Aitken touted for further commissions for Mohammed, recruiting British firms such as GEC, who would pay the Prince a percentage in order to be allowed to export to his despotic state.

In all these dealings, Said Ayas was the Prince's front man, and Aitken's conduit to him. Valerie's recollections, together with those of the Inglewood staff, now put Aitken's mysterious 1993 visit, apparently paid for by Said Ayas, to the Paris Ritz in an entirely new light. It was not the shadowy Said Ayas who was really at the centre of the affair at all – it seemed it was the Saudi royal family themselves. This was a dramatic development. But could *World in Action* prove any of it?

Some weeks later, the deceptively polite figure of Quentin McDermott, Leigh's assistant producer, came down the plane steps in Miami and rendezvoused with a local US film crew. McDermott had personally scored a coup. He had not only successfully traced the individual BAC 1-11 jet which Prince Mohammed had purchased for $3.5 million twenty years earlier – he had also found the man who sold it, and persuaded him to give a filmed interview. Wayne Hilmer, formerly of the Omni Aircraft Corporation, and now retired by a Florida poolside, was soon 'in the can' – shot rather intriguingly with a pet parrot on his shoulder – describing how the deal had been done at the Paris air show that year with a man who Hilmer took to be the Prince's attorney, or solicitor. His name, the American recalled, was Jonathan Aitken.

This was to be the first of many occasions on which Valerie Scott's powers of recall were confirmed by hard proof. She also remembered some striking details which seemed at first impossible to corroborate directly. 'Aitken got me to send Said Ayas a blue rabbit for his daughter,' she said. 'That would have been around Christmas 1974.' Years later, her dates would turn out to be absolutely accurate. Valerie also recalled that Aitken had returned to Phillimore Gardens in great excitement one day a year or two later, saying, 'Prince Mohammed has bought me a car.' She personally took delivery of the gleaming new Jaguar XJ6 when it arrived at the front door. 'It was dark blue,' she said.

To the journalists from *World in Action*, Valerie Scott was pure gold. However, although Valerie was prepared to confirm Aitken's sexual addictions to whips and canes, of which she had accurate personal knowledge, it was to be many weeks before she would unburden herself of her own personal history that she, too, had been sleeping with Aitken while he was her boss. To *World in Action*'s disappointment, Valerie Scott adamantly refused to appear on screen. She was willing to be quoted by name but, she said with a shudder, she could not bear the parents at her nursery recognizing her and pointing her out. She was far too shy.

'Never mind,' said Leigh, 'we'll use an actress.' It was not the only difficult decision he had to make.

An exuberant young Granada director, Chris Malone, was seconded to the project. Leigh and Malone cooked up between them a dis-respectful series of what they called 'living graphics'. The theme of the programme was to be Aitken's links with the Saudis – so they decided to call it 'Jonathan of Arabia'. The film was to be held together with wailing pastiche *Lawrence of Arabia* music.

'And we could have a camel,' said Malone.

'We could?' said Leigh.

'Leave it with me.'

A day or two later, Malone appeared on the chilly sand-dunes of Formby beach, near Liverpool. With him was a film crew, an actor in Bedouin robes, and a female camel called Topsy, complete with driver. 'How did you find her?' asked Leigh.

'I tried Chester Zoo first, but they wouldn't let me borrow any of their animals,' Malone said. 'So I hired her from Chipperfield's Circus.' The show-business adage says: 'Never work with children or animals' – and it proved to be sound. Filming the *Lawrence of Arabia* sequences was nightmarish, as attempts were made to persuade Topsy to patrol across the sand-dunes. Whenever she caught sight of the crashing sea, the camel froze in fear and refused to move another inch. This was perhaps to be expected in a desert animal, but it made for slow work.

Malone refused to be beaten by the cold and damp, which gave the scenes a somewhat un-Arabian appearance. He produced from his van a set of huge propane burners. These he ignited and positioned underneath the camera lens. The subsequent videotapes were excellent: they portrayed an exotic vessel of the desert swaying through shimmering columns of heat-haze – as Topsy plodded off behind dunes in the general direction of Blackpool.

Leigh was worried that the film, as it took shape, might seem racist, even though the programme-makers' quarrel was not with Arabs in general. In an attempt to redress the balance, two of the sternest critics of Saudi royal misbehaviour invited on to the film were Arabs themselves. The cultivated Palestinian author and businessman Said Aburish explained witheringly that the Saudi royal family were corrupt and levied commissions on all Western export deals. 'If you do not pay a bribe, you do not get the contract – it's as simple as that.' He explained the censorship and religious intolerance that characterized Saudi Arabia: 'You cannot possess a Bible. A Christian cannot wear a cross.' Aburish's testimony on screen – shot in huge close-up against a stark black background – made Jonathan Aitken seem desperately hypocritical. And so, perhaps, he was: a church-warden who worked for potentates who outlawed Christianity; a professional journalist whose bosses forbade free speech; and a democratically elected politician in the pay of those whose own citizens were not allowed to vote.

Aburish was followed on screen by the portly figure of Mohammed al-Masri, a fundamentalist Saudi exile in London, much detested by the Saudi regime, British arms companies with lucrative contracts, and the Foreign Office in Whitehall. Masri explained to the camera that a young prince like Saud bin Naif made his millions by levying high charges, for example, on the monopolies he controlled within Saudi Arabia, such as on international courier services: 'The price they charge is quite outrageous,' he said. 'It cost £25 to send a single packet out of the country.'

Another sequence began with a Rolls-Royce drawing up as night falls outside Aitken's house in Lord North Street. A figure in Bedouin robes slips out of the car and into Aitken's porch. The budget for actors had been exhausted – this cartoon figure was the journalist Leigh himself, dressed up. What he was reconstructing was the meeting at Aitken's home with the Lebanese entrepreneur Fouad Makhzoumi.

While he was arms sales minister, Aitken promoted an arms deal for his friend. It was a classic conflict of interests from which Aitken should have withdrawn. The minister wrote officially to the Lebanese interior minister, urging him to sign up to buy a package of 'security equipment' from the British Alvis arms company, and promising a Government 'sweetener' if he did so. Meanwhile, Alvis agreed to pay Makhzoumi between 3 and 5 per cent commission on the deal if it went through. Aitken's ministry supplied 500 free rifles to 'sweeten' the contract, and handed over 3,000 more surplus rifles, which Alvis promptly sold on to the Lebanese at a profit of 50 per cent. But, contrary to his protestations in the Sword of Truth speech, there were no records in the M.o.D. that Aitken had ever declared his history of business links with Makhzoumi before playing this questionable part in a questionable deal.

The *World in Action* film, when completed, constituted a spirited and sustained challenge to Jonathan Aitken. It depicted him as being in the pocket of the Arabs, and the Saudi royal family as being exceptionally corrupt and venal. The assault scarcely slowed throughout its twenty-six minutes, from the opening scenes of Topsy ploughing majestically through the sands with a burnoused figure on her back, to the denouement in which the actress playing Valerie Scott says crushingly of the Saudi royals and Aitken's Ritz billing arrangements: 'Wherever they went, it was always the same – Said Ayas paid the bill.'

The programme-makers now faced their main tactical problem. How to approach Aitken himself? Unlike print journalists, TV producers are obliged by the official codes to notify the subjects of a hostile inquiry in advance, and give them the opportunity to defend themselves. Obviously, this is something any fair-minded journalist would actually want to do as a rule. In practice, however, the moment a powerful person or organization is notified in advance that an attack is coming the lawyers and PR men are called in to help them decide what can be done, firstly to gain intelligence about the programme's contents, and secondly to derail it, by threats of legal action, complaints to the broadcasting authorities or the actual issuing of injunctions banning transmission. The usual tactic is to carry out these sabotaging activities while 'considering' for as long as possible whether to appear in an interview – a consideration which invariably leads in the end to a refusal. It is a game in which the influential use professional advisers to try and wrest the upper hand from heavily regulated programme-makers.

Print journalists, on the other hand, do not need to do anything, or they can merely ring up the night before, inquire, 'Anything to say?' and print the story overnight before the other side can call up their troops. Newspapers are nimble: TV must signal its punches.

Leigh, Steve Boulton and Jeffery Maunsell, Granada's battle-scarred solicitor from the London firm Goodman Derrick, agreed a strategy. Nearly two weeks beforehand, Leigh notified the Treasury press office that *World in Action* proposed to put out a programme about Aitken's business connections with the Saudis. Aitken was invited to appear and give an interview, stating his point of view. In what Leigh prided himself was a subtle twist, the formal letter went on further to invite Aitken to nominate any of his friends he pleased who he might wish to see interviewed on the topic.

This was a gamble. If Aitken had, indeed, volunteered large numbers of willing interviewees, *World in Action* would have had to walk a fine line between the demand for balance laid down by broadcasting law and the integrity – and clarity – of their story. But Aitken threw his chance away. Exactly as *World in Action* had expected, the important Tory Cabinet minister was too arrogant to accept such an offer, particularly from those he and his advisers regarded as 'hostile media'. Instead, Aitken simply ignored the programme-makers' approach altogether.

Aitken's rudeness now opened a second important regulatory door. An interview had been sought by conventional means, on a topic in the public interest, and had been refused. This refusal now entitled the programme-makers, under ITC codes, to legitimately 'doorstep' their subject. They could approach Aitken, uninvited, provided it was in a public place, insist on asking him questions, and capture on videotape the street theatre of a minister visibly failing to come clean. The ITC rules are thoroughly sensible, and designed to stop intrusive badgering with insufficient public-interest grounds to justify it. Aitken had just forfeited their protection. Underneath the suave air, Aitken was regularly prone to crashing errors of judgement.

The well-mannered assistant producer Quentin McDermott, never as nice as he looked, was the man who successfully ambushed the coy minister. As Aitken, sleek as ever, emerged alone from his Lord North Street front door and headed across the narrow strip of pavement separating him from the waiting Government Jaguar, McDermott was on the spot, wearing a radio-mike in his lapel. 'Why won't you talk about your Saudi business interests, Mr Aitken?' called out the TV journalist sternly, as his two-man crew, agile with their camera and boom-mike, captured a stony-faced and silent Aitken sliding into his car and being driven off.

The successful 'doorstep' was a model little piece of TV. It was immediately scheduled by Leigh, closeted in the Manchester editing suite, as a good sequence to kick 'Jonathan of Arabia' off. No one realized then that that particular film clip would not in fact see the light of day for more than two years – and that, when it was finally shown, it would be in even more melodramatic circumstances.

Aitken by now was plainly beginning to feel alarmed. He called in his solicitor, the veteran Richard Sykes, to bombard the TV company – and the Granada chairman – with complaints that his client was being denied a 'right of reply'. Sykes's claim that Aitken was 'considering' granting an interview under the right circumstances was deflated by Granada's discovery that his client had in fact cleared off to Switzerland for what was ostensibly a skiing weekend – although it later emerged that his patron Prince Mohammed was also in Geneva. Sykes's final ploy was then to 'offer' an appearance by Aitken – but only if it was at the end of the programme, for seven minutes, and live. A live appearance would be impossible to edit so as to focus on the relevant points. Such an appearance would occupy more than a quarter of the whole film. Aitken was the Prince of Perjury: but any seasoned politician worth his salt could evade, bluster and waffle for seven minutes on end on TV without the least difficulty. As courtroom events were later to demonstrate, even a top QC such as George Carman could not cross-examine the truth out of the slippery Aitken inside seven full days, let alone seven minutes.

The offer was obviously a bluff. If it had been accepted, Aitken might well have been in a fix. But *World in Action* were, for once, not prepared to call the bluff. The consequences of a wrong decision would have been disastrous. The TV team peremptorily refused Sykes's offer.

'Jonathan of Arabia' was now completed, the commentary dubbed and the final touches – the captions and the all-important credits – inserted. The final hurdle it faced was Granada's lawyer. Jeffery Maunsell, the solicitor from Goodman Derrick who had signed off on many intensely controversial programmes, sucked in his breath sharply at the sight of Jo Lambert talking indignantly about call-girls. When he reached the point in the script at which Valerie Scott spoke of 'brown envelopes', his suspicions were confirmed that he was in for a white-knuckle legal ride.

What convinced Maunsell that the programme was viable was the overpowering evidence that Aitken was not to be trusted. He had plainly lied, and had not sued over the Ritz. Even more significantly, he had been forced to admit – over TV-am in the past – that he had concealed his Saudi links.

'Lack of candour,' said Leigh. 'We can prove it.'

'What about the prostitutes?' asked Maunsell. 'Can you prove that?'

'Two witnesses.'

'But don't they have a grudge?'

'Of course they have a grudge! That's why they're talking!'

Maunsell passed 'Jonathan of Arabia'. So did editor Steve Boulton. Leigh, fulfilling his bargain, faxed over the pages of the script to David Pallister at the *Guardian* offices in Farringdon Road. Pallister and Leigh, two journalists who had been tweaking the tails of politicians for most of their professional lives, pushed off down the slope on what was about to turn into the most hair-raising journalistic bobsleigh-ride of their lives.

Sunday night on the newsdesk of the *Guardian* tends to be a quiet affair. On 9 April 1995 there was some mayhem from the Middle East to report: two suicide bombers had killed seven Israelis in the Gaza Strip. The main picture was of bald-pated Gazza returning to

Lazio after an injury. The splash story wrote itself: Richard Spring, the Conservative MP for Bury St Edmunds and PPS to Sir Patrick Mayhew, the Northern Ireland Secretary, had resigned after that day's *News of the World* caught him having a three-in-a-bed romp with a thirty-year-old Sunday-school teacher and a mutual male friend. The obscure Spring was the sixth PPS and the fifteenth member of the Government to resign. There was always trouble for John Major in the ministerial trouser-zip department.

But it was the second lead that caused uneasy anticipation in the Farringdon Road office as the edition went to press. The headline was blunt: AITKEN 'TRIED TO ARRANGE GIRLS' FOR SAUDI FRIENDS. Under Pallister's byline it began:

A television documentary on the business and personal dealings between Jonathan Aitken, the Chief Secretary to the Treasury, and a Saudi prince is to be screened tonight, despite Mr Aitken's attack on it as a 'despicable and cowardly breach of fair play'. Granada's *World in Action*, in collaboration with the *Guardian*, has concentrated on Mr Aitken's extraordinary life-style with his Saudi friends – and the central relationship with Prince Mohammed bin Fahd, a son of the Saudi King – over a period of nearly 20 years before he joined the Government in 1992.

The story went on to quote Robin Kirk and Jo Lambert's allegations about his attempts at procurement. It named Manon Vidal as the mysterious French woman who had actually paid the Ritz bill. And it revealed Aitken's relations with the arms-dealing Makhzoumi brothers while he was a defence minister.

For a deeply unpopular Government, wracked with divisions and battered by an endless series of sleaze stories, these latest sensational charges against a senior Cabinet minister did not come at a good time. And for Aitken himself, the article was a hammer-blow. He had assumed that this *World in Action* saga was going to be another stab at his complicated business dealings with the Saudis. He had managed, albeit evasively, to shrug off that sort of attack before. But when the first editions reached Whitehall late on Sunday night, he realized through a frantic fax to Switzerland from his private secretary that the game was a more dangerous one.

Aitken, who later claimed the article left him 'pole-axed', was in fact making a calculation about how best to regain the public-relations initiative. He made no statement at all that night. Flying back to

London early on Monday morning, he continued to keep quiet, but put about hints in the Commons that something 'explosive' was to occur later on. He was arranging to deliver the riskiest and, as events were to prove in the end, the maddest, speech of his life – on the Sword of Truth.

At 5 p.m., as Aitken began his tirade, in Manchester, 200 miles away, the *World in Action* team saw the entire performance via a live-TV feed rigged up by ITN. They watched, taut with adrenalin, as the Cabinet minister delivered his attack. Everyone on the programme knew exactly what Aitken's game was in staging this melodramatic event: he was pitching for massive coverage on the early-evening TV news, and intending to derail *World in Action*, due to transmit a short while later. The sheer ferocity of his attack, Aitken must have calculated, would intimidate Granada executives into pulling their programme. They would have no alternative.

As Aitken thundered on about how the former matron of Inglewood had been dismissed for dishonesty 'following a police investigation', David Leigh, watching in Manchester, exhaled some of his pent-up breath in relief. If this was Aitken's bombshell answer to the charges, then the team had it covered. Kirk and Lambert had not only told Leigh all about the theft accusations – they had also been recorded on tape giving their side of that story.

Leigh told a grim-faced room of TV executives: 'It's OK. There's nothing here we didn't know about.' Editor Steve Boulton and current-affairs head Charles Tremayne took a decision on the spot that was entirely quixotic. They would not see the programme cancelled or postponed: they would re-cut it, there and then, against the clock, and against all odds, to include Aitken's side of the story.

Other than that, the documentary would go out exactly as planned. 'Publish and be damned,' was to be the motto. Or perhaps 'On, into the valley of death.' Unfortunately, as Aitken had carefully calculated, there was simply not enough time to make the necessary editing changes. As Leigh sat in the flickering semi-darkness of the edit suite, watching the hands of the clock on the wall move round ever faster, and the new bits of tape re-cast themselves with terrible slowness into computerized instructions, he thought: If we don't transmit this tonight, we're finished.

The team of producers frantically trying to beat an impossible deadline felt as though the programme's whole reputation might be about to come tumbling down. The good news was there was no political interference at all from Granada's top executives. They were staunch. Granada TV's joint managing director Jules Burns appeared in Steve Boulton's office and merely asked quietly, 'Are the lawyers happy?' But the bad news was that the clock was unforgiving.

The programme was advertised for 8.30 p.m. There was a minute or so of grace for the adverts to play, before the crashing *World in Action* music opened the twenty-six minutes of the documentary. Delivery of the finished transmission tape by 8.31 p.m. was theoretically possible, although it had never been done before. As the clock approached 8 p.m., an exhausted David Leigh felt he was watching a display of such formidable discipline on the part of editors and executives that truly anything was possible. Lopped out of the programme went Quentin McDermott's doorstep at the very start. In to replace it went Aitken at his just-ended press conference, with his glassy stare and threatening words. Out went a whole interview with Peter Preston, *Guardian* editor-in-chief, to make way for Aitken abusing the Inglewood staff, followed in turn by Robin Kirk replying: 'The charges came to nothing: it was to discredit us and prevent us opening up another health hydro in opposition to him.' Out went the final allusive shot over the credits, of the ambiguous figure on the camel wielding a wicked-looking black riding-crop: it was replaced by a scroll of all the names of the Granada production team, against black, as Aitken's voice-over intoned portentously:

If it falls to me to start a fight to cut out the cancer of bent and twisted journalism in our country with the simple sword of truth and the trusty shield of British fair play, so be it. I am ready for the fight!'

By 8.20 p.m., Leigh's confidence was splintering. He thought: 'They're not going to make it.' Although Andrew Brittain, *World in Action*'s voice, had been ordered to stand by in the studio, there was going to be no time to dub on the new commentary. The entire master tape needed to be played laboriously through from start to finish for the edit changes to be copied on to it. There simply was not enough time. 'We'll do the missing bits of commentary live,' said Tremayne. 'I'll give Andrew the green light from the control room.' At 8.31 p.m. – the absolutely final deadline – the re-conformed master tape was finally being spooled back to the beginning on the film editor's deck, ready for transmission. As the reel gradually filled up, its speed of revolution maddeningly slowed.

Fifty feet away, down the corridor, the control-room technician said: 'No! That's it! You're too late. Hand over the standby programme – we'll transmit that instead.' He tried to pull it out of Boulton's hand.

'You've got to wait,' said Boulton, struggling with him.

The young director, Chris Malone, came skidding down the corridor, doors flung open for him as he ran, the new 'Jonathan of Arabia' tape in his hand. The big cassette was slammed into the slot at 8.32 p.m., and the theme music immediately started to play out from Manchester over the entire British network. Aitken's voice echoed once again across the airwaves, as his image gripped the lectern and glared around. 'I was shocked and disgusted . . .' his voice began. Tremayne, in the control room, pushed the cue button.

Andrew Brittain said, perfectly on time, and live into the microphone, 'That ringing denunciation by Jonathan Aitken earlier today, of *this* story . . .' The music swelled again and the programme ran.

Neither side had blinked. Instead, they had marched into war. It was the kind of war that would be won in the end only by the utter destruction of one of the two opposing forces. And the Granada and *Guardian* journalists, shaken by the ferocious public attack on their 'wicked lies', could be forgiven for fearing that, given the powerful nature of their opponent, and the protection provided to the mighty by the preposterous British libel laws, it was not Jonathan Aitken but they themselves who might eventually face annihilation.

....

Eight: **Sticky June**

When he remembered about Paula, Ed Chapelle – as he insisted on spelling his surname – was leading a doomed sort of life. Too much rough trade with men who might give him a kicking: too many alcoholic binges leaving him feeling like hell the next day in his East End flat. Never any money. Ed was still charming, in a lanky, balding, confiding, over-dramatic sort of way: he called himself a 'film producer', or a 'freelance journalist'. But, basically, he lived on his wits.

Now, remembering Paula, he felt his luck had begun to turn. It was a muzzy decade or more ago, but the conversation started to come back to him as he watched Jonathan Aitken on the TV, ranting and raving about prostitutes, 'wicked lies' and the Sword of Truth. 'Darling, I'm having an affair with an MP,' Paula had confided to him a touch hoarsely over the vodka: 'It's Jonathan Aitken.'

Paula had long since given up her life as a professional dominatrix specializing in bondage and chastisement. But it seemed to Ed that if he could find Paula again, and persuade her to relive those days, he would be in for a percentage of something tremendous. He felt six figures coming on, in a world where a general's mistress, or an 'actress' who had her toes sucked by a politician, could gain a fortune from the tabloids. Aitken was prominent on his Party's right wing, which swore by market forces. It was market forces that from now on were to determine all these events.

'Darling!' said Paula a little while later, opening her front door in the leafy suburb of Berkhamsted, and kissing him affectionately: 'Such a long time!' Chapelle was accompanied by Gloria Stewart, a dumpy, hard-drinking journalist with connections to the *News of the World*. They settled down to talk business with Paula Strudwick and her husband Jack Organ. Organ, an ardent trade unionist, had taken early retirement from Lambeth town council where he had worked as an aide to the Labour leader 'Red Ted' Knight. He was living on a pension, and was in no way averse to seeing his wife make a mint.

Paula herself, still handsome, good-natured and sensual, was delighted to co-operate. Indeed, she had a story to tell. She was hazy on a few details – 'I was taking amphetamines, darling' – but on the salient points much came flooding back. Christine Pickard, the 1960s sex doctor from north London, had procured Paula's introduction to Jonathan. Beating parties at an old mill, with a mysterious male sadist who had whipped Aitken, and at the Arab premises of Al Bilad – she recalled it all: 'I had to collect the birch twigs from near Inglewood, and soak them for two days in my bath until they were supple! Darling, really!' As she spoke, Chapelle happily saw a vision of hundreds of thousands of pounds. There would be plenty to share three ways.

It was ironic. Aitken, by his wild public declaration of war on the media, had woken a sleeping ghost. As a result, first blood was to go to his opponents. There were, however, a few snags Ed Chapelle encountered along the way to the exposure of Aitken as a sexual hypocrite. Stuart Kuttner, a senior executive at the *News of the World*, puzzlingly turned the story down. Gloria Stewart was forced to take it to Paul Connew at the *Sunday Mirror* – not generally such a good tabloid payer as the *News of the Screws*.

But Connew's men were competent professionals. As a first step towards substantiating the story, they set up Dr Pickard. Paula invited her round, and a video camera hidden in a table-lamp recorded some fuzzy pictures and a torrent of extremely clear words. The two women reminisced bawdily about their past sexual adventures with Aitken. This helped confirm Paula's credibility. But it did not, of course, constitute evidence against Aitken himself.

Pickard did, however, say two things of key interest. She revealed that Aitken had been ringing her up in a panic, afraid already that she was telling the truth to some of the journalists nosing around London on the story. 'He said that if I'd been talking he'd sue me, and he'd ruin me professionally and personally.'

Also, Pickard dropped the name of Valerie Scott into their conversation. She'd seen her played on the TV programme, and recalled Valerie from the Arab days. 'Jonathan was sleeping with her,' she recalled, ever the amateur sexologist: 'I think it happened during the

'74 election campaign, and she felt she had no choice if she wanted to keep her job.'

It was not long before Ed Chapelle turned up on the 17th floor of London TV Centre, guardedly ladling out his tale to Leigh and McDermott – the mystery orgies in the mill, the whippings, the Scott and Pickard connections. His manner was melodramatic, but the TV journalists knew already that his story must be broadly true. 'We can help you with one thing,' Leigh said. He tossed over a microfiche record of a small British company: 'There's your mystery sadist, and that's his address, on file as a director.'

The team had been ensconced with denizens of the demi-monde ever since their libel writ had arrived, and long talks with prostitutes and madams had already thrown up that individual's name, along with that of an executive who 'maided' for Paula wearing women's frocks; and a former newspaper editor who liked to be led about on all fours wearing a dog-collar. There were also rumours – never to be substantiated – of a party where a girl had been badly injured. The waters around the case were getting deep and dirty.

Leigh decided that there was no reason why the *Mirror* should not discreetly talk to Valerie. She was in a position to confirm much of Aitken's sexual misbehaviour, if that was what they wanted. Valerie herself was quite willing to tell the truth. In fact she was feeling angry. Aitken had tried to discredit her by circulating a story that she had been sacked from his employ after £2,000 went missing from his office safe. He failed to get it into print.

The next thing she experienced was a none-too-subtle attempt at bribery. Said Ayas, for whom she had worked for six years after parting company with Aitken, persuaded her to visit him at his Hyde Park Gate flat. He inquired tenderly after her well-being; explained that he and Jonathan – 'the poor guy' – did not want the case to go to court. His wife Danielle was finding it tiresome to administer their many homes – would Valerie like another job, working for her?

Valerie had never encountered Paula before: the Paula relationship had taken place in 1981 and 1982, when Valerie had left Aitken's employ. But she told the *Mirror* all about the whips and canes. Once again, however, she was not willing to go on the record. The *Mirror* were now satisfied that Paula's story was true. But they were left still looking for more rock-solid legal corroboration.

*

These sexual events were stirring under the surface throughout the weeks of the early summer of 1995 that followed Aitken's declaration of war on the media. But a second Nemesis, too, was arising from the mists of the past to pursue him – his involvement in the murky world of arms dealing. Ever since the collapse of the BMARC cannon company on whose board Aitken had sat, its former chairman Gerald James had been telling stories to whoever would listen about the innumerable corrupt arms deals in which he had found himself enmeshed.

James's motive was understandable enough: the DTI was seeking to disqualify him formally as a director following a critical departmental report on the financial manoeuvrings which had accompanied the firm's various take-overs and share issues. Furthermore, the chief executive Christopher Gumbley had been caught slipping bribes to Ministry of Defence officials in the hope of receiving lucrative ammunition contracts: he had been jailed for nine months. BMARC's holding company, Astra, was neither successfully nor honestly run.

James was reluctant to take the blame alone for all the shenanigans he knew had been going on in the arms business. But it was only in 1995 that he managed to obtain some BMARC company files and minutes from the receiver who had stored them in boxes in a Thames-side warehouse. The files went some way to proving what he had long claimed – that a large batch of cannon shipped from Grantham to Singapore between 1987 and 1989, with British Government approval, had then been improperly diverted on to wartime Iran. The dodge was perfectly legal – the export licence said merely that 'components' were going to Singapore. No one in Government had insisted on a proper end-user certificate, partly because Singapore was a Commonwealth country – and partly because the DTI was under pressure from Tory ministers not to make an unnecessary fuss about the destination of lucrative arms exports.

In the spring of 1995, the *Independent* newspaper obtained some naval surveillance photographs: they were able to publish a story alleging that the BMARC cannon had actually been installed on Iranian gunboats operating in the Persian Gulf. The paper pointed out that this apparent arms-smuggling had gone on while no less a Conservative politician than Jonathan Aitken had been gracing the BMARC board. Aitken responded to this embarrassing disclosure with his usual persiflage. His former chairman Gerald James, he lightly pointed out, was a complete madman: 'I had no knowledge of any Singapore contract.'

There the matter rested until 13 June 1995, when the head of the DTI and *de facto* Deputy Prime Minister, Michael Heseltine, got to his feet and told a startled Commons that his department had been investigating the matter and had discovered some very disturbing intelligence reports. These showed, it was his melancholy duty to report to the House, that cannon may very well have been smuggled to Iran from the company of which his Right Honourable friend, Jonathan Aitken, had unfortunately been a director. 'It does appear that there may be grounds for believing that the final destination of naval cannon made by BMARC could well have been Iran.' He was extremely sad, his demeanour made plain. Heseltine, who was on the left wing of the Tory Party, had reason to suspect Aitken might one day soon make a right-wing challenge for the Party leadership. He was mournful, too, as he explained that HM Customs were beginning a criminal investigation, and that the All-Party Trade Committee, if they wished to begin a similar investigation into his ministerial colleague, would have every co-operation from him. His dolour reminded one of the emotions of the oyster-eating protagonist in Lewis Carroll's 'The Walrus and the Carpenter':

> 'I weep for you,' the Walrus said:
> 'I deeply sympathise.'
> With sobs and tears he sorted out
> Those of the largest size.

Twenty-four hours later, at this tricky point in his fortunes, Aitken's secretary Lynn Fox received a phone call. 'If you tell him it's Paula – I've known him a long time. I haven't been in touch for some time. Tell him it's Paula from Islington, and a very close friend of Christine Pickard. He's a personal friend of mine. I've got something I need to tell him for his own good . . . Please tell him it's urgent.'

It was only a couple of hours later when Paula's phone rang.

'Is that Paula Strudwick? Hi. It's Jonathan.'

The fish had taken the bait. The men from the *Mirror* monitoring the spooling cassette hugged themselves in silent joy.

PAULA I've got to tell you, a few days ago I had a phone call from the press.

It was years ago, I wrote to a girlfriend and told her about – I suppose it was because I was enamoured by you, or whatever –

JONATHAN And what did you say in the letter?

PAULA Oh, I can't remember. We just had some fun. At the time I suppose it was true, I was in love with you – I thought I was, or whatever. Christine came over a few nights ago and reassured me. But what worried me was she said you'd phoned her three days ago and said you were going to sue her for every penny you could –

JONATHAN I said, in a friendly but firm way, 'Look, if you co-operate . . .' which I believe she has been. She's dropped me in it, I think. No one's offered you any money or anything?

PAULA No, they just said they wanted to see me and phone you about these letters . . . I panicked, I must admit I did, I wanted to put the phone down but I thought, I must listen, and they said, 'Your name keeps coming up.'

JONATHAN Poor Paula. I'm sorry that this . . . If I wanted to telephone you over the weekend, where would I telephone? This number?

PAULA You won't just leave me sitting here? I mean, what do you think?

JONATHAN Well, first of all, this is a very dirty, nasty game. These characters are going back twelve, fifteen years into any association I've ever had with anybody.

PAULA But why?

JONATHAN Oh, it's political. It's political and vindictive . . . They're offering huge sums of money, but don't say a word to them . . . I'm afraid they will try and say they've got anything, to put you in. Did they say which paper they were from? No? . . . I wonder if Christine . . . ? Christine is not as nice as she was –

PAULA No, I mean, Jonathan, she's been so loyal to you.

JONATHAN I wonder. I think she's been helping them a lot.

PAULA Why?

JONATHAN Money. They've been trying to bribe so many people in so many different directions. I think she might be an agent of theirs – yes – she might have had a tape-recorder on her – yeah – you'll probably find the boyfriend's selling or something . . . You've no idea what you wrote to your girlfriend? . . . That you were in love, or anything like that? . . . Do you think you went into any details?

PAULA Oh, I think maybe the first time we met, with Christine, and that I was sort of bowled over by you. I must admit I was.

JONATHAN Umm. Did they mention any other names to you at all, ask you who you knew? . . . I'll do everything to help you, don't worry . . . If everything's going to break, it'll break this weekend.

PAULA Is it really bad?

JONATHAN It's . . . I think it's very bad, yeah, I think that.

PAULA What are you going to do?

JONATHAN Tough it out.

This was the real Aitken, underneath the charm. Aggressive; stupid (it was not Christine Pickard who was betraying him, but Paula); but, above all, arrogant – 'Tough it out.'

On the same day Aitken closeted himself with a little band of advisers. Oddly, one of them was a young man called Patrick Robertson, attached to a variety of wild anti-European causes. He was a PR man for the anti-European campaign run by the megalomaniacal millionaire Sir James Goldsmith, who was occupying himself by conspiring against the existing leadership of the Conservative Party. Strange company for a Conservative Cabinet minister like Aitken.

Robertson rushed along to a morning meeting with Aitken to discover that his idea of dealing with all his looming crises was to call yet another Sword of Truth press conference and issue a further denunciation of the 'cancer of bent and twisted journalism'. This would serve only to whet the appetite of those newspapers who did not yet have a story of their own about the beleaguered Cabinet minister. Hastening back to his own office, Patrick Robertson sent Aitken a fax. He had been asking around among the tabloids, he said. They were pursuing allegations about 'Some pretty dreadful stuff: i.e. far worse than any extra-marital affair.' Robertson had picked up on the – unfounded – story the tabloids were after, that someone, possibly Aitken, had injured a girl at a sado-masochistic sex session.

Robertson warned Aitken that if he called such a press conference 'You will be forced to resign within days.' He stressed: 'Your fundamental problem is . . . BMARC'; and that as for the Paula Strudwick problem: 'You would need to talk to the other person involved.' It was not clear from his fax whether 'the other person' referred to Paula or Christine Pickard. This interesting textual question was given close study by large numbers of journalists because – in a piece of idiocy which far outdid any ill-advised course of action Aitken was planning – Robertson despatched this highly incriminating and embarrassing fax to the wrong fax number. It emerged from the fax machine of a bemused London arts producer who read it, reasoned that it was of journalistic interest, and sent it to the *Independent on Sunday*. He was confirmed in his course of action after Robertson sent him a threatening and rude fax demanding its return.

The newspaper blanked out the line that said 'far worse than any extra-marital affair' for fear of libel. They prepared to publish the rest of the text in full.

Meanwhile, Aitken was back on the phone to Paula. His agenda was – shut her up. Paula's script, on the other hand, as written by *Mirror* men, was designed to try and provoke Aitken into usable admissions about the whipping sessions. (They were comfortable by now that they could prove simple adultery, but the real circulation-builder was in evidence of perversions.) Once again, Aitken's *modus operandi* is illuminated by these extracts from transcripts, as Paula tried to persuade him that the Press have got hold of further letters with incriminating details.

PAULA Wasn't it that guy, when we went down to that place, that mill, do you remember that time?

JONATHAN No, I don't.

PAULA Years ago, we went to that party. I was crying and you threatened to –

JONATHAN I can't remember that.

PAULA She said with Doctor Someone or Other, sex sessions with someone, beatings –

JONATHAN God Almighty! Who else . . . ? I mean, this could not have been written in a letter . . . Well don't, don't speak to anybody. It's rubbish, just throw it out.

PAULA Jonathan, please try and do something.

JONATHAN I will. My lawyers are trying to move heaven and earth to do that. But honestly, nothing much can happen to you as long as you don't open your mouth to anyone.

PAULA But what do I say?

JONATHAN You just say, 'This is nonsense. I know about it – complete crap!' Just be very tough. You have to hang tough.

PAULA This is true, it's not fantasy – so where have they got it from? They must have got it from somewhere, Jonathan.

JONATHAN No it isn't true. Just you say, absolutely decisively, 'This is complete balls,' and, you know, 'This is totally untrue. This is some total invention!' and just be very, very firm . . . Try not to be frightened, and, above all, don't open your mouth.

Paula was getting the benefit of the Aitken master-class not just in Lying for Beginners, but also in the advanced version – Extreme Lying for Adepts. It was once again the technique of the Big Lie, as perfected by Hitler and boasted of in *Mein Kampf*. The essence of this technique is to realize that basically honest people are good at spotting small lies, evasions and embellishments when others perpetrate them. They are within the realms of the listener's own experience of how they themselves actually behave, and so they recognize them. But ordinary people do not go in for Extreme Lying. They do not, therefore, get the clues that point, beyond the indignance, to the Big Lie. Instead, they tend to believe it.

Aitken did not care whether what anyone said in this saga was objectively true or false. All he was focusing on, as he made clear to Paula, was the battle to preserve his political future. Typically grandiose, he talked as though the whole welter of allegations was got up by political rivals he had been conspiring against in the Conservative Party: 'This is High Politics and drama. They're trying to bring me down. That's what it's about.'

It dawned on Aitken too late that it was Paula herself who was not to be trusted. There were no more phone calls. It did not matter. His fate was sealed. A Government reshuffle was pending.

Meanwhile, four days after the Robertson leak, Peter Preston found himself shuffling uncomfortably before sixteen elderly MPs seated round a great half-moon-shaped table in a House of Commons side-room. The Privileges Committee had at last assembled to grill Preston about the cod fax and his unauthorized use of a Commons letterhead. Its chair Tony Newton, Leader of the House, and Sir Nicholas Lyell, the Attorney-General and Aitken's colleague, took a deliberately obtuse and narrow view of the Ritz affair. Over two-and-a-half hours Preston came under attack, and expressed contrition. (The meeting was briefly adjourned when the pantomime figure of Neil Hamilton was spotted lurking outside.) Eventually the Tory-dominated committee decided no further action was necessary.

But the real villain of the Ritz weekend was in grave trouble. The leak of the Robertson fax and the pending BMARC inquiry were heavy blows to Aitken. One must also assume that the Government whips followed up the clear hints in the Robertson fax of an impending tabloid scandal, and discovered that negotiations at the *Mirror* were at an advanced stage. They might print any day. (In fact, the Major Government was saved from publication for a crucial three weeks while Paula and the *Mirror* argued unedifyingly over what her story was worth, and whether a recognizable picture of Miss Whiplash herself would be included in the fee. Eventually, Paula settled for a figure in excess of £30,000.)

Ahead of the reshuffle, and with the appearance of some at least of Paula's reminiscences imminent in the newspapers, Aitken bowed to the pressure. He agreed with Major that he would step down from the Cabinet. They also agreed in an exchange of letters in which as much as possible of the blame was thrust on to the *Guardian* and Granada TV and the impending libel action.

Dear Prime Minister,
When you carry out your forthcoming re-shuffle of your Government, I would be grateful if you would allow me to step down from the Cabinet and return to the back benches. I am making this request because I have reached the conclusion that I cannot continue to carry out the onerous responsibilities of Chief Secretary to the Treasury during the coming months of the Public Expenditure Survey at a time when I also expect to be heavily engaged in preparing for legal battles with my adversaries in the media.

In these circumstances I feel it right to give priority to clearing my name of the unfounded allegations that have been made against me. I need to give my full commitment to fighting my current and possible future libel actions. I also wish to give my full co-operation to the Trade and Industry select committee's inquiry into BMARC.

Above all I have a duty to help my family to cope with the almost unbearable pressures we have had to face from elements in the media . . .

Naturally I regret the necessity of having to devote my energies to fighting legal battles but when these are won, I hope to return with honour vindicated, to the front line of public service.

Major replied in warm terms. He praised Aitken's performance as a minister: 'I have admired the way you have combined charm and patience with a steely determination to get results. I am grateful for the work you did as Minister of State at Defence before that, promoting British interests.' Major's letter, which history will now class as a foolish one, implied that Aitken would be welcome back in his Government (although a student of the small print would have observed there was in fact no binding guarantee of it).

I was very sad to hear of this, though I do understand the intolerable pressure and intrusions you and your family have had to put up with ... I look forward to the time when you have successfully completed your legal battles and are ready to return to the Government.

Yours ever,
John

It was 5 July 1995. Aitken's ministerial career had begun barely three years earlier. He had never exactly been one of the Young Meteors, as he craved, but he was certainly now in middle age emulating a meteor in one respect: he had, it seemed, finally crashed to earth.

The *Sunday Mirror* went into print four days later with a limited version of Paula's adultery story. *World in Action* and the *Guardian* then returned to the fray with a second programme and accompanying articles in December 1995 about the BMARC arms-smuggling saga.

There was one person who did not live to relish Aitken's setbacks – Ed Chapelle, the 'film producer' who had remembered Paula Strudwick. Celebrating his windfall, Ed quarrelled in his East End flat with a boyfriend – who stabbed him to death. He was one of the first casualties of a dirty affair.

It is to Aitken's great credit as a gambler that he did not retire from the table at this point. Instead, he invested in a large pile of new chips and pushed them across the baize. Double or Quits was the game, and it brought him back – astonishingly – to the very brink of victory against all his enemies.

The first of his problems, the Customs investigation, was most easily disposed of. This was a cosmetic affair, as Heseltine must have known full well when he set it in motion. Any contravention of export controls proven in the shipping of the cannon to Iran would have taken place seven years earlier. Time limits on bringing a criminal case would already have expired. Furthermore, it was common knowledge that these exports had possessed an official British Government export licence – for Singapore. The guns had indeed gone in the first instance to Singapore. And they had been purchased by the Swiss firm Oerlikon, as the main contractor on the deal. BMARC were merely the subcontractors. Therefore, the BMARC directors did not covertly smuggle the guns. They shipped them openly, with the correct paperwork for their immediate destination. A prosecution could succeed only by proving they had 'guilty minds' and knew what was really intended to happen to the guns in the end. It was relatively easy to prove a concrete event – that a crate of guns had been shipped from A to B. It was virtually impossible to prove a state of mind on the part of the directors.

Aitken, like the other BMARC directors, assured the Customs investigators that he was astonished to hear where the guns had ended up. Imagine his surprise. Only Gerald James contradicted them. And James did not have a single piece of incriminating paper to support his claim that the board knew that the Singapore destination was merely a 'dodge'. After a tape-recorded formal interview with Customs in September 1995, the inquiry into Aitken and the other BMARC board members was dropped.

In Aitken's case, his denials were probably perfectly true. It was most unlikely that Aitken would have wanted to take the risk of alienating his Saudi friends by aligning himself with their enemies in Iran. The true charge against Aitken over BMARC, however, was not that he knew about arms-smuggling, but that as a director he ought to have known.

Aitken had won the game with Customs. The next, more difficult, game to win was that with the Trade and Industry Select Committee inquiry. A criticism by them that he had been neglectful in the discharge of his duties would place him in no legal danger. But it would be a disastrous impediment to a political come-back.

Here, again, Aitken was to win because the cards turned out to be stacked in his favour. The committee was structurally incapable of carrying out any inquiry of an investigative nature. Although it had a Labour chairman, Martin O'Neill, it had, like all select committees in the Commons, a Government majority. So its efforts, and its eventual report, were dictated by the interests of the Conservative Party. It was denied the crucial information it needed. After Heseltine promised, for example, that the intelligence reports to which he had referred in his Commons statement would be passed over to the committee, the Government simply reneged on this offer, saying the material was too 'sensitive' after all.

As the MPs' eventual report gloomily observed, none of the BMARC directors and employees who came before them had a vested interest exactly in admitting malpractice. To do so would merely have incriminated themselves. The committee was to hold a few part-time sessions at which ill-briefed MPs sat around in a semi-circle, allowed to lob only a handful of questions each at the witnesses in time-limited sessions. There was no counsel to the inquiry, who could analyse documents and cross-examine witnesses. There was simply no one involved who was capable of leading Aitken through the by now numerous inconsistencies and evasions with which he had tried to cover up his incuriousness about the Singapore deal.

Aitken was allowed to reverse his position 180 degrees. When journalists first inquired, he had said, 'I knew nothing of any Singapore contract.' He had insisted that he was not briefed in any way on the deal, and that the entire contract – the company's largest contract for scores of guns being manufactured right under his nose on the albeit rare occasions when he turned up at Grantham for board meetings – was an aspect of the company's affairs on which he had remained in utter and total ignorance.

But by the time he came to appear before the committee, Aitken had decided this line plainly laid him open to criticism. All the other directors by now had admitted both that they had known of the Singapore deal, and that they had known it involved the guns going on from Singapore to some mystery destination about which they did not feel required to concern themselves. Aitken would have looked a negligent booby if he had maintained his line of virginal innocence.

So the ex-Cabinet minister turned up at the televised committee hearings in a large room on the first floor at the Palace of Westminster, and glided into a different version. He had known all about the Singapore contract, he said. Indeed, he had discussed it with company executives, as he diligently informed himself all about the firm's affairs. He had questioned them on the matter, and they – these somewhat hazy and unidentified figures – had informed him that the guns had proper export licences and were destined either for the Singapore navy or 'for export on to other friendly Commonwealth navies'. There was therefore nothing to arouse Aitken's suspicions about the contract.

Aitken's testimony was carefully given with an eye to standard definitions of the duties of a non-executive director. He presented the case that he had diligently asked the right questions, and according to conventional approaches to company law he was entitled to rely on the answers he had been given.

The committee's eventual report made no reference to the way Aitken had changed his story. Instead, they pronounced that their fellow-politician 'appears to have taken reasonable steps to familiarize himself with BMARC's business, and we believe that, in the absence of grounds for suspicion, he was justified in relying on what he was told by other directors and executives. Our conclusion is that none of the allegations made against Mr Aitken have been substantiated.'

The report represented a total vindication of Aitken on what was arguably the most grave criticism so far made of him – that he had knowingly been mixed up in arms-smuggling.

In triumph, Aitken hurled more writs at the *Independent*, who had run the original BMARC story, and at *Private Eye*, who had accused him of being an incorrigible liar, to join those he had already hurled at Granada and the *Guardian* for a second time. His gambler's nose told him that, with this parliamentary report apparently exonerating him from all crimes, his opponents were bound to concede defeat before any of the actions actually reached the courtroom door. And then, the cancer of criticism thus hacked away by his Sword of Truth, he would be back in office, a winner, a crusader, and – who knows – maybe the nation's next Prime Minister. There was no end to Aitken's self-confidence. He seemed to have acquired feelings of invincibility normally possessed only by inveterate cocaine sniffers. But in Aitken's case, the drug he was in thrall to must have been the prospect of a return to power.

BEATRICE He is now as valiant as Hercules that only tells a lie and swears it. *Much Ado About Nothing* (IV.1)

··

Nine: **Valiant Hercules**

In his epic court battle with the *Guardian* and *World in Action*, the Right Honourable Jonathan Aitken was to coin a new word: 'Carmanised'. It was one of his better neologisms. 'I have been demonised by the *Guardian* and Carmanised here in court,' he complained from the witness-box. The object of his defiance, a diminutive, bewigged figure with gold-rimmed glasses and the saintly air of an eighteenth-century divine, stared back at the former Cabinet minister unblinkingly. To be cross-examined by any barrister is an ordeal; to be cross-examined by George Carman QC, as Jonathan Aitken was to learn, is a uniquely unpleasant experience.

The pre-eminence of Carman, the son of a Blackpool furniture-maker, is built upon his reputation as the best examiner of witnesses in the legal profession. He is short, 5 foot 3 inches at a generous guess, courteous – and deadly. Like the Catholic priest he almost became, his manner of interrogation is that of a solemn catechist: remorseless, icy and calculating. He operates by attrition followed by ambush. All great barristers have an essential streak of vanity, and in this respect George Carman is no exception. Jurors warm to his stagecraft, and find themselves drawn to the Marlboro-puffing figure in the corridor. But judges profess themselves exasperated by his showmanship, privately envying both his fame and the fact he earns far more than they do. Married three times (it was women who eventually scuppered his career in the priesthood), and now sixty-seven, Carman lives alone in a giant five-bedroom house in Wimbledon. His chambers in Gray's Inn provide evidence of a brilliant life played out with gusto in the public spotlight: a crate of champagne, newspaper cartoons of himself on the walls, and a mantelpiece groaning with invitations from the many grateful celebrities he has defended in a distinguished career at the Bar.

On 10 April 1995, hours after Jonathan Aitken had declared war on the cancerous *Guardian*, its editor Alan Rusbridger held an urgent conversation with the paper's solicitor Geraldine Proudler. Proudler was herself no ordinary lawyer. Among the most accomplished and in-demand libel specialists of her generation, she worked as a senior partner for the Covent Garden firm Olswang. Over the next two years she would second-guess the hand of Aitken's grasping colleague Neil Hamilton; and see off libel actions from several other ferocious litigants. In the game of libel, where the stakes are always high, Proudler had the rare ability to keep her cool. An easygoing manner combined with a Terminator-like determination to pursue the evidence made her an invaluable combatant.

Alan Rusbridger, who took up the editor's chair after working as the *Guardian*'s features editor and diary columnist, also had a reputation for being laid-back. But his nonchalant management style and boyish features concealed a streak of brutal decisiveness in times of crisis. Jonathan Aitken was a problem Rusbridger had inherited from his predecessor Peter Preston. The affair would be an early test of his courage as editor. Aitken's blustering Sword of Truth speech had left Rusbridger unmoved; and confirmed his impression that the *Guardian* was dealing with a particularly dextrous liar.

'We better get Carman,' Rusbridger said matter-of-factly after watching the Chief Secretary's peroration, 'before Aitken gets him.' Proudler left a message with Carman's clerk saying that the *Guardian* would like to instruct him. There would, as is usual with top barristers, be a large signing-on fee. Proudler's early analysis of the situation was that the case would hinge on Jonathan Aitken's performance in the witness-box. It did not, primarily, appear to be what lawyers describe as a 'documents' case; although, in the end, it would be documents that would sink Aitken. Instead, the war looked as if it would be fought on the disputed territory of Aitken's testimony. Could an ordinary jury of twelve men and women be convinced that a senior Conservative politician was capable of lying through his teeth?

As he sat in his chambers pondering the *Guardian*'s offer, George Carman cast his mind back to a lunch he had attended at a Mayfair hotel seven years previously. The great barrister had just successfully defended Jonathan Aitken's younger sister, the actress Maria Aitken, against a cocaine-smuggling charge. Maria had enjoyed a successful career playing upper-crust leading ladies; but she had also suffered her share of scrapes. Her older brother Jonathan did not attend the trial, but thanked her legal team with a small victory party. Now, having watched Aitken's bellicose speech on the evening news, Carman wondered whether the cultivated man he had met briefly that day really was capable of procuring.

'One's initial reaction was "Good Heavens",' he said. Could this Eton-educated scion of the Beaverbrook family really be a liar and a rogue? Carman felt immediately that the stakes in this libel action were going to be extremely high. The case was a puzzle: either the Chief Secretary was a politician of integrity who had been gravely libelled, or he was a liar of great sang-froid and calculated deviousness. He could not, logically, be both.

The barrister had already built up a good working relationship with the *Guardian*. The paper had just engaged him to defend a libel suit brought by the greedy Conservative ex-minister Neil Hamilton. Carman agreed to take on Jonathan Aitken as well. Proudler's next step was to secure the services of James Price, also busy with the Hamilton brief. A junior barrister was needed who could master the huge amount of detail involved in the Aitken action. Price was a junior, just – shortly after adding Aitken to his formidable workload he was appointed a QC. A razor-sharp Old Etonian who lived modishly in Chelsea, Price had a reputation for being thorough and forensic. Later another young barrister, Alexandra Marzek, would come on board to keep order over the 300 red lever-arch files which grew into the gigantic libel action.

The *Guardian* had assembled a formidable team: Carman, the great jury-trial advocate; and Price, a cunning analyst who could absorb detail effortlessly. Granada, led by executive editor Ian McBride, joined forces as soon as they, too, received Aitken's writ – Jeffery Goodman and Claire Posner of solicitors Goodman Derrick instructed the same team of counsel. Granada TV were richer than the *Guardian*, yet in some ways they had more to lose. Their TV programme was only a small if notable part of a vast catering conglomerate business empire. Journalism was not their owners' ultimate *raison d'être*, unlike the *Guardian*'s Scott Trust. But *World in Action* did not falter. Aitken never succeeded in dividing the two sets of defendants.

In the days immediately following Aitken's declaration of war on the media, Leigh and Pallister braced themselves for his response.

In libel actions plaintiffs are obliged to supply a 'statement of claim', usually drafted by a barrister. This sets out how the client's reputation has been damaged and what compensation is sought. But from the Aitken camp there was an eerie silence. A week went by and nothing happened. Another week passed. Pretty odd, Proudler thought. Was the minister perhaps less confident of his position than he appeared? Two weeks after declaring, 'My fight begins today,' Aitken finally got round to issuing a writ to *World in Action*. Six weeks later a surprisingly late statement of claim landed on Proudler's desk. It was almost as if Aitken, the Great Bluffer, was going through the motions of litigation.

After Aitken's departure from Cabinet in July 1995, the *Guardian* met with its legal team. The venue was George Carman's then chambers at the Temple, the verdant legal enclave a short walk away from the towering Gothic edifice of the High Court in the Strand. Over fizzy water and coffee, the lawyers and the journalists discussed the implications of Aitken's writ and of his behaviour. The original article and television documentary were the result of hard work and meticulous research, Rusbridger pointed out. The paper felt it had a strong case. On the Ritz, Aitken appeared to be in terrible trouble. Using the speakerphone George Carman made a theatrical call to Mohamed Al Fayed and told him the *Guardian* would need his full co-operation to prepare its case. Fayed agreed to do his best.

The archaic system of libel law in Britain meant the defendants had a huge battle on their hands. In the American courts the onus is on the plaintiff to show that a newspaper has published a false story and acted with reckless disregard towards the truth. But in Britain it is the publisher who has to do the proving. Because of this many instances of public wrongdoing by MPs and other public servants, which ought in the public interest to be made known, never see the light of day. The huge cost of defending a libel action means that newspapers generally err on the side of caution. The European Court of Human Rights recognizes this and has repeatedly ruled that politicians in a democracy should be broad-shouldered and readier to take criticism than private individuals.

The fact that libel laws are weighted in favour of politicians has not gone unnoticed by MPs. Nor has the fact that they can supplement their comparatively meagre salaries with tidy tax-free sums from speculative libel actions. Most newspapers prefer to publish a down-page apology and fork out modest damages to the high-risk strategy of contesting even a feeble claim in court. Over the last 300 years an estimated 2,000 MPs have succeeded in bringing libel actions against publishers.

In the Aitken case, the situation was rather different. The allegations were so grave that both Granada and the *Guardian* had fully expected a writ from the cornered Chief Secretary. But they were equally confident that the allegations could be fully justified in a court of law.

In the medium term a huge amount of digging had to be done. Three *Guardian* reporters and Leigh and McDermott from Granada were assigned almost full time to assess a flood of calls and letters prompted by Aitken's denunciation, and to search for new witnesses. McDermott flew to New Zealand to interview the former air-hostess, and the paper's Kathy Evans took off for Beirut to see Fouad Makhzoumi. The south of France and Paris were scoured for Manon Vidal and a microlight aircraft hired to take pictures of King Fahd's new and secluded villa. Taking up Mohamed Al Fayed's offer of co-operation, Geraldine Proudler flew to France, returning with an intriguing sheaf of Ritz Hotel bills. These showed that Prince Mohammed himself had checked out of the Ritz just days before Aitken arrived.

Aitken, wielder of the Sword of Truth, was sitting on the back benches again, where he had spent most of his political career. He knew ministerial rehabilitation would follow only when the *Guardian* and *World in Action* had been either crushed beneath his imperious shoe or at least snared into a settlement that could be presented as a retraction. After a dilatory start, Aitken threw himself into the fight. He installed his solicitor Richard Sykes into the Great Peter Street offices of Al Bilad which, amazingly, still doubled as his parliamentary base. A large, bulky, grey-haired man who bears an uncanny resemblance to Chancellor Kohl, in recent years Sykes had worked as a one-man band – a sole practitioner.

Before taking on the case, Sykes had defended many libel actions for the *Sunday Telegraph*, where his charmingly maverick style sat well with the eccentric right-wingers who ran the paper. His intense loyalty to its editor Peregrine Worsthorne and individual members of staff was fully reciprocated for many years, even when that devotion was occasionally airily misplaced. In 1988 a *Sunday Telegraph* journalist wrote a passing reference to the fact that if a young British soldier, Private Thain, jailed for the murder of a Roman Catholic during a disturbance in Northern Ireland, had been 'luckier in his lawyers' he might have been acquitted. 'Lawyers never sue,' Richard Sykes declared. They did, and were paid substantial amounts in libel damages. His wins were notable but in the early 1990s he parted company with the paper. It should have been a short hop to retirement – but now one more case beckoned.

To do battle against George Carman, Aitken also needed a first-class courtroom gladiator of his own. He instructed the eminent libel specialist Charles Gray QC, an old Oxford contemporary whose success at the Bar had rivalled Aitken's own rise in politics. Gray had a reputation for being gentlemanly but tough – and his early assessment of the case was that Aitken should win hands down. Ironically this *éminence grise* of libel law had recently been hired by the *Guardian* to defend a writ brought by Paul Judge, the multi-millionaire former director of Conservative Central Office. The *Guardian* had reported Judge's obstructive attitude to accountants seeking to recover donations to the Conservatives made by the fugitive Polly Peck businessman, Asil Nadir. Judge was to lose his libel action, the latest in a string of notable victories for Gray. Though they were now professional adversaries, Charles Gray and James Price were old friends, and shared the same chambers at Gray's Inn. The world of libel is a small and clubbable one. Top barristers simply sit around like very expensive taxis, waiting for the next wealthy client to jump in.

As summer turned to winter, and his fellow-parliamentarians exonerated him credulously over BMARC in the Trade and Industry Select Committee report, Jonathan Aitken's mood grew increasingly martial. The libel action was beginning to take up most of his time. As he sat in his study, he must have brooded over his political fortunes. The way back to preferment would certainly be rocky: the Conservatives trailed badly in the polls; his colleagues were still at war over Europe; and Middle England was shedding its inhibitions and jumping into bed with Labour's grinning dauphin, Tony Blair. But the sooner he could rejoin the political fray, obviously the better.

In December 1995 Aitken's retaliation started with a scorching fifty-one-page document. The *Guardian* had been out to 'Get Aitken', he claimed, and had pursued an obsessional vendetta against him. It had forced his resignation from office. Over twenty scalding pages he laid out how the *Guardian* and Granada had 'maliciously' pursued 'scandalous' allegations against him. 'It was a long way away from the real issues in the case,' Proudler said.

In fact, Aitken had made a grave tactical blunder, as an excited memo circulated by David Leigh pointed out. This untenable 'malice' claim brought the chastizing Paula Strudwick and her tale of orgies, mills and beatings centre-stage into the legal drama. It was Paula, aided by the men from the *Sunday Mirror*, who had in fact forced Aitken's resignation. And the defendants would be delighted to have the opportunity to prove it.

The *Guardian* said as much in a document setting out its response to Aitken's preposterous malice claim. Paula's lurid account of her liaison with the adulterous Aitken could now be meaningfully laid before a jury. 'It went to the heart of his credibility,' Proudler explained. 'He was always painting himself as a family man and a religious man. We wanted to show the jury that was a sham.' In February 1996 a second statement of claim landed on Proudler's desk with an ugly thump. This time Aitken demanded 'aggravated and exemplary damages' for libel. 'He was clearly ramping it up,' Proudler said.

Meanwhile, Neil Hamilton's libel action against the *Guardian* was collapsing around his ears. The *Guardian* had unearthed a mountain of evidence which showed that the blustering Conservative MP had personally collected cash payments from Mohamed Al Fayed. Hamilton was another Tory MP whose love affair with brown envelopes was to cost him dear. To bring his case, the MP had forced his own amendment to a new Defamation Bill passing through the House of Lords, comparing himself ludicrously to a weed bursting through the tarmac. Now his bluff was about to be called.

Hamilton had fallen out with his co-plaintiff Ian Greer, the pomaded lobbyist and Al Fayed beneficiary whose venal tentacles had spread to the upper reaches of the Conservative Party. The day before the case was due to open at the High Court Hamilton and Greer caved in. They abandoned their libel action and agreed to pay the *Guardian* £15,000 in costs. On 1 October 1996 the *Guardian* produced its classic front-page story headlined: A LIAR AND A CHEAT, which dealt a terminal blow to what was left of Hamilton's reputation.

With the MP for Tatton out of the frame, attention focused on Aitken. Would he really go all the way to the wire? In December 1996 Aitken batted a re-amended reply to Olswang. He had realized his earlier error. The claim that the journalists had ousted him from Cabinet was withdrawn. For a plaintiff this was an almost unprecedented move, tantamount to a general marching his troops up a hill only to march them down again. The *Guardian* decided to counter-attack, and applied to have the Strudwick affair drafted back into the pleadings, the bundle of arguments which make up a plaintiff's case.

Early in the New Year, as the phoney election war between Labour and the Conservatives dominated the airwaves, a lanky, pin-striped figure slipped quietly into the High Court. This was Jonathan Aitken, now aged fifty-four and out of office; but not out of self-confidence. If his libel action was to succeed, Aitken knew he had to climb over a treacherous and difficult mountain. That mountain was George Carman Q C. Aitken's barrister Charles Gray was appearing in court 13 on behalf of a doctor who had sued the *Daily Mirror* for defamation. His opponent was George Carman. For Aitken, the case was a dress rehearsal for the drama which would follow five months later.

Sitting in the public gallery, Aitken studied Carman's methods. Unlike many barristers, Carman never gave the impression in court that he was part of the same club as the judge and his opposing counsel; rather he seemed to be saying to the jury: 'I am really one of you.' Aitken, an ex-journalist, Law graduate and instinctive phrase-maker, did not realize at all that in this Balliol scholar who had immersed himself in the cadences of Cicero, Lamb, Macaulay and Churchill he had finally met his match. Instead, Aitken arrogantly decided to press on with his case. Carman had no idea at the time that he was being watched. 'No, no, no, nothing like that,' Aitken replied disingenuously, when asked by *The Times* diary whether he was mugging up.

In the early months of 1997 Aitken immersed himself in every single document relating to the trial – of which there were thousands of pages by now. His preparations were meticulous. According to sources close to his legal team, he worked hard, sometimes as much as seventeen hours a day. At his home in Lord North Street a kind of monomania took over. He deployed his considerable intellect ruthlessly, often working late into the night. His final witness statement ran to 205 pages; a work of brilliant, seamless artifice.

New allegations were added to bump up his claim for 'exemplary damages'. Half a dozen 'scruffy journalists' had giggled, sniggered and made notes when he gave a witty sermon at a Hammersmith church in June 1995, he claimed. His children had been teased at school about their father's activities as 'a pimp'. The *Guardian* and Granada had conducted a 'vindictive and deliberate attempt' to 'vilify and discredit' him. A camera crew had made his daughter cry. 'I want to demonstrate to the world that these numerous allegations that have been placed so publicly on the record by the defendants are wholly baseless,' he wrote. The lofty moral tone never flagged. 'In the continuing absence of any apology I am driven to go to court to vindicate my reputation. I felt and feel compelled to do so in order to defend my integrity and honour.'

But the journalists did not feel much like apologizing. The *Guardian* had just won its third libel victory in a row, and the champagne was flowing in the first-floor newsroom at Farringdon Road. After the Paul Judge victory and the Hamilton victory, the case came to trial of five officers from Stoke Newington police station who had sued the *Guardian* after it reported that they had been interviewed as part of a corruption inquiry. The case had been brought by the Police Federation, which waited for almost three years before issuing a writ. The Federation had previously won all of what were known winkingly in the Force as 'garage' actions. (The damages were usually large enough to allow the officers involved to build themselves a nice garage extension.) But the jury smelt a rat. After a two-and-a-half-week trial it found for the *Guardian*. The Federation, which had won its previous ninety-five cases, and had confidently expected to win its ninety-sixth, was left pondering its cynical approach to the libel courts, and a £600,000 legal bill.

By Easter both sides on the Aitken case were encamped and digging in. Legal letters flew between Richard Sykes and Olswang, but there was no breakthrough. George Carman buried himself in the case files. Proudler's assistant Debbie Ashenhurst worked in excess of a hundred hours a week. Aitken's monster witness statement had arrived, and needed to be deconstructed. For the journalists working away on Aitken this was hard, unglamorous, exhausting slog. The legal game was moving into a new stage. As part of the 'discovery

process', both sides in a libel action are obliged to hand over copies
of all relevant documents to the other. Libel is played like a round
of children's cards, with everybody, in theory, showing their hand.
Olswang had deluged Richard Sykes with discovery of all relevant
documents. But Sykes responded with a trickle. For several weeks
the defendants' lawyers were left waiting for documentation to drop.

Aitken was playing legal hardball. As usual, he was 'hanging tough'.
He complained of the 'utterly unreasonable demands' made on him
by the defendants to 'produce tax returns, bank statements, and
property deeds' in a vain effort to fish for 'non-existent evidence' to
back up their 'false' allegations. Witness statements were exchanged.
The MP had been busy. He had ploughed through the cabinet
containing three decades' worth of useful contacts. There were
testimonials from the great and the good: two former Speakers of
the House of Commons, a Conservative MP, local Party activists, a
maverick Labour councillor, a vicar, a marchioness and a retired
intelligence expert. Most of the statements amounted to little more
than inflated character references.

But among them, more crucially, was an alarming nucleus of
statements dealing with Aitken's stay at the Ritz. David Leigh and
David Pallister read with growing incredulity as Lolicia Aitken, Said
Ayas and Manon Vidal all corroborated Aitken's fatuous explanation
of how his hotel bill was paid. Lolicia claimed to have paid it.
Furthermore, Ayas and Vidal both said they had *seen* her paying it.
Was this an organized conspiracy, the journalists wondered? Neither
of them felt the case could possibly come to court. Aitken might
give false testimony, but Said Ayas and Lolicia would surely never
give false evidence on oath. Or would they?

A month before the trial Olswang and Goodman Derrick started
to swing one of the defendants' few powerful legal clubs – the
subpoena. This potent little document commands individuals – or
institutions – to attend the High Court with whatever documents are
asked for. It was the potency of the subpoena that had helped sink
Hamilton and Greer, when the Cabinet Office was forced to offer
up some of its incriminating records. More than fifty-five subpoenas
were fired off. Out of normally locked safes, some gems came
tumbling out. From the Cabinet Office there emerged a previously
secret letter in which Aitken admitted for the first time that he had

spoken to Prince Mohammed during the Ritz weekend. From the Independent Television Commission, dozens of pages of damning detail about TV-am. And the Ministry of Defence unburdened itself of papers which showed Aitken's frantic, last-minute arrangements preceding his 'private' trip to Paris in September 1993.

In the dying days of John Major's administration, as he toured the country with his soapbox and tried to revive the election-winning magic of 1992, the defendants held a sombre meeting with their lawyers. The news, George Carman announced, was mixed. On the Ritz, Aitken faced 'formidable' problems. On TV-am a pattern of 'prolonged cunning' had emerged which now showed the unedifying picture of an MP deceiving the Independent Broadcasting Authority for 'personal gain'. But in other areas – most notably the Makhzoumi affair – the lawyers felt some of the evidence was weak, vague and untenable. James Price was notably gloomy. 'We may face large damages,' he warned, half playing devil's advocate. The costs in the action on both sides were already huge. But the worst was yet to come. Over a trial set down for eight to ten weeks, costs would roar into the sky. 'This is a classic case to settle,' both QCs urged.

The defendants agreed to heed the advice. Alan Rusbridger had already met Jonathan Aitken once previously in an attempt to broker an out-of-court deal. Sitting in on the breakfast meeting was Aitken's friend Maurice Saatchi, the Conservative Party's favourite adman, recently elevated to the House of Lords. But no deal was agreed. Standing in his first-floor office, overlooking Farringdon Road, the traffic-clogged artery between King's Cross and the City, Rusbridger phoned Saatchi again. Could the three of them meet? A table was booked at a discreet eaterie in Piccadilly, Wilton's. The British upper classes had been dining at Wilton's for 250 years; a restaurant which served wholesome portions of oysters, fish and game, and where service was of the old school.

But, for reasons which still remain mysterious, Aitken pulled out of the lunch at the last minute, leaving Maurice Saatchi to act as a go-between. The editor and the peer sat down to eat. 'Jonathan Aitken is going to be destroyed by this case,' Rusbridger began, pouring out a glass of wine. 'You ought to tell him that.' The new TV-am documents were damning, the editor explained. Both sides would get knocked around if the case went to court. Rusbridger calmly proposed a new deal. Each side would walk away from the libel action and pay their own costs, already large. The *Guardian* and Granada would not apologize, but would agree to a face-saving formula which would leave Jonathan Aitken's reputation substantially intact. The *Independent* newspaper – sued by the MP over BMARC – may have been prepared to pay damages into court. Payment into court was one of libel law's more arcane strategies. If Aitken pursued his action against a newspaper, and was awarded *less* than the payment into court in damages, he would be liable for *all* costs incurred after the payment was made. This way the newspaper could protect some of its costs. Alternatively, if Aitken abandoned the action he could walk away with the sum paid into court by way of damages.

Rusbridger's pitch was this: Aitken could take any money the *Independent* might decide to pay into court. He could then announce he was discontinuing his action against the *Guardian*/Granada team to spare his family from further distress. The MP could then claim he had been paid large damages by the media and trumpet that his reputation had been restored. Jonathan Aitken was, after all, no stranger to the black arts of spin. An election was looming; and there were few certainties ahead for any candidate wearing a blue rosette.

The *Guardian* would not challenge any gloss Aitken decided to put on the deal. He could make the announcement on the eve of polling-day, and the story would sink without trace. 'It seemed to me a brilliant deal,' Rusbridger said. Saatchi, who knew little of the detail, agreed to relay the message faithfully to Aitken. But Aitken never rang back. Later that day the Right Honourable Jonathan Aitken must have rolled the Rusbridger offer around in his mind. He faced several problems. The first of these may have been the holdall full of cash which Lolicia had collected from the enraged Prince Mohammed. An out-of-court settlement hardly amounted to 'getting Fayed'. To back down would involve considerable loss of face. It might also necessitate an ugly confrontation with the Prince at some stage.

The MP was also in an embarrassing position *vis-à-vis* his lawyers. If he had told them the truth, they would have urged a swift and discreet settlement. As it was, they had believed all his lies. Having been fed false evidence they had reached the erroneous conclusion that he would win his action easily. And then there was Aitken's gambling instinct, the reckless boyhood streak which kept him at the casino long after it would have been sensible to cash in his chips and flag down a taxi home.

Meanwhile, across the verdant Shire counties of Middle England, in suburban streets lined with neat semi-detached houses and Ford Sierras, and in the increasingly tatty commuter hinterland of Thanet, a bloodless British revolution was going on. There was a general election to fight. The country was fed up, and was about to deliver the Conservative Party a well-aimed punch on the nose. Future historians will doubtless come up with numerous explanations for why the ruling Party suffered its worst defeat since 1906: arrogance, sleeze, complacency, weak leadership, exhaustion, contumely, intellectual bankruptcy, and a resurgent opposition piloted by a young, almost Kennedyesque leader. Like the volcano on the Caribbean Island of Montserrat, which would shower the British dependency with ash over the summer, the democratic cycle was about to undergo a mighty tectonic upheaval.

In the markets of Ramsgate and Broadstairs, and among the wistaria-clad bungalows of Sandwich, Jonathan Aitken was doing his best to resist this great psephological explosion. In the three weeks before polling-day on 1 May 1997 Aitken took time out from his legal struggle and descended on his constituency with his teenage daughter Victoria and a team of young helpers from Conservative Central Office. His team were kitted out in blue waterproof anoraks and baseball caps which bore a one-word logo in capital letters: AITKEN. (Later the new Conservative leader, emerging from the catastrophic debris of a 179-seat defeat, would toboggan down a watershoot wearing a similar baseball hat emblazoned with: HAGUE.) Some elderly residents mistook the YCs for itinerant vigilantes as the Aitkenites arrived in dozens of villages across Kent and fanned out across well-swept pavements. But then a grinning Jonathan Aitken would emerge from his campaign Land Rover, the net curtains would stop twitching, and all would apparently be well. Aitken was no fool, however: two weeks before election night he confided to an old journalist contact: 'I think I'm going to lose my seat.'

In the end the night of 1 May was a disastrous one for the Conservatives. Front-line casualties were heavy: Malcolm Rifkind, the Foreign Secretary; David Mellor, the toe-sucking former Heritage Minister; Michael Forsyth, the Scottish Secretary; and, most dramatically, Michael Portillo, the Defence Secretary, and coiffed darling of the Thatcherite right. The Tories were wiped out in Scotland and Wales, and reduced to a depleted rump in the English Shires. The evening began with Jonathan Aitken apparently in buoyant mood in the Winter Gardens, Margate. The dilapidated former ballroom had seen better times. The main hall, which once resounded to the waltzing of immaculately groomed couples, now played host to dreary provincial celebrities like Chas 'n' Dave and Hinge and Bracket.

At first Aitken chatted amiably with his Party agent and a large group of supporters. But when the first BBC exit poll spelt out the nature of the Labour landslide he moved to another table and sat quietly with Lolicia and Victoria. In the main hall, with its green chairs, red walls and blue stage, bundles of votes were being laid out. 'It was like a train moving down a table,' one observer said. The count was delayed after a ballot-box was wrongly delivered to Dover and had to be fetched back. Two lines were running neck and neck, and then one of them stopped. The winning line was restarted on a second row. For five minutes nothing happened. And then the returning officer grabbed a handful of votes from the largest pile and glanced at them. A whisper went through the hall. Labour had won – by 2,878 votes on a swing of 15 per cent.

Across millions of television screens the words 'Thanet South Labour gain' flashed up. The gain meant Labour had an overall majority in the House of Commons: Tony Blair was to be Prime Minister. Aitken had represented Thanet for twenty-three years. As a young man he nursed ambitions to be Prime Minister himself. Now he had lost his seat; he was an ex-politician as well as an ex-minister. At 2.30 a.m. the returning officer formally announced the result. Aitken made a gracious speech and paid tribute to the victorious Labour candidate Dr Stephen Ladyman, a 44-year-old local councillor. 'He fought the whole election like a democrat,' Dr Ladyman said afterwards. 'He was always polite to me. There was no bitterness. He is the sort of person that when you meet him you want to like him. He has a twinkle in his eye.' And then, incredibly: 'Tories have written to me saying they can't believe the things that have been said about him. It would not surprise me if they had him back again.'

Aitken was down but not out. One more great battle beckoned.

'"I'll be judge, I'll be jury;" said cunning old Fury.'
Lewis Carroll, 'The Mouse's Tale',
Alice in Wonderland
'This may be a complex story but it is not one based on a web of deceit. There are good, honest explanations for all the points put to me.' **Jonathan Aitken, 10 June 1997**

....

Ten: **High Noon**

S eated in the solemn splendour of the High Court in the Strand, the Honourable Mr Justice Popplewell, knight, judge and cricketing enthusiast, peered over his half-moon spectacles, and said cheerfully: 'Yes, Mr Gray.'

Sir Oliver Popplewell had come to hear an application from Jonathan Aitken regarding his forthcoming libel trial against the *Guardian* and Granada television. The general election had come and gone. For several heady days the whole country had seemed to be *en fête*: the pubs were full, and groups of young people spilled out on to the pavements to drink in the May sunshine. Tony Blair's son had worn a Ted Baker shirt for his father's first photocall outside 10 Downing Street. Gordon Brown, Labour's rugged Iron Chancellor, had granted the Bank of England independence with a click of his fingers. In the practice nets, the England cricket team glowed with a new and mysterious confidence.

Mr Justice Popplewell, who had reconciled himself to spending most of the summer on the Aitken case, was no mean cricket fan himself. Admittedly, he had met his wife Catharine on a lacrosse pitch at Cambridge almost half a century earlier. (The first thing she had said to him was: 'Would you care for a cup of tea, Mr Popplewell?' He had given her a Parker-Knoll chair for her twenty-first birthday. Upper-class dating etiquette was different in the 1950s.) But cricket remained his abiding passion. The judge had only just stepped down as President of the MCC – the Marylebone Cricket Club – the ultimate Establishment accolade. Colleagues at the Bar regarded him as decent and kindly. They had even bestowed upon him a joshing nickname, which might have echoed round the dormitories of Charterhouse where he was a pupil during the war: 'Opple-Popple'. 'Not a high, high intelligence,' one said, 'but a jolly nice chap.' Called to the Bar in 1951 Popplewell's progress had been stately rather than meteoric: a QC in 1969; made a knight and High Court judge in 1983; and authored a report into the Bradford and Heysel football tragedies three years later. He now ambled along in what the legal profession regards as its retirement lane, hearing mostly libel cases. His wife, meanwhile, had busied herself with 'good' works: prison-visiting, the Open University, the magistracy and the Conservative Party. For almost a decade Lady Popplewell represented the Conservatives on Buckinghamshire County Council; for five of those she chaired the council's education committee. Lady P felt *very* strongly about the importance of selective education. Most mornings, it would be fair to assume, a well-thumbed copy of the *Guardian* did *not* lie on the Popplewells' neat Home Counties breakfast-table.

Nine days after Labour revellers partied into the dawn on London's South Bank, the lawyers involved in the Aitken trial gathered at the Royal Courts of Justice. Charles Gray QC stood up. He wanted to make an unusual application on behalf of his client. The case was too complicated to be heard by a jury, he argued. And, more especially, the documentation involved was huge. Instead the interests of justice would be better served if the judge heard the case by himself – a rare but entirely permissible option for a judge presiding over a civil action. The *Guardian* and Granada team listened in mute disbelief. They had been royally outflanked by Jonathan Aitken. The defendants had pinned their hopes on an ordinary jury seeing through his Etonian *désinvolture* and grasping that the man was a liar. No jury! In his great Sword of Truth speech, Aitken had pledged to defend his reputation 'not only before the jury of the courts but before the wider jury of all fair-minded people'. Now he was trying to defend his reputation before one rather elderly judge. Surely, though, Mr Justice Popplewell would realize there were wider public issues involved in the trial than the number of lever-arch files? After all, juries were frequently entrusted with complex fraud trials like that of the Maxwell brothers, the sons of the late media tycoon and overweight crook Robert Maxwell. There was no precedent for a libel action brought by a senior politician being heard without a jury.

But Sir Oliver agreed with Mr Gray. He would hear the case without a jury. And he alone would decide whether Jonathan Aitken was telling the truth. It would be a 'reasoned judgment,' he purred.

As the *Guardian* and Granada team trooped out of court, they felt shocked and despondent. It would be an uphill struggle, they felt, for the judge to denounce one of his own. George Carman – the famous jury advocate hired by the defendants for just that reason – regarded losing the jury as a 'mortal blow'. 'It was disastrous,' Proudler said. Over at Carman's new set of chambers in Gray's Inn, the lawyers and journalists kicked around the implications of Popplewell's ruling. A jury would have been well qualified to assess Aitken's credibility and would not have been easily taken in by his charm and confidence, Carman felt. It would not have been impressed with his convoluted commercial links with a golden circle of wealthy Arabs. Popplewell, a member of the Establishment down to his slippers and striped pyjamas, was likely to be more sympathetic. Six days later the defendants went to the Court of Appeal.

'The ordinary layman and the media will say "This is a bit of a whitewash, it should be left to a jury,"' Carman told the Lord Chief Justice, Lord Justice Bingham, perched up above him in court 4. 'There will be criticism which will diminish public confidence in the administration of justice.'

But Lord Bingham was having none of it. 'I do not believe public perception is a reliable guide,' he sniffed grandly. There would be no jury.

The *Guardian* had already decided it would not blink. With a month to go, Alan Rusbridger had pulled aside a team of anxious executives to discuss the Aitken crisis. The barristers had advised the *Guardian* to make some kind of payment into court. This would involve the paper in a huge loss of face, but would also protect some of its spiralling costs. Caroline Marland, the paper's managing director, Brian Whitaker, the managing editor, and Paul Naismith, the hard-headed finance director, listened grimly as Rusbridger, Pallister and Leigh outlined the worst possible scenario: the case would drag on all summer; Popplewell would award Aitken massive damages; the *Guardian* would be left with a £2-million legal bill; and there would be savage editorial cuts across all departments. Rusbridger, who was forty-three but looked much younger, had a reputation for keeping his cool in difficult times. This was one of them. If Aitken really had lied over the Ritz and Inglewood, and if he was about to be hammered over TV-am, he did not deserve one penny in damages, libel's famous raspberry. He had no reputation, Rusbridger argued. The question was formally put to everyone in the room. Should the *Guardian* make a payment into court? 'No', the first voice said. And then: 'No.' 'No.' 'No.' 'No.' 'No.' 'No.' 'No.' It was unanimously agreed. There would be no climb-down. The *Guardian* would fight on.

On Wednesday 4 June 1997 the Right Honourable Jonathan William Patrick Aitken swept into the High Court with his wife Lolicia at his side. Aitken was wearing an immaculate grey wool suit; his wife was kitted out in bright checks. The Aitkens smiled at the photographers loafing around outside the Royal Courts and walked into the darkened sanctuary of the main atrium. He placed his black briefcase on to the conveyor belt gurgling towards an X-ray machine and strolled through the rectangular metal detector into the entrance lobby. The Aitkens then moved through the vast main hall which doubles as a badminton court in the evenings and disappeared to the right up a white stone staircase to the first floor. At the top, still smiling, they turned right down an echoing corridor musty with stale cigarette smoke, and right again. This was court 10, the terminus of Aitken's deadly battle against 'the cancer of bent and twisted journalism'.

Inside, waiting for him, were the journalists whom he regarded as his mortal adversaries: Rusbridger, Preston, Leigh, Pallister and McDermott, all sitting four rows back. Aitken took a seat right at the front, on the far left in the well of the court, beneath the witness-box. The two jury benches to his right had been converted into a commodious press-box. Most national newspapers had decided to send reporters to cover this intriguing contest. Curious members of the public were ushered into an upstairs balcony. Leigh turned to Pallister and whispered: 'I don't believe this is happening. How can he go ahead with this? How can he put Lolicia in the witness-box?' Surely this was all part of an elaborate bluff. The normally dishevelled Leigh had decided to buy a new suit for the trial and had chosen a light beige one from Next, reminiscent, he hoped, of TV reporter Martin Bell's white one worn during his recent dramatic 'anti-corruption' general election candidature against Neil Hamilton.

Charles Gray QC sat with his legal team on the left of the court, directly behind his client. Carman, his opposing counsel, seemed unusually nervous.

'Mr Aitken sues the *Guardian* over an article entitled "Aitken tried to arrange girls for Saudis,"' Gray began. He gave a brief description of the *Guardian* article and the *World in Action* programme. 'It is no exaggeration to say they have butchered his personal, political and professional reputation,' Aitken's QC said. The defendants had claimed that Mr Aitken had 'pimped' for Arab clients and 'deliberately concealed' the fact that he was 'in the pockets of the Saudi royal family'. But these allegations were 'false, utterly false', he told the court. In the press-box, biros scratched furiously.

Alan Rusbridger was in fatalistic mood. 'It's preposterous,' he had murmured to Leigh as the court filled up with bewigged men talking nonsense. As editor there was now little he could do. An accomplished doodler, in the corner of his notebook he started sketching a rather inflated Mr Justice Popplewell: a large torso in judicial regalia, a round head and tight frizzy hair, against a suitably Gothic backdrop. 'The first few days of a libel trial are always the worst,' Rusbridger said later. 'You sit there and have buckets of wet brown stuff tipped all over you.'

The morning session ended, and the defendants gathered for the first time in a large ante-room to the left of the court. Nobody felt very upbeat. Downstairs, Jonathan Aitken and his wife sat in the main hall watching the barristers and solicitors, the clerks with their trollies and the foreign tourists glide past. As the *Guardian* journalists talked gloomily through the morning's events, they noticed a floppy-haired public schoolboy hovering on the edge of the conversation. The young man, it transpired, was Aitken's spy. For the duration of the trial he would shadow the *Guardian* journalists like a bungling Viennese secret agent, lurking hopefully for some damaging titbit. At the end, when his master was unveiled as a villain, he would complain darkly about the *Guardian*'s *schadenfreude* at Aitken's fall.

In the afternoon of the first day, Gray jogged lightly through Aitken's account of his Ritz weekend. The following morning the headlines made grim reading for the defendants. EX-MINISTER'S REPUTATION 'WAS BUTCHERED' the *Daily Telegraph* read. The page-3 photograph of Aitken and his wife summed up the mood: a grinning ex-minister striding confidently into court.

On Thursday the Right Honourable Jonathan Aitken mounted the steps into the witness-box for the first time. Over at Edgbaston, the English cricket team – a national laughing-stock a few months earlier – was busy demolishing the Australians in the first day of the opening Test of the Ashes series. Professionally, Mr Justice Popplewell's mind was fixed on the proceedings before him. Spiritually, he hovered somewhere in the humid skies above Edgbaston where Andrew Caddick was to take five wickets and help dismiss Australia for 118 runs shortly after lunch.

Aitken's performance in the witness-box over eight days was awesome. His eyes twinkled, he was confident, fluent and charming. A bemused half-smile, almost a smirk, played on his face, lending him an aura of good-humoured stoicism. 'We had always expected him to be a very good witness,' Gray said later. 'He was intelligent, seemed to me very credible, and performed extremely well. I don't think Carman really laid a glove on him.'

After giving a brief résumé of his career in finance and politics, Aitken launched into a tear-jerking tableau he had prepared with some care before the trial. He had read the *Guardian* front page which accused him of pimping while in Switzerland with his family, he said. The article left him 'pole-axed', 'horrified' and 'astonished'. 'It was the equivalent of having a heart attack in terms of the shock and pain I felt on reading it,' he added. There followed a characteristically bogus embellishment which he calculated would cause huge favour-able publicity the following day: 'I remember burying my head in my hands and saying, to nobody in particular, "The *Guardian* have said, on the front page, I'm a pimp." I remember my son saying, "What is a pimp, Daddy?" He would have been twelve.'

The journalists filling the press bench exchanged incredulous looks. This was fantastic stuff. Mr Justice Popplewell peered down approvingly.

Aitken went on: 'I felt that the *Guardian* had moved from their vendetta, which I felt they had been running for some time against me, to all-out war. I had a sleepless night once I had read the *Guardian*'s story and I said to myself in the long, dark night of the soul, "I have got to stand and fight these lies and I will do so."' His worst fears had been 'confirmed' when he flew back to London and watched the *World in Action* documentary 'Jonathan of Arabia' screened later that day. 'Clearly this was a hatchet job. This was character-assassination television, not current-affairs television. There was no attempt at fairness or objectivity – it was destroy Aitken time,' he declared.

Aitken was a truly brilliant witness – plausible, quick and entertaining. As Aitken got into his stride, Popplewell leaned admiringly towards him as if he were listening to an amusing companion across a dinner-table at the Garrick. The lofty moral tone never wavered. Questioned about Inglewood, for example, Aitken feigned entirely predictable outrage. Mr Gray asked: 'Did you in 1981 or at any other time ask the matron, Jo Lambert, to procure prostitutes for Arabs visiting Inglewood?'

AITKEN No, I most certainly did not.
GRAY Did you make any such request of Robin Kirk?
AITKEN No, I did not. I was appalled by both those allegations.

The 'What's a pimp?' line went down a storm among Fleet Street news editors. The *Daily Telegraph* obliged with a large article on page 3 the following day with the headline 'WHAT'S A PIMP, DADDY?' ASKED AITKEN'S SON. Next to it, a stagey photo of Aitken *en famille* in his Lord North Street home, with his arm placed solicitously round the shoulder of his twelve-year-old son, William. The *Daily Mail* devoted page 5 to the story with the same headline: 'WHAT'S A PIMP, DADDY?' and another photo of loving father with son. The fact that the *Guardian* had never used the word 'pimp' in its original article did not matter. This was a deadly battle of soundbites.

On Friday 6 June, Jonathan Aitken faced his test. Over the next eleven days, with a break for two intervening weekends, the former Cabinet minister was to be cross-examined by Carman. In his long career Carman had never interrogated a single witness for so long. Aitken's twin strategy was clear. He would combine charm with mockery – sometimes flattering the great advocate, and on other occasions trying to crush him with public-gallery sarcasm. Aitken was aided by his encyclopaedic knowledge of the case – he had read and memorized everything – and his own formidable cleverness. 'He was a witness in a thousand,' James Price QC said later. 'I don't expect to see a better liar in my career. Most witnesses who have constructed a false story find themselves caught out fairly early on.'

Carman began with great solemnity, and some wit. Was Mr Aitken, a 'truthful and honourable man', with the privilege of a first-class education, aware of the importance of 'probity and integrity' in political life? 'Yes,' Aitken replied. Was it imperative for a Cabinet minister to behave with total truthfulness to the Cabinet Secretary and Prime Minister? Aitken: 'I would certainly hope so.' Then why had he lied to them both? Aitken admitted he had been guilty of 'sharp editing' in his letter to Sir Robin Butler, which gave the impression his wife had paid all of his Ritz bill. But he claimed his intention was not to deceive Sir Robin but simply to 'throw the *Guardian* off the scent'. This was a major concession, but one Aitken had calculated would not damage him fatally. Carman pressed on. Would Mr Aitken accept he was 'totally unfit for public office' if the judge had to make the 'melancholy decision' that he had lied to the Cabinet Secretary, the Prime Minister, the House of Commons and the court over his Ritz stay? Aitken: 'I don't accept any of these melodramatic hypothetical allegations you are putting to me.' Then, a prophetic foretaste of the disgrace which lay ahead:

AITKEN If his Lordship were to make those dramatic judgments it would be a shattering blow to me, yes.
CARMAN It would butcher your reputation.
AITKEN My reputation is already butchered.
CARMAN It would butcher it again.
AITKEN It would.

As the defendants poured out of the court, they felt uneasy. Aitken had held up remarkably well in the witness-box. Where he was weak – in his letter to Sir Robin Butler – he resorted to the 'verbal subtleties' which had got him out of trouble during the Biafra affair twenty-seven years earlier. Otherwise, he had given no ground at all. And there were ominous noises emanating from Mr Justice Popplewell. The judge had decided to make an early ruling in the case on the *World in Action* programme and *Guardian* article which dealt with Aitken's role as a director of BMARC, the British defence firm. This was covered by Aitken's second writ. The defendants had argued that the programme implied Aitken *should* have known about the illegal arms sales to Iran. Aitken's team counter-argued that the programme claimed he *did* know. Normally, such nuances were left to a jury. But Mr Justice Popplewell had got rid of the jury. He was going to take a video of the programme home for the weekend and decide what, exactly, it meant.

On Monday 9 June the judge came back with his ruling. After three days of evidence, the decision would clearly be a crucial indicator as to Mr Justice Popplewell's state of mind. Did he realize he was dealing with an exquisitely gifted liar? Mr Popplewell came crushingly down in favour of Jonathan Aitken. The programme conveyed the meaning that he *had* known about arms shipments to Iran.

The defendants were appalled; that was never their intention. Aitken was cock-a-hoop. This meant he had already won a significant part of his libel action, and the trial would be shortened by at least two weeks. When giving his judgment, Sir Oliver forgot to invite the press back into court to listen. It was left to the former Cabinet minister to break the news in the corridor. 'I hope you guys realize,' he said grinning, 'this means I'm not an arms dealer.' That lunch-time, Aitken celebrated with his wife in the lawyers' haunt over the road from the High Court, Daley's wine bar. Daley's felt off-limits to the defence team; instead they munched miserably on Pret a Manger sandwiches.

And Aitken had another card to play. Back in the witness-box, he was cross-examined about his infamous stay at the Ritz. He had been 'set up', he told the court. The 'original' registration form he had filled in on his arrival at the hotel had gone missing. The defendants were staggered. Gone missing! All relevant documentation from the Ritz Hotel in Paris had been disclosed and made available to Jonathan Aitken. The form could not have gone missing – because it did not exist. 'I have asked myself many times over the years whether I have been a victim of a set-up or a cock-up in this saga,' Aitken mused from the witness-box. 'I inclined towards the latter, but the fact this registration document I signed has not been produced, makes me wonder.' The trick worked perfectly. That afternoon, the *Evening Standard* splashed a front-page story with the headline: AITKEN: MY RITZ 'SET-UP' FEARS.

Later that evening, as the journalists analysed the evidence and prepared new lines of attack, an anonymous fax arrived at the *Guardian*'s office in Farringdon Road. Dated July 1988, it thanked a prominent Arab, Dr Abdul Masri, for his hospitality and passed on 'warm thanks' to a brother-in-law of the Saudi King, Sheikh Abdulaziz al Ibraham, for 'his most generous gift of that magnificent watch'. The letter had been written by Jonathan Aitken. The watch, which had never been declared in the Register of MPs' Interests, was another intriguing jigsaw piece in the puzzle of Aitken's venal commercial links with the Arab world. But it was not a breakthrough. The following morning, when confronted with the letter in court, Aitken simply said he did not regard the watch as a form of personal enrichment.

Mr Justice Popplewell, meanwhile, was rapidly losing patience with George Carman. The watch letter did not impress him. 'I am sitting here without a jury, Mr Carman, and I have got the point,' he said.

The QC spent the day minutely examining Jonathan Aitken's unwieldy account of his stay at the Ritz Hotel. Carman's forensic attention to detail would help sink Aitken later. The minister had constructed a 'web of lies' in which 'improbability was heaped on improbability', Carman told the court. Aitken had 'weaved a tangled web' to conceal the fact that he had improperly held a business meeting with Arab associates and allowed an Arab friend to pay his hotel bill. 'When you add it all up, that catalogue of improbability, do you not realize how scandalous, incredible and preposterous your story is?' Carman asked.

But Aitken, who by this stage felt he was getting the upper hand, was characteristically robust. 'I don't realize any such thing,' he snapped. 'I flatly reject these flamboyant allegations made to me. This may be a complex story but it is not one based on a web of deceit. There are good, honest explanations for all the points put to me.'

Seated on the front bench, Lolicia Aitken grew restless and dabbed her forehead and wrists with pungent aromatic oils. Her agitation whenever the Ritz bill was mentioned was noted by the press bench. Why was she so nervous?

Every morning, lunch-time and afternoon the team of defence lawyers and *Guardian* journalists would gather in the ante-room overlooking the main hall to analyse the evidence and discuss tactics. Lolicia was clearly going to go into the witness-box with some reluctance. Before the case came to court, Lolicia had twice been asked by journalists to confirm that she had paid her husband's hotel bill. She declined to do so. Perhaps she would now fall 'sick' and be unable to testify. No stunt would be too outrageous for the Right Honourable Jonathan Aitken, the defendants felt. George Carman had already asked Aitken whether his close friend Said Ayas was intending to turn up to court. He was abroad, Aitken said, adding with entirely predictable melancholy, 'but not so well'.

Most afternoons at 5 p.m., Aitken and Sykes would gather in Charles Gray's chambers in Gray's Inn where they discussed the case bullishly. During the next two days Aitken weathered cross-examination over TV-am and Inglewood. There were more Aitkenian synonyms for lying – 'lack of candour' in his dealings over TV-am; 'dissembling' over the ownership of Inglewood. But these admissions had no discernible impact on the judge. When George Carman tried to read from a damning *Daily Mirror* exposé of the TV-am affair, Mr Justice Popplewell intervened to stop him. The report, written by reporter Graham Brough, was serious, thorough, and impeccably sourced. In addition, Jonathan Aitken had extraordinarily not issued a writ over it. 'This is simply Mr Brough's view of Mr Aitken,' the judge said. Clearly he did not think much of journalists.

Sitting in his one-bedroom basement flat in the Oval on Thursday evening, *World in Action*'s Quentin McDermott pulled out a video tape and slotted it into his machine. McDermott was the TV journalist who had ambushed the minister outside his Lord North Street home four days before 'Jonathan of Arabia' was transmitted. The doorstep sequence which showed Aitken leaving home by himself had ended up on the cutting-room floor. But in his witness statement, Aitken had transformed the innocuous encounter on 6 April 1995 into a piece of melodramatic theatre. The MP claimed he had left his home not alone but with his daughter Alexandra. They had been 'stampeded' by the *World in Action* team, he claimed – a ridiculous untruth. Alexandra had been 'visibly upset' by the crew's 'aggressive behaviour' and had burst into tears. He and his daughter had got into the ministerial Jaguar and set off to Heathrow airport for a skiing holiday. But, according to his witness statement, they had been pursued in a dangerous 'Keystone Kops' chase by the Granada journalists driving a van and were eventually forced to swap vehicles at the Spanish Embassy.

This absurd piece of fiction had been crafted by Aitken in November 1996, before he realized *World in Action* had kept a copy of the original clip. The unedited television rushes shot on 6 April 1995 revealed an entirely different picture. Alexandra Aitken was not there. The minister got into the car by himself. The car drove off. No attempt was made to pursue him. The film showed Aitken had lied, using one of his teenage daughters to exaggerate the distress caused to his family, in an attempt to bolster his fraudulent claim for exemplary damages. On Thursday afternoon the unedited clip was played to Aitken for the first time. There was a moment's hiatus while the judge watched a Bugs Bunny cartoon instead. 'No, I do not think this is quite . . .' Sir Oliver faltered. 'It looks more like Children's Hour, if that still exists.' Eventually the clip was shown – revealing that there was no daughter and no chase. For the first time in five days in the witness-box Aitken looked acutely embarrassed. But he was saved further distress when the afternoon session ended minutes later.

The following day, Friday 13 June, Carman returned to the attack. 'Where on earth is your daughter in the film that we saw yesterday?' he asked.

Aitken was in trouble, and his syntax fractured. 'We were shouted at, we were, my daughter was upset and there was a car chase . . .' Seated in the front bench his wife Lolicia mouthed at him: 'Another time.' Sykes was looking agitated. Aitken took the hint. 'A different film,' he ventured, explaining that he had been approached by camera crews several times that day.

Sitting in the living room of his south London flat that evening, McDermott had another look at the tape. As he chased the minister along the pavement, the camera wobbled up and down. He froze the picture. At the top of the frame he spotted something new: a clock on the face of the church opposite Conservative Central Office in Smith Square, which could perhaps confirm that this was not a 'different film' but a contemporaneous recording of the unremarkable doorstep. The clock's hands were faintly discernible. McDermott got on the phone to a producer friend in Manchester and asked her to blow up the film in an editing suite in the hope that a magnified shot would pinpoint the time exactly.

The doorstep fiasco was Aitken's worst moment. Otherwise, Jonathan William Patrick Aitken was to survive twenty-three hours of cross-examination by Britain's toughest and most remorseless advocate. He had told more lies on oath than any other senior British politician in living memory; and, about the Ritz, had indeed woven a web of deceit in which improbability had been heaped on improbability. But the edifice of mendacity, though it creaked from time to time, was holding firm. Mr Justice Popplewell may have had the odd doubt, but he still seemed to incline towards this charming former

Tory minister. The judge had already thrown out the *Guardian* and Granada's argument on BMARC. By Friday afternoon, on 13 June 1997, George Carman was exhausted. Aitken was also in poor shape. He had privately been indulging in 'scream therapy' – a form of intense massage – after court, to relieve stress. Like two weary gladiators they circled round the arena for one last exchange of blows.

CARMAN A long time ago, it seems, you said in a moving public speech that you were going to take out the Sword of Truth to prosecute these claims for libel. Do you recall that?

AITKEN I do.

CARMAN Mr Aitken, as a man who claims to take up the Sword of Truth my last suggestion to you is this: before this court case, and during it, you have proved yourself – and I want your comment on this to see if you accept it – a stranger to the truth whenever it suits you.

AITKEN My comment on that is that it is an unfair and unjust comment and I stand by what I said in my press conference of April 10th, namely that I believe that the issues which have been raised in the *Guardian* that morning and were raised that evening in the Granada television programme would in the end be vindicated by what I rather rhetorically called the Sword of Truth and the shield of fair play.

And that was it. On the press benches the verdict on the contest held without a jury was less wordy. 'The *Guardian*,' one hack said, 'is buggered.'

....

Eleven: **The Fragrant Witness**

S hortly before midnight, reporter Owen Bowcott turned off uphill towards the Swiss town of Villars and accelerated through the dark. As the road narrowed and twisted into switchbacks, his rented Fiat Brava emitted a low groan. The steamy night air wafted in the scent of damp meadows. Outside, the grass slopes were illuminated by pale moonlight; the village streets passed through, utterly deserted. At 12.06 a.m. Bowcott drove into Villars past the sign for Aiglon College. Of all the missions he had been sent on in connection with the Jonathan Aitken saga this, he thought, was one of the least likely to produce results. Could his unpromising trip to this picturesque Swiss ski resort possibly turn up a vital piece of evidence to precipitate Jonathan Aitken's downfall and reveal him as a perjurer and a cheat?

Twelve hours earlier, on Sunday 1 June 1997, Bowcott had been returning home from a late-morning swim with his girlfriend when his pager, lodged in his pocket, began emitting its plaintive electronic bleep. A former Northern Ireland correspondent for the *Guardian*, he wondered whether an IRA bomb had gone off. Instead, when he phoned the *Guardian* office from a call-box, he was greeted in apologetic tones by the enigmatic David Pallister. 'How'd you like to go to Switzerland?' Pallister volunteered. 'On the next flight today.'

The Hotel Bristol in Villars, where Lolicia Aitken had stayed during the infamous Ritz weekend, had recently gone bust. It was now entangled in an international fraud inquiry, Pallister explained. The hotel records had probably been destroyed, seized by police, impounded by accountants or eaten by mountain goats. But if not, however, there was a tiny chance that they retained sufficient evidence to demolish Aitken's unbelievable account of his wife's travel arrangements.

Both journalists agreed it was worth a final throw. Before heading off to Heathrow airport that evening for a flight to Geneva, Bowcott had a hurried conversation with the *Guardian*'s solicitor Geraldine Proudler. 'It could be the killer-point for the whole affair,' she suggested, ever dogged. 'If we can prove that Lolicia was never at the Ritz, the entire edifice of his explanation collapses. There's no evidence to show that she even made it to Paris.'

Telephone records from the Ritz revealed that the last call made from Aitken's room to the Hotel Bristol was at 10.15 a.m. on Sunday 19 September 1993. So Lolicia would have had to have checked out afterwards to fly to Paris. Even then, it seemed improbable she could have arrived in Paris by Sunday lunch-time. Could she have driven from Villars back to Geneva in time? Could Bowcott time the journey?

Pallister had himself visited the Bristol two years previously. But the receptionist had not been helpful, and had shown him only a registration card for a visit by Jonathan Aitken in November 1993. 'You do realize this could be a complete wild-goose chase,' Bowcott told Proudler gloomily. The Aitken libel trial was due to start at the High Court in two days' time. Speed was vital. But BA flight 732 sat obstinately on the runway for fifty minutes, stalled by an industrial dispute. As he waited in his business-class seat, Bowcott mused on the Swiss predilection for client confidentiality and the diplomatic storm breaking over the missing wartime millions lodged by Holocaust victims in the country's bank vaults, the details of which had apparently disappeared for ever. He did not greatly fancy his chances of getting any co-operation.

At Geneva Bowcott picked up his Fiat and sped off along the dual-carriage motorway towards Lausanne and Villars. Leaving the airport he recorded that it was 10.54 p.m. As he accelerated through the dark, rain swept in, obliterating the view of Lac Leman. Oncoming headlights dazzled through the glistening windscreen. At Villars he checked into the Hotel Eurotel, then went out again immediately to look for what was left of the Hotel Bristol. The local guidebook pictured the wooden building resplendent in crisp, bright snow and listed its facilities as the Arc-en-Ciel and Le Chalet restaurants, Bar l'Horizon, banqueting rooms, a heated swimming pool, sauna, solarium and squash courts. But there was no sign of life, not a single light on in the dark, emptied hulk which he found.

Up early the next morning, he donned a suit, snatched a quick breakfast, and set off for the Bristol expecting it to be shuttered up. Instead, he found two men outside, admiring the snow-capped peaks which glimmered serenely at them from across the valley. The Aitken investigation was a complex story to explain at that time in the morning, let alone in imperfect French. But the tale of plots, lost receipts and impending legal catastrophe at least sharpened the sense of intrigue.

'Come inside,' the caretaker beckoned, and introduced Bowcott to two others busy conducting a financial inventory of the hotel's contents. Yes, they explained, the reception records were still in the building, stored in a deep basement. No, they were not authorized to allow anyone to examine them. No, he couldn't glance at them.

Badgered for permission, the two accountants agreed to drive him to the Hotel Panorama down the road. Owned by the same collapsed Belgian company that had run the Bristol, it too had been closed by the mysterious disappearance of 3.5 billion Belgian francs (£65 million) – a financial disaster entirely unconnected to the Aitken case. In the lobby of the emptied Panorama, the former manager Stephane Coeckelenbergh listened attentively to Bowcott's unusual request but apologized that he did not have the authority to permit a trawl through 'les archives'. He would, however, ring the head accountant's office in Lausanne and see if he would agree. The phone call was peremptory; the inquiry rebuffed.

'Could I speak to him,' Bowcott pressed.

'No, but I will give you the fax number,' M. Coeckelenbergh proposed, 'and you can send him a message.'

Back in his room at the Eurotel, Bowcott waited for the accountant to call. So close. Swiss bureaucracy remained one frustrating step ahead. It would probably be a matter of hiring local lawyers, he speculated, court applications for access, and a legal process which could grind on for months – long after the juryless libel trial in London had ended in gloating triumph for the villainous Aitken. Then the phone rang. The senior accountant was curious; he asked about details of the story. 'OK,' he sighed eventually, sounding as though he had been persuaded against his better judgement.

Bowcott bounded out of the door and was back at the Hotel

Bristol within minutes. It was already mid-morning. The caretaker, instructed by now to help, took him down in the lift into the darkened basement. In one room to the right, the hotel's supply of sheets and pillowcases were being ironed and counted. Along a dim corridor, through heavy metal security doors, lay the storeroom. It was lined with tall wooden lockers. No natural light percolated down from the bright summer's day outside. The room reverberated whenever a tram passed by on the street overhead.

Unlocking four of the cupboards, the caretaker revealed piles of printouts, cardboard boxes and overflowing ring-binder files stacked up to above head height. Some of the papers were loose, some in dated bundles. Thank God computers generate so much paperwork, he thought, and that someone hoarded it all away. But where to start? Squatting down on the concrete floor, he pulled out files from the top of the first locker and began reading.

The papers dated back to 1988 when the Bristol began trading. There were even telephone logs by room, but they stretched back only to 1994, a year after Lolicia and Victoria had swept into reception. A neat box of 'fiches de police' – registration cards – arranged alphabetically sent his heart racing. Lolicia Aitken's card should be there, showing when she had arrived and left that weekend.

Flicking through the As, skimming from name to name, at last an 'Aitken'. But not Lolicia, only Jonathan. It was the same card as the one seen by David Pallister two years earlier, dated 20 November 1993 – many weeks later. And on it the same immodest flourish as at the Ritz: for profession, the MP had written 'Minister of Defence'. Of Lolicia's earlier visit, however, there was no trace. Nothing either under L or O for Olivera, the other Christian name she used. Had it been removed?

More boxes, more folders, more files. Eventually a bulging dossier labelled 'Reservations de Chambres, 1993'. Bowcott turned sheet after sheet, sometimes doubling back in case he had missed a name, until 'Aitken' stared up from the page. The room number, 234, was scrawled across one corner of the paper. 'Adultes: 2; 1 plus 2', the receptionist had written, 'Aiglon College, vers 22h 00'. No date, but it was wedged between other reservations for the weekend of 18–19 September. 'Eureka!' he exhaled. 'A first sighting.' It was the first proof that Lolicia had ever even stayed at Villars.

At lunch-time, the caretaker returned to close the hotel for an hour and a half; everyone would have to leave. Faxing what he had gleaned back to the *Guardian* in London, he descended again in the afternoon into the gloomy basement. The tightly packed boxes of computer printouts came in innumerable forms. There were guests listed by room number, bar bills, restaurant slips, and even a list of no-shows. None of the bills, he noticed, had check-out times. And then came another breakthrough. 'Aitken, Olivera' was listed as a late arrival on 17 September 1993. She was due to stay until the 19th. 'Changer prix pour demain pour 1 pax,' someone had added to her entry. This showed that the notoriously stingy Lolicia had asked for, and got, a single-occupancy discount on her room for the Saturday night. This was later to prove a crucial piece of evidence for the defendants, albeit not clinching. At 6 p.m. Bowcott was forced to abandon the search when the hotel was locked up for the night.

Early the next morning, the day before the libel case opened at the Royal Courts of Justice, the caretaker unlocked the door again. Several cupboards remained unexplored. There were piles of neat white cards produced by tills in the hotel's bars and restaurants, including one which recorded what Lolicia had for breakfast on Saturday morning. (Cornflakes and apple juice, 8 Swiss francs. A healthy choice.) There was only one cupboard left to examine. And in it, a vital clue of which the defendants had been kept deliberately ignorant. A 'Liste de Codes de Facturation' turned up Lolicia's name among those who had paid their bill by American Express card that day.

But Mrs Aitken did not have an American Express card. Or at least this is what she had told Mr Justice Popplewell via her lawyers at a pre-trial hearing two weeks earlier. Jonathan Aitken had been served with a court order in April which compelled him to reveal credit-card statements relating to the crucial Ritz weekend. On 30 April 1997 Lolicia had been served with a similar court order which obliged her to disclose 'bank or credit-card statements of all accounts held by you or jointly by you and the plaintiff showing expenditure during the month of September 1993'. The Aitkens simply ignored the court orders. Unlike Nixon, who vacillated over whether to burn the incriminating White House tapes which recorded his bungled attempts to cover up the Watergate scandal, Aitken had no compunction about burying the evidence. In the months before the libel trial Aitken had abused the 'discovery process' which obliges both sides to hand over copies of relevant documents to the other. The defendants played by the rules and handed over everything – internal memos, records of phone calls, journalists' notes. But Aitken had played dirty. He concealed the existence of his Amex card, on which he and his wife had joint signing rights, knowing that its discovery would have cast serious doubt on the credibility of his flimsy Ritz story. For three years it had remained hidden. By the time Aitken decided to face down his enemies in the High Court, he had wrongly concluded they would never find it.

As Bowcott scooped up Lolicia's final bill from the Hotel Bristol for 575 Swiss francs he could not have known of the crucial role it would play. But he realized the documents opened up fresh – if desperately belated – areas for investigation. Over at Aiglon College, the international college where Victoria Aitken was educated for just one lachrymose term, nobody could remember whether the blonde Mrs Aitken had put in an appearance four years earlier that Sunday afternoon. But new possibilities swirled everywhere. At the airport, queueing for his return flight, Bowcott asked the British Airways staff how many airlines flew the Heathrow-to-Geneva route. 'Just two,' they replied, 'us and Swissair.' And would the flight records from four years ago still exist? 'Of course,' they assured him, 'ours will still be on computer in London.'

Back at Olswang, Proudler leafed excitedly through the bundle of documents which Bowcott had retrieved from the Hotel Bristol. They confirmed for the first time what Aitken had said in his witness statement to the court: that his wife *had* stayed at Villars on the Friday evening with their daughter, and on the Saturday evening by herself. Perhaps, Proudler thought, Aitken was telling the truth about his wife's movements. But given his track record of mendacity and concealment, this seemed unlikely.

And then there was the intriguing detail of the undisclosed American Express card. Before the trial Lolicia had turned up in court to hear her barrister tell the judge she had complied with the subpoena 'in full'. She handed over her Swiss passport and a bundle of choicely irrelevant Barclaycard statements. The passport showed she had returned to Heathrow on Monday 20 September 1993. Although it bore an entry stamp, Lolicia's place of departure remained a mystery.

Proudler wrote immediately to Aitken's solicitor Richard Sykes and asked him to hand over full details of the former minister's

American Express records. The following day, Wednesday 4 June 1997, the case kicked off in the High Court. Sykes's response was dilatory. Two days passed. In exasperation, George Carman raised the delay with the judge. The judge had already ordered that the statements should be disclosed. He agreed Aitken's team should hurry up. Sykes eventually wrote back and said that Aitken had 'no record' of his American Express transactions and could not help. Proudler then wrote directly to the legal department of American Express asking them to supply the records. Nothing happened. On Monday 9 June she resorted to the nuclear option – and fired a formal subpoena at Amex. 'This was a very good example of how this case went. The crucial evidence was not made available by Mr Aitken. We had to work to get everything. It was like extracting teeth,' Proudler remarked.

The following day Amex replied. The firm said it had dug up three relevant pages relating to Aitken's Amex expenditure in the months of August, September and October 1993. But when the documentation arrived at Olswang the crucial page – the October statement which showed September's expenditure – was missing.

Over in the High Court, meanwhile, Aitken was doing his best to try and discredit Owen Bowcott's new Hotel Bristol evidence. 'Mysteriously, despite the hotel being shut, the *Guardian* is able to enter the basement of the hotel and do the equivalent of what in the East End is called "finding something that has fallen off the back of the lorry",' he told George Carman from the witness-box. 'These are rather odd documents, and they are contradictory in certain parts. Forgive me for being a little suspicious of your clients.'

Aitken had previously moved elegantly out of check as Carman had attacked the former Chief Secretary to the Treasury over his wife's movements. His wife had clearly spent the Saturday evening of the Ritz weekend 500 miles away in Switzerland, Carman said. She could not have returned in time to pay his hotel bill at the Paris Ritz, arriving the following lunch-time, because Aitken's Paris hotel phone records placed her still in Switzerland, at Villars, at 10.15 a.m. the following morning.

No, no, Aitken replied smoothly. When he phoned the Hotel Bristol that morning at 10.15 a.m. his wife had indeed already left for Paris. He spoke instead to his mother-in-law who also went to stay in Villars that weekend.

'The mother-in-law?!' the *Guardian* team exclaimed. This was incredible. In his 205-page witness statement Aitken had made no mention of his wrinkled Yugoslav mother-in-law staying at the Bristol. Under cross-examination, Aitken was solving the problem of the damning telephone call by popping granny, too, into the bedroom of the Hotel Bristol at the requisite time.

'The story about your mother-in-law occupying the room for a second night with your wife is untrue,' Carman suggested.

'I spoke to her not only in the morning but also in the [previous] evening,' Aitken lied. Like a reckless Porsche-driver faced with a stop barrier, Aitken had simply pulled out on to the wrong side of the road and accelerated past. But the documents from the Hotel Bristol now clearly put him in check again. If there had been only 'single occupancy' of the hotel room that night, the mother-in-law could not have been sharing the room. Check again. But never checkmate.

Nearly a week had gone by, and the defendants were no nearer to getting their hands on Aitken's Amex bill. Joel Barry, the solicitor at Olswang dealing with Amex, bombarded the company with faxes, letters and telephone calls. On 12 June Amex wrote back to say: 'We have still been unable to obtain the documents you would require.' There was a technical problem, and records' staff would have to go back to microfilm records. Barry groaned. Later that day another letter arrived. 'We still have been unable to obtain from our system copies of the October statement,' Amex's legal department wrote. Barry groaned again. 'However,' it went on, 'from a manual search we have been able to put together the attached lists of transactions billed in the October statement.'

An incredible breakthrough. At the bottom of the statement of 'Cardmember: Mr Jonathan Aitken MP' there were two separate entries for a 'Supplementary cardmember: Mrs L. Aitken'. The first read: 'Hotel Le Bristol, Switzerland' for 575 Swiss francs. Date debited '21/09/93'. The second was wholly unexpected: 'Budget Rent-A-Car, Ankunftshalle, Switzerland' for 420 Swiss francs. Date debited '29/09/93'.

Both entries clearly related to the same weekend. They had simply been debited at different times. What did they mean? The bill corroborated exactly what Bowcott had discovered in the vaults of the Hotel Bristol: that Mrs Aitken's bill total confirmed she had requested a single-occupancy discount on her room for the Saturday night. That exploded the 'mother-in-law-in-the-room' gambit. Lolicia must have taken that call.

But what was this Budget Rent-a-Car entry? Proudler burst into a colleague's office and asked if anybody spoke German. Nobody did, but had she tried looking in the office dictionary? Proudler turned to A and 'Ankunftshalle'. The English translation jumped off the page: 'arrivals hall'. 'It was obviously an airport,' Proudler said.

This single word opened up a shimmering new vista of inquiry. By this stage Aitken had given evidence claiming he was 'unsure' how his wife had first travelled on from Paris to arrive in Geneva – but that he thought it was 'by TGV'. If she was at the airport how did she get there? Proudler thought. Where was she going to? Did she fly back after that? When did she arrive at the airport? And what happened to the car on that crucial Sunday when she was supposed to be in Paris paying her husband's bill at the Ritz?

After a week of frustration and delay, the *Guardian* and Granada troops were finally going on the offensive. But there were still more questions than answers. In the *Guardian* newsroom, surrounded by a mountain of lever-arch files, empty polystyrene coffee cups and lurid-green pot plants, the paper's researcher Jamie Wilson pored over airplane timetables and road-maps. Aitken was clearly lying about the 10.15 a.m. call on Sunday morning. He had claimed Lolicia had arrived in Paris 'late to mid-morning'. There was a plane at 11.15 a.m. which would have taken her from Geneva airport to Paris in time to pay his hotel bill – just. But Bowcott had already timed the journey from Villars to the airport: 1 hour and 12 minutes, with no traffic. 'There was no way she could have done that,' Proudler reasoned.

After conferring with Leigh and Pallister, the *Guardian* team decided to look again at Lolicia's extraordinary travel movements between Paris and Geneva. Joel Barry telephoned Swissair's London office to try and establish whether Mrs Aitken had been on a flight between Paris and Geneva that weekend. The airline initially said it might be able to oblige. But then a call came back saying: 'Sorry, we can't help.' The relevant documents existed but were all in Switzerland, beyond the reach of a British subpoena, which was not legally enforceable abroad. Brick wall. What, then, about British Airways? Aitken had still not been able to supply any evidence at all – tickets, restaurant receipts, bank statements – which proved his wife had ever even been in France. The evidence, his solicitor Sykes claimed, had been destroyed. Aitken's story was desperately thin.

Proudler turned to British Airways. She wanted all possibilities covered. She subpoenaed the airline to see whether Lolicia and Victoria had flown not just between Paris and Geneva but also between London and Paris and London and Geneva several days either side of the Ritz weekend.

Then there was more frustrating bureaucracy. On 11 June 1997 BA wrote back: 'I fully understand the importance of the information asked for and also our obligation to comply with the order,' Stephen Parker, BA's manager (operations), began portentously. 'It is, however, an enormous task because much of the information you require has been placed in the archives and it has been estimated that it will take in the region of 33 man days to complete.' Thirty-three man days! This was too slow. Proudler offered the services of two legal juniors to help BA expedite the search. The airline appointed a senior British Airways criminal investigator to oversee the process, Wendy Harris. But she was not available for another five days.

Nothing could be done to move the process on more quickly. On Monday 16 June two Olswang legal assistants, Anthony Ponsford and Emily Hohler, turned up at Vanguard House, the grey Lubianka at Heathrow airport which houses BA's Security and Investigation Service. They jumped into Wendy Harris's Ford Escort and drove for a mile through the airport complex – past grounded jumbo jets, refuelling hangars and fuel dumps. At a vast, windowless warehouse they got out. It was here that BA's internal records were kept, on spools of microfiche stacked on 3-foot-tall metal shelves. Some had been jumbled into heaps, and tossed into discard bins. Others were stacked in orderly chronological lines. Wendy Harris briefed Ponsford and Hohler and the team got to work.

Back in the High Court, a tall man with a broad forehead, thinning hair and a frank-looking oval face stepped into the witness-box to give evidence. In a different era, his integrity and unswervable opinions might have made him a Quaker preacher or a saintly mendicant friar. As it was, Richard Charles Scrimgeour Shepherd was the Conservative MP for Aldridge-Brownhills, and he had come to courtroom 10 to try and help out his old friend Jonathan Aitken. In a freethinking political career Aitken, the consummate networker who remembered everybody's birthday and the names of their wives, had built up an unusually wide range of cross-party friendships. In his hour of need, several faded political figures, including former Commons Speakers Lord Weatherill and Viscount Tonypandy, had rushed to his aid. Shepherd described Aitken as a 'good and kindly' man and explained that the two were friends who had fought several 'bonny' fights together. Of Aitken's Saudi links Shepherd was profoundly ignorant. 'Never been there,' he said, of Saudi Arabia.

Another FOJA (Friend of Jonathan Aitken) also tried to help out his old chum as best he could. Lord Pearson of Rannoch had been at Eton with Jonathan, a bond which obviously still counts for much in modern Britain. A silver-haired Conservative grandee with the high-pitched voice of a suburban manicurist, Lord Pearson told the court he was godfather to Victoria Aitken and sometimes met Jonathan for dinner. An insurance broker, he had also helped insure the plane bought by Prince Mohammed with Aitken's assistance at the Paris air show back in 1977. He had met the Arab fixers Said Ayas and Wafic Said at parties thrown by Jonathan. But of Aitken's secret money-making activities he knew little. 'Thank you very much,' Mr Justice Popplewell remarked, as the peer made his cameo exit.

Watching the drama for the first time was the gazelle-like Victoria Aitken, brought in to sit next to her father on the front bench of the court. Victoria, whose photo sometimes graced the society pages of *Tatler*, darted animated glances at the judge and the press gallery. Of Lolicia, on the eve of her fiftieth birthday, there was no sign. Her place had been taken by Victoria's fearsome grandmother, Lady Aitken, whose rigid gaze bored through the doodling court usher into the bookshelf behind the judge, laden with dusty legal tomes. In front of her she placed a crisp new copy of *Country Life*. Why, the press wondered, had Aitken bothered to bring his seventeen-year-old daughter to court on the ninth day of the trial, in this stage-managed simulacrum of family unity? The answer became clear soon enough.

Over at the BA warehouse, at around 1 p.m., Anthony Ponsford fed another spool of microfiche into his reference-library-style viewfinder. The next batch of coupons blurred for a second, then sharpened into exactitude. The names Mrs L. Aitken and Miss V. Aitken stared brazenly out of the screen. It was the Aitkens—mother and daughter.

Excited, but still somewhat confused, Ponsford reached for the phone and dialled Joel Barry at Olswang. Barry was taken aback. 'Get hard copies!' he yelled. The coupons *proved* that mother and daughter had flown directly from Heathrow to Geneva at 8.30 a.m. on Friday 17 September 1993. Lolicia flew back alone from Geneva at 19.05 p.m. on Monday 20 September. They had never been to Paris at all.

Coming out of court, Proudler found an urgent message on her mobile phone from Barry. There was a two-minute delay before she got through to Olswang. 'We've found it!' Barry exclaimed.

'What?' Proudler said, trying to hear over the shuffling and muttering of Carman lighting up a cigarette, and the lawyers and journalists milling around her.

'Flight coupons from Geneva.'

'*What?*' Proudler said again.

'Flight coupons to and from Geneva,' Barry replied.

Proudler was thunderstruck. 'I think we've just had a breakthrough,' she said quietly. The *Guardian* and Granada team, who had gathered in the ante-room overlooking the cavernous main hall of the Royal Courts, watched in bemusement as Proudler pointed mutely at her phone. Pallister handed Geraldine a buff folder and a pen. As the details came down the line she wrote: 'Br Airways. 17 Sept 8.30 a.m., Heathrow/Geneva. Lolicia & Victoria. 20 Sept 7.05 p.m. Geneva/ Heathrow. Flight coupon.'

Carman took control. 'Quiet, please, tell me details exactly,' he said. Proudler read them out and a gasp of astonishment and relief went round the room. Carman looked like a cat with a gallon of cream.

This was impossible. This meant neither Lolicia nor Victoria had been in Paris on Friday. Lolicia had flown home from Geneva. The implications were hard to digest. This was potentially a total destruction of the Cabinet minister's entire testimony about the payment of the Ritz bill. Aitken, the man who declared war on 'the cancer of bent and twisted journalism', had spent the last three years lying to his colleagues; and had unpacked the same lies in the High Court on oath.

In a state of shock, euphoria and incredulity, Pallister went over to Leigh. 'I think we can shake hands on this, that's it.'

'Not quite yet,' Leigh replied dourly. Indeed, as the defendants walked dazedly out into the Strand their high spirits began to evaporate. After all, Aitken was a supreme wriggler and liar *par excellence*. Could he wriggle out of this one?

Over at 75 Farringdon Road, the offices of the weekly international edition of the *Guardian*, Alan Rusbridger was sitting in front of a flickering computer screen. His phone rang. It was Leigh. 'There is something we need to talk to you about. Not over the phone,' Leigh whispered conspiratorially. By now paranoia was setting in.

Ten minutes later Leigh and Pallister rolled up by taxi and briefed the editor about the new development. Rusbridger was ecstatic. Aitken, he felt, was sunk. 'It seemed too good to be true,' Rusbridger later said. 'But by that stage of the case you get superstitious. Aitken had been masterly at wriggling out of everything so far.' If Aitken was given any advance warning, Rusbridger reasoned, he might adapt his 'preposterous story'. Like a fast-changing virus, Aitken's story mutated before one's eyes. He invented a fresh lie to replace an old, exhausted one. There was only one way to catch him out: cold-blooded ambush.

Later that evening Proudler peered at the documents which were to destroy Aitken two days later. Two blurred photocopies of flight coupons in the names of Mrs L. Aitken and Miss V. Aitken, and a mysterious document marked 'batch header'. The quality of the microfiche records was poor, Proudler felt. What, exactly, did they mean? And did they leave Aitken a way of escape? It was immediately clear that Wendy Harris's evidence would be of crucial importance. She would have to give a detailed witness statement, and would probably have to appear in court. Sinking into her chair, Proudler reached for the telephone and dialled Wendy Harris's number. Could they meet, urgently? Ms Harris said she was not available the following day, Tuesday 17 June 1997. Nothing would persuade her to change her plans. But she would give a statement on Wednesday.

Over at 45 Great Peter Street, Jonathan Aitken and Richard Sykes were also talking strategy. Aitken's credibility over his Ritz story had been badly knocked by the Hotel Bristol printouts. Their significance would not have escaped Mr Justice Popplewell who, like a bowler taking a long run-up, finally seemed to be getting the measure of the case. It seems that Aitken decided that what was needed was a grand gesture. More specifically, an invincible witness who could restore the former minister's sinking credibility over the Ritz affair.

In a private briefing paper for his lawyers Aitken had already declared that he did not feel obliged 'to play by the Queensberry Rules' in his dealings with the *Guardian*. 'This was war between us,' he wrote of his combative correspondence with Peter Preston. And so into the field of battle Aitken decided to despatch a witness whose purity and goodness could not seriously be questioned in a court of law: his pretty seventeen-year-old daughter Victoria. Carman could not usefully tear Victoria apart in the witness-box. In the event of an Aitken victory this would infuriate Mr Justice Popplewell, and probably add tens of thousands of pounds on to the figure for damages. She would probably spend only five minutes in the witness-box at most, Aitken calculated.

Victoria would be the trial's 'fragrant witness'. Every libel trial worth its salt has one, named after the politician Jeffrey Archer's wife Mary. (After she once testified on her husband's behalf, a besotted libel judge murmured: 'Is she not fragrant?') Sykes and Aitken decided to decorate the plan with a PR motif of their own. Victoria was due to give evidence on Thursday 19 June, together with her mother Lolicia. Over at Ascot racecourse, Britain's champagne-guzzling aristocracy would be gathering for Ladies' Day, a silly annual orgy of extravagant millinery, short skirts and tabloid photography. Why not dub Thursday 'Ladies' Day' at the High Court? The hacks would love that. Aitken and Sykes were agreed.

But before putting Victoria on the stand, the seventeen-year-old public schoolgirl needed to make a formal witness statement. This required some care. Victoria had inherited her father's good looks and her mother's alleged dyslexia. Her statement needed to sound credible, but should also tug on Mr Justice Popplewell's avuncular heart-strings. That evening, Aitken (probably aided by Sykes) drafted the statement which Victoria would sign the following morning. Aitken, of course, knew his daughter had flown directly from London Heathrow to Geneva. The former minister had never shown any hesitation in the past about exploiting his daughters when it suited him. He had cynically calculated that Victoria's homesick letters would go down well with a jury, and he had lied about the *World in Action* camera crew making his other daughter Alexandra cry. He had also taken Victoria to the Sword of Truth press conference, giving rise to *Private Eye*'s celebrated front cover and imaginary bubble: 'Can I go now, Dad?' Now Victoria was going to have to make the ultimate sacrifice for her father. If this meant telling a grossly false story so be it. Her statement read as follows:

Statement of Victoria Spasa Aitken
of 8 Lord North Street, London, s.w.1.

1. I am the daughter of Jonathan and Lolicia Aitken. I am a student at present at Schule Schlossstein, near Munich, studying for 'A' levels in German, Russian and Politics.

2. In September 1993 I was due to join a new school, Aiglon College in Villars, Switzerland. On Thursday, 16 September, my mother and I left Sandwich and drove to Dover where we caught the ferry to Calais and the train to Paris. We arrived there in the late afternoon/early evening of Thursday. We stayed at the flat of one of Said Ayas's daughters. Those present in the flat on Thursday night were my mother and I and Rima, another daughter of Said Ayas. I believe that Said joined us for dinner.

3. We were expecting my father to join us in Paris on the Friday but we received a message that he was going to be delayed in Poland. I told my mother that I would like to get down to the school as quickly as possible. We left Paris in the middle of the day or early afternoon. We took the train to Geneva and my recollection is we went by car to Villars where Aiglon College is. My mother and I stayed in the Hotel Bristol that night sharing a room.

4. On the Saturday morning my mother and I went up to the school where I tried on my uniform. At some time during the day we met my grandmother, Madame Nada Azucki. My mother and I then went to the school where after saying goodbye, she left me. This would be some time in the afternoon and I slept the night in the school. The following morning I felt very unhappy and telephoned the Hotel Bristol. My mother was not there but my grandmother was there and I spoke to her and told her how miserable I was. She came out to see me at the school and tried to comfort me. My mother had already left Villars by the time I phoned.

5. My father came to see me in the evening.

6. The contents of this statement are true to the best of my knowledge and belief.

   Dated 17/6/97.

   Signed: Victoria Aitken.

'We always wondered how low he would stoop,' Alan Rusbridger said after the case collapsed. 'That was the moment we knew.'

'Jonathan Aitken seems to have impaled himself on the simple sword of truth. For three years he has lied to newspapers, lied to the Cabinet Secretary, lied to the Prime Minister and lied to his colleagues. Now he has made his fatal mistake by lying on oath to the High Court.' **Alan Rusbridger, 20 June 1997**

Twelve: **He Lied and Lied and Lied**

On Tuesday 17 June 1997 the lawyers trooped into court a little later than usual. Over at the press bench, attendance had fallen off. Early in the case the gallery where the jury usually sit had been full. Journalists had jostled good-humouredly for space, swapping anecdotes and leafing through huge piles of newspapers. Most lunch-times the press pack would decipher their shorthand notes collectively in the smoke-filled office of the Press Association downstairs, before walking out of the back entrance of the High Court to the Seven Stars pub for a pint and a ham sandwich. This particular morning only *The Times* and *Guardian* reporters were left, and they were losing interest. The case looked as if it would stretch across the hot expanse of summer into August, an eternity of sunless after-noons punctuated only by judicial breaks for tea and chocolate biscuits. There was no reason for them to know a melodramatic denouement worthy of a Sherlock Holmes thriller or a Grisham novel lay just around the corner, or that the Right Honourable Jonathan Aitken was about to be impaled rather nastily on his own rococo phraseology.

Two court cases were unfolding that morning: the official one inside the courtroom, which was dull, slow and often obscure; and the secret one outside in the ante-room where the defendants gathered, which was tense, heart-stopping and irascible.

'I think Miss Victoria Aitken's statement has just been handed to your Lordship; may I suggest tab 81 for that?' Charles Gray QC said helpfully as the session began.

The blown-up *World in Action* tape of the clock facing Smith Square had been sent back from the Manchester editing suite. It showed the doorstep incident with Quentin McDermott had indeed taken place at 1.15 p.m. – confirming Granada's version of events and disproving Aitken's assertion that the clip was of a 'different time' – as Aitken set off alone for Heathrow and his skiing holiday. The minister had clearly lied about the car chase. His daughter Alexandra, the magnified video proved, was not there. That morning Aitken had called in Peter Beaumont, his ministerial driver, to give evidence which would corroborate his wholly fictitious story of a car chase outside his Lord North Street home. George Carman primed the ambush, stepped back, and watched Peter Beaumont fall helplessly in.

With some drama, the barrister played the new blown-up video to the court, freezing the frame on the Smith Square clock. The time on the dial was 1.15 p.m. Aitken had lied about the presence of his daughter and the 'Keystone Kops' car chase. Beaumont realized he was stuck in a hole. 'I am sorry, Sir, but I cannot agree that that . . .' he floundered desperately.

Aitken's QC Charles Gray intervened to try and rescue the situation. 'Have you come here to tell lies for Mr Aitken?' he asked Beaumont.

'No, certainly not, Sir,' the driver replied, looking pained and uncomfortable. The case was turning like a giant ocean liner, wheeling slowly away from the plaintiff and towards the defendants.

During the lunch-time adjournment Proudler and Carman discussed the new evidence turned up by British Airways. Britain's premier libel lawyer was becoming increasingly agitated. 'You *must* get a witness statement *imm-ed-iate-ly*,' he bawled at Proudler. But there was no witness statement to be got; Wendy Harris was out of London. Carman was not satisfied. Proudler would have to go *in person* and take the statement as soon as possible, with full details, career history . . .

Tempers were beginning to fray. 'I know how to take a witness statement, George,' Proudler sniffed.

Thirty feet away, through soundproof double doors, the giant figure of Richard Sykes could be seen briefing reporter Mike Horsnell of *The Times* about 'Ladies' Day'. Could he pass on the message to the rest of the press? Of course, of course, Horsnell soothed. Nobody wanted to miss Lolicia giving evidence.

Carman, Price and Marzek retreated to their temporary chambers across the Strand for a quick bite to eat. Carman needed Wendy Harris to be interviewed urgently so Aitken could be dramatically confronted with her testimony. And then there was Victoria's astonishing witness statement which had just been circulated to the defendants. The statement prompted no gloating – only dismay among the barristers, and the journalists. The girl had lied at the instigation of her father in a quite flagrant way, Carman felt. If Aitken insisted on putting her on the stand, Carman would be forced to intervene with the judge to prevent her from committing perjury. The intervention would have to happen before the damning BA evidence was given to the court.

Downstairs in the gents' lavatory Aitken bumped into Quentin McDermott. The two had a surreal exchange. 'I recognize you now,' Aitken quipped, standing at the urinal.

'I am that man,' McDermott replied.

'You are that man,' Aitken said thoughtfully, zipping up his flies.

At 1.50 p.m. court resumed. John Hemmingway, Aitken's solicitor at the time of the TV-am affair, took the stand. A large, completely bald man who resembled, uncannily, the stage actor Harold Innocent, Hemmingway spent the entire afternoon in the witness-box holding forth on the intricacies of off-shore trusts, the Netherlands Antilles, and the Independent Broadcasting Authority. Mr Justice Popplewell, whose wife was a member of the IBA, took a lively interest in the witness. But over in the press-box there were stifled yawns. 'My Lord, we are very grateful you sat a bit late,' Charles Gray said with characteristic courtesy after two-and-a-half impenetrable hours. Later, at Olswang, Proudler hammered out a template which would form the basis of Wendy Harris's statement the next morning.

A new tactic had been agreed between the barristers, solicitors and journalists: No Way Out. There was to be no way out for Jonathan Aitken. It was imperative that Wendy Harris's statement closed down every single avenue of escape for the former Cabinet minister. Aitken was as slippery as an eel. He could not be allowed to argue that a blurred flight-coupon entry was not sufficient evidence to prove that his wife and daughter had actually flown to Geneva. Back at the *Guardian* offices in Farringdon Road the mood was mellowing. Pallister had already taken the paper's deputy editor in charge of news Paul Johnson aside. 'Don't tell a soul, but I think the case is about to collapse,' Pallister confided. 'It's not clear yet what we will be able to publish, but we'd better be prepared.' Officially, the line was still one of scepticism. 'George is doing his best,' Pallister told colleagues. He wandered over to Luke Harding, who had been covering the case for the *Guardian*, and told him to expect an 'interesting witness' the following day. Harding, who had no idea of the latest developments, made a couple of telephone calls and alerted his colleagues on other newspapers. The Fleet Street tom-tom drums were beginning to beat.

Five hundred miles away, in an industrial estate near Zurich, Muriel Bailey (not her real name) reached for another roll of microfiche and slotted it neatly into her viewfinder. Ms Bailey had agreed to use up her lunch-breaks and evenings to sort out a peculiar query relating to an intriguing legal dispute over in England. Three days earlier she had had a call from Jeffery Maunsell, the solicitor who represented Granada Television. Did her company have records of car-hire agreements dating back to September 1993? Yes, she replied. A woman called Lolicia Aitken had hired a car over the weekend of 17–19 September 1993 and paid with American Express. Could she find the car-hire agreement? Ms Bailey said she would – but the search would have to be done in her own time. At first the task seemed unfruitful. Nobody in the name of Aitken had taken out a car from Geneva airport that month. She switched off her viewfinder and decided to resume her efforts early the next day.

Over at the Hyatt Hotel that evening, George Carman was finding it difficult to contain his excitement. Earlier he had solemnly decreed that the BA records should be treated as a state secret. 'Nobody outside this room should know,' he intoned. They should not be discussed on the phone. But at 12.30 a.m. Carman was himself on the phone to Pallister in a clearly euphoric mood. At 2 a.m. he was talking volubly to Leigh.

The following morning, Wednesday 18 June 1997, was Waterloo Day. The Right Honourable Jonathan Aitken breezed into court as usual and took up his place on the far left-hand side of the front bench. One hundred and eighty-two years earlier, on the fields of Waterloo, the Duke of Wellington had famously vanquished the French and seen off a superior enemy through clever military strategy. Aitken always knew this was his Waterloo. But he had imagined himself Wellington; in fact he was about to become the defeated Napoleon. Soon he would be going into exile.

Aitken's wife and daughter were not there to see the battle, and his formidable elderly mother Lady Aitken was away from the fray having her hair done. Aitken's main adversary throughout the trial, George Carman QC, whom Aitken had tried both to prickle and charm, was on truly withering form that day. Carman knew the BA statement would arrive later. This lent him what he described a trifle mystically as 'inner strength'.

The first witness was a former junior civil servant by the name of Andrew Thomis. Thomis had worked as an assistant secretary for Aitken at the Ministry of Defence. In normal circumstances, this callow young man would have made a half-decent witness. But under Carman's scrutiny, he wilted and drooped. In a burst of cross-examination, Carman managed to establish that Aitken had helped Thomis find a job with the defence firm Alvis, an obligation which seemed to explain Thomis's uneasy presence in the High Court. Of Aitken's long-standing commercial links with the arms dealer Fouad Makhzoumi, Thomis, who professed to know everything, knew little. 'Thank you,' Carman concluded, sitting down with theatrical emphasis.

The pantomime continued with Irene Maggs, an elderly Conservative activist who, like thousands of others in her dwindling tribe, had spent a lifetime licking envelopes and making jam in support of the cause. For eighteen years Mrs Maggs had been the chairman of Jonathan Aitken's constituency Conservative Party in Thanet, Kent. Unable to mount the stairs into the witness-box, she gave evidence from the press bench instead. Of her former MP's deep and venal connections with the Arab world, she knew nothing. Asked about Al Bilad UK, Mrs Maggs replied: 'Never heard of them, Sir.'

'Thank you very much,' Carman replied, sitting down again solemnly.

By the time Aitken's secretary Lynn Fox took the stand, George was conducting his own legal master-class. Mrs Fox had come to explain why entries in Aitken's ministerial diary had been mysteriously Tippexed out. Wriggling, she was forced to admit that she worked out of the London offices of Al Bilad, Prince Mohammed's company, and had done so secretly while Aitken was a minister. 'Very interesting,' Carman growled.

*

Over in Switzerland, Muriel Bailey suddenly found something. She had turned up Lolicia's car-hire agreement papers. They revealed that Mrs Aitken had hired a Volkswagen Golf at 12.02 p.m. on Friday 17 September 1993 at Geneva airport. According to her husband, she was still in Paris at that time. Another lie. The car had been taken out in her maiden name – Azucki. Ms Bailey briefed Jeffery Maunsell by telephone as soon as she made the discovery. At 10 a.m., just before dashing into court, Maunsell and his assistant Clare Posner stood in some trepidation by their Canon fax machine on the fifth floor of Goodman Derrick in Fetter Lane. Through their office window, in the middle distance, the bleached Gothic spires of the High Court sparkled in the sun. At 10.02 a.m. the documents chugged through on yellow fax paper. 'Fantastic,' Maunsell said. The car hire coincided exactly with the flight coupons showing Lolicia and daughter flying into Geneva. Ms Bailey had offered to go back to the archives to pull out another document which specified when Lolicia had returned the car. Did he want it? Maunsell dialled Switzerland to say yes he did, very much.

In Covent Garden, in the marbled lobby of the First Chicago building, where Olswang is based, a young, briskly efficient woman announced herself to the security guards as 'Wendy Harris'. It was 11 a.m. She took the lift up to the third floor and walked into Olswang's reception: a bright, airy lobby of fresh flowers, designer furniture and bold monochrome prints. Geraldine Proudler ushered Harris into a conference room. The statement took longer to complete than expected and sandwiches were brought in for lunch. Ms Harris meticulously checked every fact. Proudler's secretary typed – and retyped – the six-page draft.

Back in court, George Carman was becoming increasingly agitated. Where was Geraldine? During a brief adjournment he stomped into the corridor. He wanted to phone Geraldine immediately. Debbie Ashenhurst, Proudler's indefatigable assistant, dialled the number of Olswang on her mobile phone and clamped it to Carman's ear. (Carman, Britain's greatest living advocate, could not work a mobile phone.) 'Geraldine, what's *happ-en-ing*?' the barrister asked.

'She's still working on it,' Proudler replied.

Fuses were blowing. 'You *must* get it here,' Carman went on.

'He really was being unbearable,' Proudler said later.

Inside courtroom 10 at 2 p.m., the atmosphere was becoming increasingly surreal. Alan Rusbridger, who had long given up trying to concentrate on a revamp of the *Observer*, sat at the back of the court with a grim Peter Preston and the *Guardian* and Granada team. The public benches were crammed. Heads twitched every time the swing-door into court opened. Where *was* Geraldine?

Over in the witness-box, a man by the name of 'Mr X' was giving evidence. Tall, etiolated, with lank black hair and a demeanour the ancients would have called melancholic, Mr X had clearly spent most of his life in the shadows. There were dark bags under his eyes. A retired MI6 officer, Mr X had come to give evidence anonymously about Aitken's patriotic information gleaned from his talks with Fouad Makhzoumi. The presence of an ex-intelligence officer clearly excited Mr Justice Popplewell. 'I have directed that this gentleman need give neither his name nor his address for good reason,' the judge announced sternly.

'Spook,' the press bench sniggered.

Almost an hour passed and there was still no sign of Geraldine. Sir Alan Thomas, the former head of the Defence Sales Export Organization at the Ministry of Defence, was in the witness-box. Sir Alan had worked at the ministry when Aitken was Minister of State for Defence Procurement; naturally the two had liaised closely. Sir Alan, his hair plastered Bobby Charlton-style over his round forehead, was a man clearly used to having his commands obeyed. His replies to George Carman's interrogation were suitably laconic. 'Yes.' 'Yes.' 'Usually him,' he barked.

At Olswang, Wendy Harris was at last signing her witness statement. Proudler had several copies run off, stuffed them into white envelopes, and jumped into a taxi. The document itself was a model of lucidity. On the opening page, Ms Harris explained that she worked for British Airways Security and Investigation Services and was responding to a subpoena. She had supervised the search of microfiche records which had produced two flight coupons in the names of Miss V. Aitken and Mrs L. Aitken. They had flown from Heathrow to Geneva at 8.30 a.m. on 17 September 1993. Mrs L. Aitken had flown back at 19.05 p.m. on 20 September. Mrs Aitken's ticket had cost £147; Victoria's £242 (more, because she flew back later). Ms Harris's damning conclusion was wryly written:

It follows from what I have said in this statement that the only way it would be possible for the Plaintiff's wife and daughter to demonstrate that they did not in fact travel on the flights referred to in 'WDH1' [the flight coupons] would be if the following events occurred:

A. By coincidence two other ladies by the name of Mrs L. Aitken and Miss V. Aitken travelled on these flights.

B. If there was a transfer of tickets, for example if these ladies gave their tickets and passports to two other similar-looking ladies who travelled under the names of Mrs and Miss Aitken, and this was not identified by passport control.

The *Guardian*/Granada strategy had worked. There was no way out. Aitken, the great Houdini of modern British politics, had made his last death-defying escape.

As Proudler's cab crawled through the Covent Garden traffic, Jeffery Maunsell was examining another damning document. Muriel Bailey had by now retrieved Lolicia's closing hire rental agreement which showed the car had been dumped in downtown Geneva at 6.25 p.m. on Sunday 19 September 1993. At the very time Lolicia was supposed to be in Paris, having paid her husband's hotel bill. The fat lady was beginning to sing.

At 3 p.m. Geraldine Proudler swept into court 10. She handed copies of the statement to Leigh and Pallister at the back of the court. The two men grinned. Proudler walked to the front of the court and handed George Carman a white envelope containing Wendy Harris's statement. She passed copies to James Price QC and Alexandra Marzek. Carman was on his feet, cross-examining Sir Alan. For several heart-stopping minutes the envelope lay there smouldering on his lectern. Eventually Carman sat down, and Charles Gray bowled a few more questions at the witness. 'Is it good?' Carman whispered.

'Brilliant,' Proudler replied. Gray sat down.

Carman then rose to his feet for what he later described as the most dramatic moment of his distinguished career at the bar. His knockout blow was wrapped in the vellum of legal etiquette.

'My Lord, before any further evidence is called by my learned friend, I am now in a position to provide the plaintiff's solicitors, Mr Gray and your Lordship with a signed witness statement of a lady called Wendy Dawn Harris, who was employed by British Airways. I think, my Lord, if I may respectfully say so, it might be very important for Mr Gray and your Lordship to read it immediately.'

'Very well,' Mr Justice Popplewell replied grumpily. Not without a certain sense of solemn theatre, Carman opened the envelope and handed one copy to the judge and another to Charles Gray. The court rose. The Budget Rent-A-Car documents arrived five minutes later, to make a second course for the judge. Aitken, Gray and Sykes all stood up, and scrutinized their single copy of the Harris statement resting on Gray's podium. Aitken was utterly impassive. Outside, word ricocheted through the long Gothic warren of the High Court that something sensational was going on. The sleepy press room downstairs, strewn with empty plastic sandwich cases and fag ash, jolted into action. In the corridor David Leigh was briefing reporters as to what it all meant. For the first time the word 'perjury' was being murmured. It was, Leigh explained, almost certainly curtains for Aitken.

In the ante-room James Price quietly digested the BA statement while Carman tried to gauge from Proudler whether Wendy Harris would make a good witness. How would she play on the stand? 'Excellent,' Proudler said. 'Clear, thoughtful and authoritative.'

Sitting alone in his oak-panelled chambers, Mr Justice Popplewell arched his bushy grey eyebrows. The man was a bounder after all, he must have reflected, reaching for a biscuit. And he seemed such a charming chap.

When the court reassembled at 3.30 p.m., Carman had two applications for the judge: to call Wendy Harris as a witness; and to cross-examine Mr Aitken again. The subtext was clear: you are finished. 'If he can get out of this I will applaud,' Jeffery Maunsell whispered.

The former Conservative minister was slumped in the front bench with the statement beside him. He sat in a crumpled diagonal posture, legs crossed, reading and re-reading every page. The press bench was buzzing. Aitken's barrister Charles Gray decided the best strategy was to pretend nothing had happened, although he later admitted he was fully aware of the significance of the document.

He called what turned out to be the trial's final witness, the arms dealer with the appropriate name of David Trigger. Aitken had fixed his previous witnesses with a look of studied politeness. But he ignored Trigger completely. Instead, the man who had pledged to fight falsehood with the Sword of Truth lay buried in his own inscrutable misery. When he finished giving evidence, Trigger moved to the back of the court and produced some memento for Aitken from his briefcase. The former Cabinet minister turned on his usual puckered grin, and affected a friendly interest. Inside, his gut must have been knotting in disbelief.

At 4.05 p.m. the court went into private session, and the journalists poured excitedly into the corridor. The fat lady was singing loudly. George Carman guided Mr Justice Popplewell through the significance of the car-hire documents. Eventually, the penny dropped. 'Yes, I see,' the judge said. There was a long pause. 'Thank you very much. No doubt, Mr Gray, you will want to consider the position overnight,' he added, a not-so-subtle hint that one side had struck the other a mortal blow. Aitken slipped quietly out of the back of the court with his solicitor. Nobody knew it then, but he was not coming back.

One hour later, at the offices of the *Guardian* in Farringdon Road, an editorial meeting was hastily convened in a side-room next to the editor's office. There was high excitement. The case looked as if it would collapse imminently, probably tomorrow. There would be huge national and international interest. More dirty linen of the Major administration was about to be aired in a very public way. Aitken had lied to the Prime Minister, to the Cabinet Secretary, to the House of Commons, to the High Court. He had committed perjury, attempted to defraud the *Guardian* and Granada of at least £2 million, and had tried to save his skin by sending his own daughter into court to lie on oath. It was important that the *Guardian*'s coverage was powerful – and definitive.

Paul Johnson, the deputy editor in charge of news, marshalled a platoon of reporters and writers. Five pages would be cleared. Johnson recruited Charles Nevin, a feature writer, to pen a sketch, reporters Kamal Ahmed and Richard Norton-Taylor to profile the man, and old Aitken hands Jamie Wilson and Christopher Elliott to compile an inventory of the lies Aitken had told. There were also other considerations. The following day was already a huge news day. The longest civil trial in English legal history, between the $30-billion burger chain McDonald's and two unemployed anarchists, was due to end at the High Court. The case had already run in court 35 for 313 days. Over at Westminster, the battered and much diminished Conservative Party was about to choose itself a new leader. Would it be the balding 36-year-old wunderkind William Hague, or the portly Kenneth Clarke and his newly acquired Vulcan sidekick, John Redwood? Both stories demanded space.

Back in the newsroom, Luke Harding hammered out a front-page story for the first edition. Headlined SURPRISE TWIST TO AITKEN CASE AS DOCUMENTS SURFACE the article sent a clear signal to the rest of Fleet Street that the former Cabinet minister was on the brink of a spectacular fall. Over at Olswang, Geraldine Proudler and her colleague Debbie Ashenhurst knocked off early. In previous weeks both women had worked flat out. Proudler had rarely returned to her fashionable Chelsea town house before midnight, grabbing a snack and then crashing out. Now they were going to the pub. Over a scotch, they discussed a new possibility: life after Aitken.

That night Aitken did not sleep. Instead, he and Lolicia, it appears, had a furious row; their cavernous home must have resounded with marital shrieking.

At 8.30 a.m. the next morning, Jonathan Aitken left Lord North Street and jumped into a black cab. Did he have any comment? He smiled thinly and shook his head. The former Cabinet minister emerged at Gray's Inn, the cloistered legal Mecca near Chancery Lane, for a sombre meeting with his lawyers. Things did not look good. Until the previous day, Aitken's QC Charles Gray had been supremely confident the former Conservative MP would win his libel action handsomely. He and the rest of the legal team – Richard Sykes, Aitken's solicitor, Mark Warby and Justin Rushbrooke, the two other barristers in the case – had believed everything Aitken told them was true. 'We were doing jolly well,' Gray said. The ex-MP's Ritz story was so curious and implausible it could not have been made up, Gray had reasoned to friends.

Now the barrister was having to confront the uncomfortable possibility that his client was a liar. The man himself seemed disorientated. He appeared to have lost all stomach for a fight. Gray decided the best strategy was to play for more time. Perhaps the BA documents were not as conclusive as they appeared? The meeting broke up.

Over at the Royal Courts of Justice, court 10 was filling up. The press benches, which forty-eight hours earlier had been virtually deserted, were packed. The public benches were full. The *Guardian* and Granada had turned up in force. At Ascot, Britain's blue-blooded classes were gathering for a day of racing and preening. But in the Strand, Ladies' Day had been cancelled indefinitely. At 10.30 a.m., when the judge normally sat, nothing happened. The mood of intrigue was deepened by the non-appearance of the trial's star turn, Jonathan Aitken. For the first time since the case had kicked off fifteen days previously, the plaintiff was not there. So where was he? At 11.05 a.m. the barristers swept in. Gray looked shattered. He took his glasses off and rubbed his face. Aitken's QC then stood up and applied for a day's adjournment so further 'investigations' could be carried out into what Lady Aitken later dubbed 'Carman's stick of dynamite'. The defendants were 'sympathetic' to the adjournment, George Carman said. But would his Lordship ensure that Mr Aitken turn up tomorrow so he could be cross-examined? His Lordship agreed Mr Aitken should be there. The court broke up.

The case was rapidly moving into a new and deadly phase: a quick-deal poker game. Plaintiffs who withdraw from a libel action have to pay most of the costs of the other side. Aitken had nominally 'won' on the second action concerning some of the arms-dealing allegations after the judge had made the technical legal ruling in his favour. But the cards were not laid equally between George Carman, for the *Guardian* and Granada, and Charles Gray, for Aitken. Carman had all the aces. Aitken had lied in court and his evidence was discredited across the board. Gray could conceivably invite the judge to award Aitken costs in the second action. This would not lessen his client's humiliation, but might shave something off the huge legal bill Aitken now faced. Back at the *Guardian* the mood was uncompromising. 'Why should we back off when we have our foot on his windpipe?' Alan Rusbridger said.

Over at the Garrick, the theatrical watering-hole in Covent Garden frequented by Britain's elderly bohemian intelligentsia, four lunch-time diners were in a convivial mood. George Carman had invited James Price, Alex Marzek and Geraldine Proudler to eat with him at his club. Women were banned from the Garrick's main dining room, so the four ate downstairs in a private room. Sooner or later, Carman knew, Charles Gray would be forced to come seeking terms. Sure enough, when Carman returned to his chambers in Gray's Inn there was a message from his clerk: 'Call Charles Gray.' Negotiations began at 3.30 p.m. Carman's opening position offered Aitken little cheer. The *Guardian* and Granada wanted all their costs paid in full. Nothing less. 'You are asking for blood,' Gray said, on behalf of his client.

'The truth is indivisible,' Carman replied.

Gray made a counter-offer of sorts: Jonathan Aitken would with-draw his first libel action, which covered the most damaging allega-tions: that he had lied over his Ritz bill; procured women; and become financially dependent on the Saudis. This in itself was an astonishing climbdown. But Gray wanted a fig leaf to cover his client's modesty. He would ask the judge to rule in Mr Aitken's favour over the arms-dealing charges.

Carman, Proudler and Rusbridger conferred by phone. It would be monstrous, Carman reasoned, for a man who had perjured himself in the witness-box to be awarded any damages at all. But grave doubts remained about Mr Justice Popplewell's view of the BMARC affair. The *Guardian* and Granada team felt he had inclined towards Aitken throughout the trial. At crucial moments during Aitken's cross-examination, the judge had appeared buried in his notes. Would he now make a perverse narrow ruling in Aitken's favour, and ignore the broader canvas of deceit, amorality and calculated deviousness?

Unbeknown to the *Guardian* camp, Jonathan Aitken had already decided to raise up the white flag. That afternoon, a tall, loping figure strode into the private back garden of 8 Lord North Street and unlatched the wicket gate which led directly to the flat of the Honour-able Lady Aitken MBE. He was getting a divorce from Lolicia, who two days earlier had celebrated her fiftieth birthday, Aitken told his mother. Lady Aitken had never liked her dizzy, weight-obsessed daughter-in-law, and gave a small inward cheer.

Later Aitken drove down the M4 to see his son William at Eton College. His mind was not focused on the legal machinations taking place on his behalf back in Gray's Inn, only on the mechanics of escape. By 6.30 p.m. negotiations were still at an impasse. The discussions were becoming increasingly fractured. Proudler suggested all the interested parties gather at Olswang. George Carman was against the idea. He reluctantly asked Charles Gray for his home phone number. Then the switchboard at Carman's chambers closed down for the night. Eventually Proudler managed to reach him via a mobile phone belonging to Alex Marzek, his junior barrister. This was farcical, Proudler reflected. At 8 p.m. Carman, Price and Marzek trooped into a large conference room at Olswang where everybody else had already gathered. The *Guardian* team included the editor

Alan Rusbridger, his deputy Georgina Henry, and the paper's lawyer Siobhan Butterworth; Geraldine Proudler and Debbie Ashenhurst from Olswang; for Granada, Steve Boulton, the editor of *World in Action*, and Ian McBride, Granada's managing editor; as well as their solicitors Jeffery Maunsell and Claire Posner.

This was end-game. Alan Rusbridger was still not in the mood for compromise. Aitken had been caught out lying, he argued, and his position was as bad as it could be. 'We were all for stamping on him,' he said. But the lawyers were urging magnanimity. Carman's feeling was that if Gray was pushed too far he might ask for judgment on the second action. This would leave the defendants exposed to a rogue ruling from the judge. And nobody on their team had much confidence in Mr Justice Popplewell in relation to the murky arms-brokering allegations.

Carman set out a new position, which would give Gray an incentive to settle and leave nothing to judicial discretion. Aitken would pay 80 per cent of the *Guardian* and Granada's costs, a huge sum. The defendants would pay 20 per cent of their own costs, relating to the second action. Aitken would withdraw both writs. This formula still amounted to a complete triumph for the *Guardian* and Granada, and left the Right Honourable Jonathan Aitken with a £2 million legal bill.

George Carman retreated to the adjoining room and phoned Charles Gray with the offer. 'Take it or leave it,' he said. Five minutes later, at 9.10 p.m., the phone rang in the conference room. It was Charles Gray. On behalf of his client, he accepted the offer unconditionally. Carman instructed Marzek to take a note, and repeated aloud the terms of Aitken's surrender.

'They were biting our hands off,' Proudler said. Rusbridger got on his mobile phone to break the news to Leigh and Pallister. Downstairs, fridges were scoured for bottles of champagne. Georgina Henry, the *Guardian*'s deputy editor, whooped. The paper had pulled off what was destined to become a famous victory.

Over at the sleepy, lightless offices of the Press Association in Victoria, the night news editor had been puzzling over a fax from the Right Honourable Jonathan Aitken. In a terse one-page statement Aitken announced that he was separating from his wife Lolicia for personal reasons. 'Recent events have shattered me and broken our family,' he said. The story was obviously true – Aitken's secretary

Lynn Fox confirmed it on the phone – but what did it all mean? At Olswang, where the party was in full swing, there were a few uncharitable explanations.

Earlier in the day Aitken had walked into his Great Peter Street office and coolly dictated the release to Mrs Fox. She was to fax it to the press later that evening, he told her. It looked like a cynical ploy to distract attention from the impending collapse of his libel case. Perhaps Lolicia had refused to lie for her husband at the last minute from the witness-box? George Carman had known about the development earlier in the afternoon but had said nothing to anyone except James Price. 'I'm telling you this counsel-to-counsel,' he told him with solemn drama. 'Jonathan is leaving Lolicia.'

The following morning, the lawyers gathered at the Royal Courts of Justice for the last time. The rite they were about to perform was purely ceremonial: Charles Gray and George Carman had already briefed Mr Justice Popplewell in private as to the terms of the agreement. The public and press benches were full again, but of the Crusader for Truth there was no sign. The entire front bench, where Aitken usually sat, was deserted. Richard Sykes, his solicitor, was not there. Neither was his wife, nor his daughter, both of whom had signed statements they knew to be false. In the *Guardian* and the Granada camp, there were huge smiles. After four years of claim, denial, painstaking investigation, slog and despair, it was all over.

'I'm instructed by my client to ask for the action to be discontinued on the terms which, subject to your Lordship, have been agreed relating to costs,' Charles Gray said. And that was that. Pallister turned round to Peter Preston, sitting on the bench behind. Since the autumn of 1993 they had had this great albatross round their necks. Now it had flown. 'It's over,' Pallister murmured. Preston gave a wan smile and nodded. Mr Justice Popplewell, who might have been expected to refer the case to the Attorney-General with a view to prosecuting Aitken for perjury, merely thanked both sides for the clarity of their documentation. At the back of the room, a courtroom artist for Sky television sketched the judge's greying profile. Earlier in the week, Mr Justice Popplewell had spotted the artist's sketch of himself and George Carman QC on Sky. Via his clerk, he had asked her to draw him another sketch as a personal memento of the trial. 'The same as last time,' he specified vainly, 'but without George Carman in it.'

Outside, in the corridor, Alan Rusbridger, Peter Preston and Ian McBride were crushed by reporters wanting to know why, exactly, Aitken had caved in. Gradually, the enormity of Aitken's deceit was explained. He was a 'serial liar', Preston said grimly. 'Mr Aitken was lying about the Ritz from the start and the lies unravelled and unravelled and are lying on the floor. If there is one thing that sticks in my gullet, it's that anyone would use a schoolchild to back up a story like this. It's disgraceful by any standards.'

'Jonathan Aitken seems to have impaled himself on the simple Sword of Truth,' Rusbridger added, in a statement fed out by the *Guardian* press office. 'For three years he has lied to newspapers, lied to the Cabinet Secretary, lied to the Prime Minister and lied to his colleagues. Now he has made his fatal mistake by lying on oath to the High Court.'

There was no triumph at Aitken's fall, merely a feeling of emptiness. A talented and brilliant man had been destroyed by his own hubris. Inside the court, George Carman found his progress to the door, and his Marlboro cigarette, blocked by the scrum. 'I do hope they are not saying anything defamatory,' his fellow counsel James Price quipped.

Outside, on the steps of the Law Courts, TV cameras and photographers waited impatiently. Three miles away at Associated Newspapers in Kensington, the headline on the *Evening Standard* was being laid out, which set the tone for much of the press coverage over the next twenty-four hours. It read: THE RUIN OF AITKEN. The press caravan outside court 10 was eventually moved on by a police constable. Rusbridger and Preston swept down a helical staircase, through the cavernous entrance lobby, and emerged blinking into a wall of arc lights and flashbulbs. 'It was a bit like Oscar night,' Rusbridger later said. One of the lessons the *Guardian* editor had learned from the Neil Hamilton libel action was that the game of television soundbites was almost as important as the written story. Television is an effective medium for an accomplished liar when the story is difficult and hidden. Hamilton had dropped his libel suit against the *Guardian* at the last minute – only to then parade his innocence in a succession of television studios, claiming, incredibly, that the victory was his.

Rusbridger, Preston and McBride repeated on camera what they had said on the first floor of the High Court. The case demonstrated how ineffective official procedures were at exposing dishonesty at the heart of public life. Britain's libel laws made such reporting dangerous and potentially prohibitively expensive. The Lord Chancellor should move urgently to reform the laws which make London the libel capital of the world, Rusbridger stressed.

Back at the *Guardian* offices in Farringdon Road, the newsroom hummed with delight. A succession of television crews, dragging long tripods and spotlights, arrived to interview Preston and Rusbridger. A letter from the *Guardian* editor was on its way to Dame Barbara Mills, the Director of Public Prosecutions, and Sir Paul Condon, the Commissioner for the Metropolitan Police. It read:

You will be aware that Jonathan Aitken today discontinued his libel action against the *Guardian* and against Granada TV in the High Court. He did so because incontrovertible evidence from British Airways, obtained on subpoena, showed that Mr Aitken had perjured himself on oath.

Witness statements from his wife, 17-year-old daughter and from a close family friend – all of whom Mr Aitken had been intending to call to give evidence – were also directly dishonest. There is, therefore, the clearest evidence of a well-laid and carefully co-ordinated conspiracy to pervert the course of justice.

Our solicitor, Geraldine Proudler, of Olswang, has all the documents to support this charge and would be happy to assist you in any enquiries.

Yours sincerely,
Alan Rusbridger

Bizarrely, that afternoon, Rusbridger and Pallister found themselves drinking tea in an Embankment hotel with an Arab source who insisted he would talk only to the paper's editor. The source brought the news that Said Ayas, Aitken's friend and co-conspirator, was under house arrest in Saudi Arabia. Across the open-plan office, Atex keyboards clacked as the Aitken team got to work. At 6 p.m. Rusbridger wrote a 1,500-word editorial for the front page, while Paul Johnson, the deputy editor in charge of news, devised a headline. At 9 p.m. the first page proofs glided off the newsdesk printer. The following morning, Saturday 21 June 1997, a historic front page in contemporary British journalism hit the news-stands. The headline, above a four-column photo of the former Conservative Cabinet minister, the Right Honourable Jonathan Aitken, read simply: HE LIED AND LIED AND LIED.

'As I leave you I want you to know – just think how much you are going to be missing. You won't have Richard Nixon to kick around any more, because, gentlemen, this is my last press conference.' **Richard Nixon after his defeat in the election for the Governorship of California, November 1962**

···

Postscript: **Exile**

On the weird and wild coast of northern California, in a ranch ringed with Monterey pines, Jonathan Aitken put his feet up and gazed out of the window. Across the meadow from his bedroom, Pacific breakers fell rhythmically on to a deserted cove. There were few humans around to trouble the one-time Cabinet minister or his son William. Deer grazed all around the rented property, while the occasional mountain-bike rider skittered past a dirt track before vanishing into the distance. Over in the Northern Mountains, black bears padded primevally through evergreen forests humming with eagles and hawks. On the scenic Highway 1, nobody had appeared to be in pursuit as the former MP motored wordlessly along the West Coast in a rental car, through the Giant Redwood forests to Gualala, 110 miles north of San Francisco.

Aitken had calculated correctly that his media tormentors were unlikely to find him here. The house was accessible only through a network of private roads. Besides, Aitken had taken the precaution of getting a friend to book into a Sea Ranch Vacation Rentals property, which bore the quaintly English name of 'Peel'. Aitken's name figured nowhere; he was a non-person. Only Lord Lucan had managed to vanish more successfully; and Lucan, of course, never came back.

The holiday must have inspired thoughts of another trip made by Aitken in happier times to the West Coast of America in the spring of 1975. The newly elected MP paid homage to Richard Nixon, six months after the Watergate scandal, at his home in San Clemente near Los Angeles. The ex-President was deeply depressed, frail, and at the nadir of his fortunes. At that time the very word 'Nixon' was a synonym for disgrace, obloquy and mendaciousness; and yet this young-ish British parliamentarian turned up to what had been dubbed 'the Western White House'. Over a two-hour chat and a cup of coffee, Aitken enthusiastically sought out Nixon's views on foreign policy. 'I almost expected to meet a monster complete with horns and a tail,' Aitken wrote in his overly complimentary biography of the 37th President of the United States who, he concluded, 'had been excessively maligned for his faults and inadequately recognized for his virtues'. Now the roles were reversed. Nixon had acquired in death the kind of respectability that had eluded him in life. Aitken had himself become a synonym for the worst kind of Nixonian perfidy. And here he was once more in California, enjoying his own peculiar exile. Had he troubled to read the British newspapers, he would have found little in them to cheer him up. The word 'disgraced' hung round his name like an albatross. The trip was made more bearable, perhaps, by the presence of his fourteen-year-old son William, down from Eton for the holiday. But Nixon, the misty-eyed presidential hero who asked Aitken despairingly for advice in the dark days of 1975, could offer only limited posthumous help.

Since slipping quietly out of the High Court on Wednesday 18 June, Jonathan Aitken had done everything he could to ensure his departure from Britain went unnoticed. On 19 June, while his lawyers accepted a humiliating settlement on his behalf, Aitken flew out of Britain to Paris by private jet. There, he booked a one-way £1,089-club-class Air France ticket from Paris to New York, where he stayed at the home of an old friend. Back in London, meanwhile, Fleet Street's finest were on his trail. Reporters were sent spinning across the globe: to the summer home of his mother in Ibiza, and to properties owned by his Saudi business friends in France and Spain. Others were despatched to the jungle palace of the terminally ill Sir James Goldsmith in Mexico, a network of scorpion-proofed villas bounded by rough seas. Rumours swept the *Daily Telegraph* newsroom that Aitken was holed up at the Florida home of its right-wing proprietor, Conrad Black. Some lucky soul was sent to the Barbados home of Aitken's cousin John Kidd. By the time hacks caught up with him in New York, he and his son (who joined him a week later) had moved on — as is the case in all the best films —

flying to San Francisco with United Airlines. By the time they reached Gualala, their pursuers had been shaken off. Aitken *père et fils* were left unmolested to wander along misty, sandy beaches or take the car up-country to the tiny timber-and-fishing towns which stretch up the coast towards the foggy Oregon border.

While Aitken kept his head down, and did a serviceable impression of Lord Lucan, the Friends of Jonathan Aitken (the FOJA) were busy making the best of a bad job. It did not look good for their man, it was true. He had told a few fibs in court, which made the whole thing tricky. But the patrician view among the members of Aitken's snobbish Conservative Philosophy Group was that Jonathan was essentially a good chap whose tussle with the *Guardian* had left him badly, but not fatally, wounded. They took a bafflingly indulgent view of the fact that he had committed perjury and per-suaded his teenage daughter to lie for him. A new theory also started circulating at the Beefsteak Club, White's and around other high Tory tables: that he did it for his wife (or, expressed less charitably, between clenched teeth, for *that awful woman*). Others hinted darkly that his stay at the Ritz may have been on hush-hush MI6 business.

The suggestion that Aitken had lied in court to *protect* Lolicia was given a kind of credence by an extraordinary interview with his loyal but confused mother, Lady Penelope Aitken. Unlike some of Aitken's most fervent supporters in the media, Lady Aitken had at least bothered to attend some of his doomed thirteen-day libel action. Little of it seemed to have percolated into her head, however. In an interview with the *Mail on Sunday* the aristocratic Lady Aitken blamed her parvenue of a daughter-in-law for her only son's horrible downfall. In an exquisitely deranged syllogism, she declared:

Years ago Lolicia made a statement to say that she had paid the bill so, even though nobody really remembered what had happened, Jonathan felt he had to stand by her. I suppose she thought she was helping him because he'd done nothing wrong. But it just all ended up in unnecessary muddle.

Warming to her theme, Lady Aitken also accused Lolicia of neg-lecting her husband during their eighteen-year marriage. 'She doesn't cook for him,' she said, adding memorably: 'I don't even think she knows what a saucepan looks like.' Lady Aitken's considered view of her only son's seemingly traumatic decision to divorce his wife –

announced just three days earlier – was 'cheap at the price' and 'the best thing to come out of all this'.

Over at the *Spectator*, the Conservative Party's cuddly house journal, the veteran columnist Paul Johnson clapped on his rusty armour and got ready to do battle. Johnson was one of the distinguished group of academics and politicians whom Aitken invited to meet Richard Nixon in 1978, when the MP hosted Nixon's visit to Britain. The two men talked about philosophy. Johnson and Aitken have a longstanding friendship. In his book, *Nixon: A Life*, Aitken paid this dyspeptic Whig moralist, and admirer of Thatcher and Blair, the ultimate compliment when he wrote that Johnson's *Modern Times* was the contemporary history book that Nixon most admired. Even by the usual standards of Johnsonian vitriol, however, his article of 28 June 1997 was extreme. Johnson began by claiming Aitken had been laid low by the 'abuse of power by the media' before asking, rhetorically, why journalists had behaved with 'such malice' towards his friend. 'The answer,' he wrote, 'is lamentably simple – envy.'

He continued in similar ranting vein with an earnestly intended piece of sub-Dickensian parody: 'Journalists tend to be ugly, stunted – or if tall, uncouth – poor, because they spend all their money on drink or in the betting shop, with bedraggled wives and unwelcoming homes, to which they return late and reluctantly.' Aitken was the 'cynosure of media envy', 'tall, handsome, irresistible to women' etc., etc. Johnson had not bothered to attend court himself, but felt himself sufficiently well informed to air the fashionable right-wing theory that Aitken had lied to protect his good wife. 'Any gentleman, to protect his family from harm or a lady from exposure, may tell a lie under pressure,' he opined. In the deeper recesses of the same magazine, the playboy gossip-columnist Taki complained about the 'self-satisfied hyenas' of the press and the 'assorted body snatchers' of the *Guardian*. The media hysteria which accompanied Aitken's demise was 'unparalleled since the fall of Milton's angels', the cocaine-loving Taki snorted.

But while Aitken's hysterical apologists in the media fought a high-profile rearguard action, his old political allies vanished into the shadows. Eleven days before Aitken's reputation sank like a soufflé in the High Court, a group of merry MPs and peers gathered at 8 Lord North Street for a party hosted by his former Cabinet colleague Michael Howard, one of the least appealing survivors of the ousted

Major dynasty. The catastrophe of the general election had done nothing to dim Howard's vaunting ambition. The former Home Secretary commandeered Aitken's home as a swish base for his campaign for the leadership of the Conservative Party. On the eve of the poll of Conservative MPs, Howard supporters sipped Laurent-Perrier Champagne, and munched on Pringle crisps and peanuts. Yards of tin foil had been unfurled to protect Aitken's carpets and cherished antique furniture. The swanky party, though, proved a waste of time. Howard finished a dismal fifth in the Conservative beauty parade, out of five. Surely, though, having so recently enjoyed his friend Jonathan Aitken's hospitality, Howard would have an informed view on the collapsed libel trial? 'No comment at all,' he snapped.

Diane Abbott, Aitken's Ritz Hotel interlocutor, was unavailable. Scarcely more forthcoming was Alan Duncan, the Tory MP who had described Aitken as a 'good and honourable man' when he made his great Sword of Truth speech, adding: 'Good for him for taking a stand.' 'I have no comment to make in any respect,' he now said.

Only Richard Shepherd, the libertarian Tory MP who had attended Aitken's wedding, was prepared to put a brave gloss on the catastrophe. 'He served his country, his constituency and his party with distinction,' he said. 'It is a terrible tragedy.'

Meanwhile, from his secret base in Manhattan, Jonathan Aitken kept himself well briefed in the days immediately after the trial. He sought reassurance from his secretary Lynn Fox and his solicitor Richard Sykes, who had been devastated by the collapse. They almost certainly faxed him press cuttings; and must have told the ex-MP over the phone that things looked bleak. Another row was brewing – over Aitken's membership of the Privy Council, the august body of senior politicians and ex-politicians which advises the Queen. Aitken had become a Privy Councillor on his promotion to Cabinet. Could he now be stripped of the title which allowed him to add the words 'Right Honourable' to his name? In the present circumstances the prefix had rebounded somewhat mockingly upon him.

Those who had resigned from the Privy Council in the past were a pretty ignominious bunch. John Profumo, the Cabinet minister who lied to the Commons about his relationship with Christine Keeler in 1963, voluntarily offered up his resignation. So, too, did the former Labour minister John Stonehouse after his conviction in

1976 on eighteen counts of theft and false pretences. The last person to have been struck off the Privy Council list was Sir Edgar Speyer, a philanthropist, financier and friend of the Liberal Prime Minister Herbert Asquith. Speyer's crime was treason: in 1921 he was convicted of having collaborated with the Germans in the First World War.

Five days after the end of the trial, Aitken let it be known via friends that he was going to fall on his sword. The alternative was to face the humiliating prospect of being struck off. Pressure was also building from within his own Party to do the decent thing. William Hague, the Conservatives' new leader, had already signalled he would be seeking additional powers to sack MPs who embarrassed the Party. Lord Parkinson, meanwhile, the new Conservative chairman, who had sparkled with remarkable good humour at the Conservative meltdown on election night, did his best to distance the Hague regime from the former minister. It was a 'personal tragedy' he said, 'but Mr Aitken may have been a fool.'

On 26 June 1997 a brief announcement appeared in the official *London Gazette*, which said the Queen had approved 'at his own request that the name of Jonathan William Patrick Aitken Esq be removed from the list of Privy Councillors'. Aitken had faxed his request to the clerk of the Privy Council, Nigel Nicholls. A short meeting of the Council at Buckingham Palace, attended by the Prince of Wales and the Duke of York, confirmed the ignominious request. Jonathan Aitken had become only the third member of the Privy Council to resign this century. More than that, though, the move had huge symbolic significance. It was the first time Aitken had shown any signs of a Freudian virtue which had figured little in the story previously – guilt. This was the first, and possibly the only, admission that he had done anything wrong.

On 25 June 1997 two gentlemen waited calmly in the bright entrance lobby of Olswang, the *Guardian*'s solicitors in Covent Garden. Alan Rusbridger's letter had landed in the in-tray of the Commissioner for the Metropolitan Police, Sir Paul Condon. The wheels of justice were turning. Two senior Scotland Yard detectives had been appointed to investigate the murky Jonathan Aitken affair. Their politically sensitive task was to establish whether the former Conservative Cabinet minister had committed any crime – perjury, conspiracy to pervert the course of justice, or indeed fraud. The officers, Detective Chief

Inspector Geoff Hunt and Detective Inspector Greg Faulkner, both belonged to Special Operations, a small but powerful branch of the Met which deals with serious and organized crime. Their boss David Veness is regarded as the most senior operational detective inside Scotland Yard. The unit has a special brief to operate extra-territorially, going beyond normal departmental boundaries. The appointment of DCI Hunt and DI Faulkner made it clear that the Met was treating the affair seriously.

Over coffee and biscuits, the men from Special Operations were briefed on the case by the *Guardian*'s Geraldine Proudler and Debbie Ashenhurst. Three lever-arch files of documents were later sent off by courier and taken through Scotland Yard's marble-floored reception lobby up to the organized-crime group on the fifth floor.

Meanwhile, in Saudi Arabia, Aitken's friend Said Ayas was experiencing justice of a rather more summary kind. Ayas was in trouble. The former Lebanese medical student had fallen out with the man who, over a quarter of a century, had made him very rich, Prince Mohammed.

According to the *Sunday Times*, the Prince had accused Ayas of plundering £25 million from one of his bank accounts. In a fury, he had placed him under house arrest at Ayas's Saudi home in Dhahran. While Aitken enjoyed the Californian sunshine, Ayas, his co-conspirator, found himself a prisoner in his own house. Watched by two security men, he fretted about his high blood pressure and made increasingly desperate telephone calls to his French wife Danielle back in London. At one stage he even vanished – later emerging, grimly, from a Saudi jail. According to impeccable sources, Ayas was reluctant to give false evidence at Aitken's libel trial; although, it has to be remembered, he had no scruples about lying for Aitken repeatedly in his witness statement.

Over at the San Tropez playground where Ayas and Aitken had frolicked three summers previously, there was more bad news. Ayas's £20-million luxury yacht *Katamarino* had been impounded off Antibes. Behind the scenes Prince Mohammed, it is understood, was making discreet inquiries as to its resale value. The 184-foot yacht moored in Port Vauban looked not unlike the *Marie Celeste*. The vessel's white-suited crew were occasionally spotted, but the yacht's fabulously wealthy owner was nowhere to be seen. Instead he was stuck in Dhahran; desperate, bitter, unhappy and trapped.

While Ayas languished miserably in front of his television, a middle-aged woman wearing a black wig and dark sunglasses boarded a flight from Portugal and flew quietly back into Britain. Lolicia Aitken vanished for two weeks after the débâcle of 18 June, the day documents from British Airways proved that both she and her husband had lied. On her return she launched herself back into the life beloved by chic, unemployed, upper-class, middle-aged, metropolitan women everywhere. She had lunch with friends in a smart South Kensington café, and splashed out on anti-cellulite treatments for her wobbly thighs at a fashionable clinic in Chelsea. For a few days, the handful of hacks who loitered outside the Aitken home in Lord North Street failed to recognize her. Eventually a reporter from the *Mail on Sunday* penetrated her pantomime disguise.

Lolicia then agreed to give an interview. She told the pro-Conservative *Mail* she was standing by her husband, adding, bafflingly, that 'Everything comes in its own time, and we all pay for our sins'. Describing herself as a 'spiritual person', Lolicia seemed to suggest that her husband's announcement that they were to divorce was a cynical ploy. 'I'm not going to tell you whether Jonathan and I are separating. We might. But I am with my daughters now, and all the children are all right. We are together as a family and leading a quiet life.' There was a glimpse into Lolicia's curious lifestyle ('I do yoga, I meditate, I pray a lot.') and into her religious beliefs ('I have inner peace.'). But what of her husband? Why had he lied to the High Court? Why had *she* lied to the High Court in her witness statement, and to the world in general, for almost four years? 'No comment,' she said. 'I do feel that Jonathan was holding the sword of truth,' was the best she could manage.

Back in California, Jonathan Aitken was preparing to face the music. Via the sympathetic conduit of the *Daily Telegraph*, Aitken had already let it be known that he did not plan to remain in exile permanently. Exile did not really suit a worldly Etonian. Aitken had been in touch with Scotland Yard and agreed to be interviewed by detectives. Sooner or later he was going to have to fly home. He wanted a bit of peace and quiet first, he told friends. But on 11 July 1997 Aitken telephoned the manager of the Sea Ranch property he was renting and told him 'something had come up' and checked out. Journalists who had been tracking the former minister missed him by a matter of hours – and discovered his unmade bed, a half-made fire, lights left on and a newspaper lying on a table. The great man himself, meanwhile, was motoring back to San Francisco with his son.

At San Francisco airport, as he tried to arrange his flight back to Paris, he was confronted by reporters. It was the first time he had been seen in public since the shattering collapse of his court case twenty-four days previously. 'How did you find me?' he stuttered. Aitken's legendary *savoir-faire* then returned. 'I've been on holiday with my son,' he said breezily. 'We had a great time, lots of sun. It was very enjoyable.' Aitken did not exactly look like a man who had spent three weeks being tormented and jabbed by the demons of remorse. Suntanned and relaxed, he had dumped his trademark pin-stripe in favour of an unministerial pair of jeans and a blazer. He was not going to say very much, though. 'I've been advised not to make any comment whatsoever on legal or family matters,' he declared. And that was it. From then on the former Conservative MP would behave like a Trappist monk in public.

At the United Airlines check-in desk Aitken did his best to dodge his pursuers. His son William flew directly to Heathrow, popping up back at home on 13 July 1997. But Aitken changed his flight and decided to return to Britain via Paris. One would have thought Paris, scene of the Ritz fiasco, would be the last place on earth Aitken would wish to visit; and yet the city had always held a kind of fatal magnetism for him. After touching down at Charles de Gaulle airport, Aitken jumped into a taxi and headed for a mid-range hotel at the Gare du Nord railway station. Cheaper and less baroque than the Ritz, the £100-a-night Hotel Terminus Nord afforded Aitken little respite. After bedding down for a couple of hours, he grabbed a bite to eat from a brasserie and checked out without even staying a night.

Aitken's covert return to Britain was carried out not by air but by land. He jumped on the 9.23 p.m. Eurostar destined for Waterloo. As a back-bench MP Aitken had vigorously opposed the construction of the Channel Tunnel; now it afforded him an easy way of eluding the media. He slipped off the train at Ashford, Kent, and vanished into the night.

Jonathan had begun his libel action against the *Guardian* thirty-seven days earlier with his reputation somewhat dented but structurally pretty much intact. As he strode into the echoing amphitheatre of the High Court's central lobby, he was a Privy Councillor, former

Cabinet minister and pillar of the Conservative Establishment. Now, as he looked up at the starry Kent sky, he was simply a liar and a vainglorious con-man who had been found out.

It was Winston Churchill who once observed that 'No one can guarantee success in war.' Jonathan Aitken would have done well to heed the advice of Churchill who, during his wilderness years in the 1930s, often dossed down at 8 Lord North Street on the sofa of his bachelor crony and sometime Minister of Information Brendan Bracken. During Aitken's absence media interest in his story had built up, gradually, like the gurgling juices in a bottle of fermented homebrew. After the first pictures of Aitken at San Francisco airport were published, the bottle started to tremble with excitement, and the cork was ready to blow off. Outside Lord North Street photographers gathered at dawn to try to catch the first snap of the disgraced ex-minister. They stayed until midnight. The man himself was nowhere to be seen. The day after his arrival home, however, a press release fell from the fax machines of Fleet Street.

'I have decided,' Aitken announced portentously, 'not to make any immediate public statement on matters relating to my recent libel case. I will therefore not be giving any media interviews or statements for the foreseeable future.' The press release typed by his loyal secretary Lynn Fox was headed: 'From: Jonathan Aitken.' The Right Honourable prefix had been chopped off; a sop to his enemies. But how was Aitken to handle the siege situation outside his home, and get rid of the noisome photographers slurping coffee on his pavement?

Aitken decided to hold a photocall. This was not a wise move. The event was to become one of the great bungles *de nos jours* and was to go down in contemporary media folklore as 'The Battle for College Green'. The idea was a simple one: a stroll for the cameras across College Green, the narrow grass rectangle opposite the Houses of Parliament. Once satisfied, the photographers would bugger off and leave him in peace. A briefing note at the bottom of the press release stated that Jonathan Aitken was 'aware' of the large numbers of photographers 'stationed' outside his home and was 'letting it be known' that he would be walking across College Green at 5 p.m. on Wednesday 16 July 1997.

But the stunt was to backfire horribly. Walking unarmed across no man's land into the enemy's deadly machine guns would have been less risky. Some one hundred photographers, camera crews, and journalists assembled well before 5 p.m. in the pleasant July sunshine to watch the bizarre spectacle. At 4.58 p.m. one photographer shouted, 'There he is!' All hell broke loose. Aitken found himself mobbed as he tried to navigate between a wall and a blue Transit van. His driver Peter Beaumont tried to beat a path through the scrum. But there was no way through, and Aitken turned back a few yards short of the Green. 'If this is how you are going to behave, I'm going back,' he said petulantly.

Realizing they had missed their shot, those who had waited politely on the Green howled with frustration, then dived into the mêlée. Michael Brunson, ITN's portly political editor, fell over with a thud. 'Sorry, Michael,' Aitken murmured, 'but it's not my fault.' A photographer and an ITN producer started fighting and tumbled on to the pavement. The dwarf firs outside the Victoria Hotel on Great Peter Street quivered as the swirling media swarmed past. Aitken inched forward.

Brunson got up. 'Did you commit perjury?' he shouted. Others had been asking Aitken the same question. But he refused to reply, and simply smiled wordlessly.

'Why did you do this?' a bemused snapper asked.

'I was trying to be helpful,' Aitken ventured.

Eventually the sanctuary of 8 Lord North Street was reached, and Aitken let it be known that he had had enough. He retreated behind his black front door. The media clapped and shouted, 'Bye bye!' The former Cabinet minister, whose Sword of Truth press conference had been a garrulous model of stage-managed pomp, had been reduced to an embarrassing and mute scramble outside his own house. He had said nothing; and by saying nothing had compounded the now widespread impression that he was as guilty as hell.

Over at a semi-pedestrianized shopping centre in the heart of Ramsgate, above a shop selling cheap dresses and shoes, the small plastic plaque which once bore the name of THE RIGHT HONOURABLE JONATHAN AITKEN had vanished from South Thanet Conservative Centre. Four screws still holding little bits of the plaque are all that remains. As July turned to August, Aitken repaired to his windswept seaside home in Sandwich with his family. There, he wrote letters of apology to his friends; and eased himself gradually back into what eighteenth-century novelists called 'society'. Over a congenial dinner, Aitken entertained two rather elderly figures: Lord Runcie, the former Archbishop of Canterbury, and E. W. Swanton, the nonagenarian former cricket correspondent of the *Daily Telegraph* and Sandwich neighbour. Here was living proof (just) that no sin is too great for the British Establishment not to forgive one of its own.

Aitken's return to Britain in the summer of 1997 threw up many questions, and provided few answers. How, he must have asked himself, should a disgraced ex-politician behave? Richard Nixon, Aitken's tarnished hero, played golf, fretted darkly about his place in history, and plotted his return to public life after being driven from office by what he regarded as a low media conspiracy. He also wrote voluminously, getting up at 6 a.m. every morning to work on his memoirs. Back in 1960 the victorious John Kennedy had written to Nixon after defeating him in the American presidential election by the slimmest of margins. 'There is something about being an author,' Kennedy wrote, 'which really builds up the reputation of a political figure.' It is advice Aitken appears to be heeding. Latest reports say he is busy writing a novel; a form of therapy which offers some relief from the torment of sleepless nights.

But a work of fiction will not answer two stubbornly perplexing questions: what *was* Jonathan Aitken doing at the Ritz Hotel during the weekend of 17–19 September 1993? And why was he prepared to gamble away his entire reputation to keep the real purpose of his trip secret?

There are several explanations of differing plausibility. It has been suggested that Aitken shared his bed at the Ritz with a woman who was not his wife. But this theory, even if true, would not be sufficient to explain the great edifice of lies which Aitken was to construct over the next three-and-a-half years. He had always treated infidelity as an act of no consequence. Besides, Mrs Aitken was no stranger to his philandering, nor to his weird fondness for 'correction' and swishy canes.

Aitken's friends have also put it about that he was on secret service business in Paris. The suave Etonian figure who joined the James Bond club at Oxford University lied for Queen and country, they maintain. There are precedents. Dick Helms, a former director of the CIA, and Oliver North, President Reagan's national security adviser at the centre of the Iran-Contra scandal, proudly admitted to having lied 'in the service of the state'. At the time of his trial Aitken was chairman of the Cercle, a secretive, far-right-wing group run by former intelligence agents. The Cercle meets twice a year, frequently as the guest of the rulers of oil-rich Gulf states. And yet this beguiling explanation, conjuring up the romantic spectre of espionage, MI6, and seduction by female foreign agents, has no substance to it. Ministry of Defence documents disclosed to the *Guardian* on subpoena make clear that the visit to the Ritz was a 'private' one. These letters were strictly for internal Whitehall consumption. They give the lie to the theory that Aitken was some kind of Martini-drinking super-spy.

According to better-informed sources, Aitken flew to the Ritz to confer with his Saudi cronies over an arms deal. The Conservative MP met Prince Mohammed three or four times a year in Paris and Geneva; the Prince always paid his hotel bill. The plan was that the 'board' including Said Ayas should meet at the George V Hotel in Paris. But the venue changed after the Prince remarked that the girls in the Ritz Hotel health spa were 'more appealing' than those in the George V. According to an informed Arab source, the gigantic Al Yamamah Tornado contract lies at the heart of the Ritz mystery. King Fahd of Saudi Arabia was reluctant to distribute £600 million in commission to the middlemen who had brokered the Tornado contract. The plan, elaborated at the Ritz, was to persuade King Fahd to approve these vast bribes. In exchange for an even larger chunk of commission, Prince Mohammed would lean on his father to approve the vast payments. Meanwhile, Jonathan Aitken MP would tie up the British end and propose a business tour of the Persian Gulf to John Major. Aitken, as usual, would be rewarded for his efforts.

The reality is that the mystery is never likely to be solved. Prince Mohammed has no incentive to explain the riddle; Said Ayas, still under house arrest, is in no position to come clean; Wafic Said never met any of the protagonists; and Jonathan Aitken, the man who unscabbarded his Sword of Truth only to find himself ignobly impaled upon it, is pathologically incapable of telling the truth.

Index

'JA' refers to Jonathan Aitken.